An Accidental
Sportswriter

also by robert lipsyte

An Accidental
Sportswriter

a memoir

ROBERT LIPSYTE

An Imprint of HarperCollinsPublishers

HarperCollins books may be purchased for educational, business, or sales promotional use. For information please write: Special Markets Department, HarperCollins Publishers, 10 East 53rd Street, New York, NY 10022.

A hardcover edition of this book was published in 2011 by Ecco, an imprint of HarperCollins Publishers.

FIRST ECCO PAPERBACK EDITION PUBLISHED 2012.

Photograph on title page courtesy of Barton Silverman

Designed by Mary Austin Speaker

Library of Congress Cataloging-in-Publication Data has been applied for.

ISBN 978-0-06-176914-6

12 13 14 15 16   OV/RRD   10 9 8 7 6 5 4 3 2 1

For Lois, my format

The ball I threw while playing in the park
Has not yet reached the ground.

—Dylan Thomas, "Should Lanterns Shine"

contents

introduction: **accidents happen**

I lined up a summer job in 1957 as helper on a city water truck that would cruise Manhattan filling troughs for the dwindling number of working horses in the city. I had just graduated from Columbia and was headed to Claremont College in California, which was as far from the borough of Queens as I could imagine myself. I had sent a dorm deposit. Once out there, I would fulfill my destiny as a novelist, either starving on the beach because my fiction was too avant-garde or luxuriating by the side of my pool because I had sold out. Both scenarios involved dangerous women. I was an English major.

But I needed a summer job to raise cash for the trip. When the water truck job fell through—it was canceled, I think, for lack of funding—I bought my first copy of *The New York Times*. I'd heard the paper had good classified ads and quickly found one for "editorial assistant" at the *Times* itself.

The personnel people at the *Times* were pleasant enough when I showed up at West Forty-third Street that June morning, but patronizing. These jobs are extremely coveted, they said, because you assist *New York Times reporters and editors*. You get to share their air. It sounded as though I were applying to be a squire for King Arthur's Knights of the Round Table. One of my interviewers waved toward the invisible line of Rhodes Scholars, Fulbright Scholars, and Ph.D.

candidates waiting for a job and implied that my B.A. was a dime a dozen. But my last interviewer suggested I fill out an application anyway. Who knows? Something might come up in a few months. I almost didn't bother since I would be going west in a few months. But I was a polite boy then, and I filled it out.

I went a block south to seedy old Forty-second Street and saw a cowboy double-feature. I loved Westerns. When I was a kid, my dad and I went to a shoot-'em-up every Tuesday night in the summertime, and the Lone Ranger has been a role model of mine since childhood. He protected weaker people by beating up bullies without becoming a bully himself. (I still love Westerns. In some ways, I think, sports have replaced Westerns and jocks have replaced gunslingers in our national imagination, not necessarily to our advantage.)

After the movies, I took the subway to Rego Park. I had moved back home after graduation. My mother looked up from the stove to say, "You got a crank call, Bobby. A man said if you show up tomorrow and pass a physical, you can start work immediately at *The New York Times*."

The physical consisted of showing up.

That "editorial assistant" job was copyboy in the sports department. It seemed like an odd place for me, and I wondered if I could handle it. I didn't know much about sports. A fat boy growing up, I didn't even start playing sports seriously until I was in my teens. My dad was no fan; we never talked sports at home. I was, at best, a casual fan, enough to understand what my friends were talking about. (I actually didn't become a fan until I left daily sportswriting for the first time in 1971 and could watch a game without having to think about covering it.) And not only had I never read the *Times* sports pages, I had barely read the *Times* at all. (My parents, being public school teachers, got the *New York World-Telegram & Sun*, which had an education page.) But I needed a job.

My shift was 7 P.M. to 3 A.M. My nights off were Tuesday and Wednesday. My first night on the job, I almost stopped the presses.

The copyboy who broke me in was in a hurry to get out for a long dinner break at Gough's, the bar across the street, to talk sports with the printers and pressmen. What he was supposed to train me to do was simple enough: hover near the copydesk—actually a dozen dirty blond cigarette-charred wooden desks lined up so the cranky old bullies could face each other and chuckle as they butchered reporters' stories—until one of them yelled "Boy!" This could be a call to get coffee, sharpen pencils, refill pots of library paste, or, most important, snatch a page of edited copy, roll it up, snap on a rubber band, and slip it into a plastic-and-leather canister that would be launched like a mortar round up a metal pipe in the pneumatic system to the fourth floor, where it would pop out of the pipe and thump into a rubber well. Someone would unsnap the leather strap of the canister, pluck out the copy, and hand it to a Linotype operator, who would turn it into lines of hot metal type to be fitted into the frames of printing press pages on huge stone tables.

Whether it was a failure of communication in the five-minute training session or, more likely, one of my enduring techno screwups, I skipped the stage in which I was supposed to slip the copy into the canister. I slipped the rolled-up paper directly into the sucking mouth of the hydraulic pipe. There was a whoosh, and the lid of the pipe snapped shut.

After a while, the sports makeup man on the fourth floor began phoning down: *"Where's the fucking copy?"* The head of the sports copydesk screamed back, *"Look up your ass!"* This was common, but the long absence of copy was not. As deadline approached, someone thought to check the system, actually put an arm up the pipe. It was lined with paper. Most of that night's sports report was stuck in transit.

Had it happened a few minutes later, they might have had to stop the presses or release part of the first edition with no sports section. Small loss, I say in retrospect, but unthinkable then (not unthinkable now, of course, when the *Times* apparently has toyed with the idea of further downsizing the sports report, even dropping the section entirely, as did the *Washington Times*, to save money). With the exception of Gay Talese's pieces, the *Times* sports section in 1957 was at best mediocre, perhaps by design. The editorial side of the *Times* seemed faintly embarrassed by sports, although Business appreciated the car and boat ads it anchored, and everybody enjoyed the free tickets that flowed in. A survey later revealed that *Times* readers interested in sports took a second paper, usually the *New York Post* or the *Daily News*, to satisfy their jock jones.

But on my first night, the pipes were jammed with the faux Homeric mythmaking of rosy-fingered Arthur Daley, the "Sports of the *Times*" columnist; the plodding game detail of the ambassadors to baseball, John Drebinger, Roscoe McGowen, and Louis Effrat; John Rendel's yacht-racing stories with their long tails of agate-type results; and the symphonic tennis summaries of the courtly Allison Danzig. All were respected students of their games, all were determinedly dulled down in the style of the *Times*. Years later, writing feature sidebars to Danzig's coverage, I was impressed (and, yes, proud) at how tennis stars lined up at the press table after their matches to respectfully ask what *Mister* Danzig had observed and how well or poorly they had played.

But that first night at the *Times*, I was made to feel as though I had almost let the only illuminated pages of Genesis slip out of my hands into a fire.

The hydraulic system was shut down until the pages, some still rolled, tumbled and fluttered back into the sports department. I stood there dumbly as the deskmen glanced at me, rolled their eyes, and shook their heads. Smirking, one of them, with exaggerated movements, filled the canisters and fired them upstairs. They chuckled, then asked me if I understood what I had done, how close we had come.

I felt like crying, but didn't know how anymore. I was nineteen. Should I walk out into the night right now or wait to quit until the other copyboy returned?

I'm not sure why I decided to wait. It was not as if this were going to be the start of a career. Was it because I thought it was the right thing to do or I wanted to hang tough or I was frozen in place? After the other copyboy returned, I decided to finish my shift because I didn't want to slink off. The next day I decided to go back because I didn't want to let the bullies win. All night I had brooded over that deskman's smirk and his elaborate gestures. I went back that next night with a stony look and my fists in my pockets. No one mentioned the incident that night or ever again. Old news.

Fifty-three years later, time contracts. The humiliation of that first night is more vivid than today's breakfast. And the lesson as well. Don't quit. Gut it out. Try to hold on till the buzzer. It will work out, somehow.

Doggedness was the first of many lessons I learned as I began, accidentally, my career. I'm sure I would have learned many of them as a doctor (in my mother's dreams) or as a college professor (my dad's). Mine came from a lifetime ducking into and out of locker rooms chasing Muhammad Ali, Mickey Mantle, Billie Jean King, myself, and, ultimately, my dad.

In the protective environment of the *Times*, in those days more powerful than most of the sports organizations the *Times* covered, I got the chance to develop a distinctive voice that has drawn supportive fans and furious critics. Some thought I was a clear voice of reason, some thought I was a clueless contrarian. The label *cynic* often cropped up; I saw myself as a *skeptic*. I came to despise the common practice, in the great sports editor Stanley Woodward's term, of "godding up" the ballplayers.

Some in friendly fashion (Bob Costas, Dick Schaap), some not, wondered why I couldn't kick back and enjoy the games. Why couldn't I appreciate the joy? Why couldn't I accept these accomplished men and women in sports as my heroes? Why did my work have to be so relentlessly political? (At first, perhaps defensively, I would try to trace that question back to the discussions about social justice at my parents' dinner table. Then I thought—now I always think—why isn't everyone else's work more political?)

The question begs, Bobby: *What held you in sports for so long, and what kept bringing you back?*

For starters, I fell in love—with the paper. Though I never liked the copyboy job or the grumblies on the desk, I came to love the *Times*, especially at 9 P.M., when the giant presses in the subbasement roared to life with the first edition. More than fifty years later, the hot-type presses long scrapped, the paper now housed in a glass skyscraper a few blocks south of the Disneyfied Times Square, I can feel the old building shuddering in its nightly rebirth. When the tremors reached the sports department on the third floor, I could feel them in my loins. Maybe it helped to have read too much Romantic English poetry, but I felt connected to something grand and important. I had dabbled in journalism as an ironical columnist for the Forest Hills High School *Beacon* and as a lackluster reporter for Columbia's *Daily Spectator*, which I quit, bored, after a year or so. Truth was in the sweep of fiction, I thought, not in a string of little facts. But at the *Times*, there was a sense of mission to find the Truth.

There were heroes at the *Times* who had that calling, role models you could actually talk to: the great war and civil rights reporter Homer Bigart; the artistic, compassionate cityside columnist Meyer Berger; the bold foreign correspondents Harrison Salisbury, David Halberstam, and Gloria Emerson. There was also Charlotte Curtis, whose incisive, witty dispatches on society and fashion transformed the style pages; she proved you could make your points and launch a big-league career from a *Times* department that was considered secondary to Foreign or National. Her example certainly helped me. I rejected offers to move to other departments at the paper or to the Washington or Tokyo bureau.

There could be no denying, even if not always understanding, sports' hold on me. It was heady to interview my heroes' heroes ("What's Yogi Berra really like?" Halberstam asked me) and attend the front-page games and fights. But after a few years, that was no longer glamorous. Other people's envy of my job wasn't enough. I'm still figuring out how much of what kept me on the job was the pull of sporting events themselves and how much was the perspective that sports gave me on the larger world. I could enjoy the Kentucky Derby, for example, as a great horse race, a splendid party, and a vignette of Americana only the first couple of times I covered it before issues of class, race, and equine exploitation became impossible to ignore. The first two Super Bowls I covered (II and III) were bang-up football games. What fun I had, drinking with Coach Vince Lombardi, hanging out with Joe Namath, meeting sportswriters from all over the country! But after that, the glorification of real and symbolic violence in a time of war, the corporate involvement, and the defining of manhood through the game seemed at least as compelling as the play-by-play.

Eventually, in all the events I covered, I began to perceive the shape of a social infrastructure that at first I called SportsWorld, now Jock Culture, because it is based on a model of manhood in the arena and it extends into business, politics, and family life. I'm more and more convinced that Jock Culture is a defining strand in American life and has helped create many of its values—positive ones such as hard work, bravery, and fellowship, as well as negative ones such as intimidation, domination, and cheating to win. In Jock Culture, the opponent must be beaten but ultimately respected. Contempt is reserved for those who are not of the team, not one of the righteous, focused, disciplined insiders who play or cheerlead or comfort or boost. Contempt is reserved for the Outsiders, the nerds, wimps, burnouts, band fags. The English majors.

In this company of men, male sportswriters are honorary jocks, their manhood certified by their locker room access (which has been diminishing for years). At first I preened in my faux jockhood, but that got harder when I realized that what we did was hardly manly, sniffing around athletes for news crumbs, boosting them when they were winning, kicking them when they were down, dismissing them when they no longer mattered for our stories, meanwhile convincing ourselves and others that the outcomes of games were important. The games *are* important, as Jock Culture dramas, as signifiers of a time, as definers of values. The scores aren't important.

As an ambitious sportswriter on a major-league paper, I acted like a jock in pursuit of victory, which in my case meant filing the best story. Yet I felt like an outsider among most of my subjects and even some of my colleagues. I rarely cared who won or lost, except for how it affected my travel plans or the drama of my story.

Covering orchestrated commercial spectaculars such as the Final Four college basketball tournament, I felt I was wasting my life. Covering the political and racial aspects of Muhammad Ali or the paradoxes of Sandinista baseball in Nicaragua, I felt like a real reporter. Once I became a columnist in 1967, ten years after the happy accident, the job became a lot more fun. Not only could I express my own growing opinions, I could follow stories off the beaten track—lacrosse on an Indian reservation, a youth league in Brooklyn, gay athletes coming out. Even while covering the mainstream events I could filter the story through my own developing sensibility. Sometimes I tried too hard and became tiresome and didactic. But I couldn't help myself. At the Olympics, at the World Series, at the heavyweight championships, I kept looking for a story beneath the story, always sure that if I found it I would be able to enlarge my own and my readers' understanding of our world.

I never understood until I began to write this book that sports would also reveal my own story to me. And maybe that was what I was looking for all along.

Sports helped confirm my sense of myself as an outsider, a lurker in the shadows, a spy gathering intelligence in an alien world for people who want to know the truth. "That's pretty gaudy," as Jim Roach, the sports editor who nurtured my early *Times* career, would describe the most overheated of my most painfully know-it-all prose. But outsider was the way I had come to feel as a fat kid, and as a sportswriter. I also thought of myself as smarter and a better writer than my colleagues, free to leave for higher pastures when I felt my mission of wringing truth from the locker room was completed.

Because of this sanctimonious attitude, I knew, I would never be a universally beloved scribe. In the 1960s, after I wrote about boxing's cynical use of racial and ethnic rivalries to boost the box office, Madison Square Garden demanded that the *Times* take me off the beat. I was thrilled and thought of President John F. Kennedy demanding that the *Times* bring Halberstam home from Vietnam—his boots-on-the-ground reporting was giving the lie to the generals' falsely optimistic press conferences. I didn't equate my judgmental stories with David's brave dispatches, but the Garden's reaction confirmed my belief that there was a calling in sports journalism.

(Forty-odd years later, in 2008, I had a welcome flashback when the Professional Golfers' Association of America mounted a campaign to have me removed from *USA Today*'s Board of Op-Ed Contributors. I had written what I thought was a somewhat tongue-in-cheek piece about the Masters tournament being "all that's retrograde in American life." Fortunately, *USA Today*, as had the *Times*, seemed gratified by the attention.)

I wonder now if that outsider armor was something I wore as

psychic protection in the planet of the jocks. Or did I stay a sportswriter because I felt more comfortable as an outsider?

In 1971, I left the *Times* to write fiction. After twenty years that also included television journalism, screenplays, and young adult novels, all unforeseen opportunities, I was called back to the paper. Joseph Lelyveld was about to become the executive editor and Neil Amdur, another friend, the sports editor. They wanted an edgy voice among the columns. That was 1991, and I thought I'd write the column for a year or two, tops. Another summer job. But I fell in love with the *Times* all over again and was entranced anew by the looking glass of sports. That time, the summer job lasted twelve years and ended with another lesson in Jock Culture.

In the summer of 2001, soon after he was named executive editor, Howell Raines invited the sports department upstairs to an executive dining room for lunch. He contemptuously dismissed the Lelyveld administration ("wussies" was the implicit criticism) and promised a new era of hard-driving, zone-flooding, competitive tension in which he would run the paper the way Coach Bear Bryant had run the University of Alabama football team. College sports, he said, was the mortar that held America together.

Being sportswriters, we assumed that this Coach Bullfrog was merely trying to out-jock us. Sportswriters are used to that, and, like jocks, we tend to offer sly servility to alpha males. We were wrong. Raines was serious. He was ruthless, capricious, and inaccessible, and for all his micromanaging, he was careless. Maybe he was scared, in over his head. He ignored warnings about a young reporter, Jayson Blair, who was ultimately fired for plagiarisms and fabrications. Using that as a weapon, the newsroom rose up and drove Raines out of the arena. But not before he got me. At the end of 2002, Raines, who may have felt personally defied by my columns on the corruption of college football, refused to renew my thirteenth consecutive annual contract. Hurt and angry, but not surprised, I slinked off.

Less than six months after I left, right after Raines was fired, Lelyveld returned as interim coach and the *Times* sent me a new contract. I never signed it. I had moved on again, back to young adult fiction and TV, ahead to online sportswriting. But I never stopped thinking about Jock Culture and manhood, about the psychosocial-political aspect of games, and about the people, most of them subjects, whose stories had informed my career and my life. Their stories begat my story.

Sixty years later, we still meet a few times a year. I'm in the third row, seventh from the left.

ONE | My Bully

At Stephen A. Halsey Junior High School 157 in Rego Park, Queens, New York City, I belonged to a group that was a bully magnet. We were members of the Special Progress (S.P.) class, selected for our above-average IQ scores (120 was supposedly the threshold), a fact we flaunted like a varsity letter. Not only were we smarter, but we were too cool for this school; we would leave for high school after completing the three-year curriculum in two. There were some good athletes among us, but we were clearly nerds.

We were easy to spot. We moved from class to class in a clump and were individually identified by heavy brown leather briefcases filled with books. The non-S.P. boys called our briefcases "fag bags" and tried to kick them out of our hands. They also shouldered us in the halls and pushed us around on the streets.

There were ways to minimize the damage. Most S.P. boys kept their mouths shut and heads down when the bullies called them "fag." I thought that was giving in to them. You could also join them. One of my S.P. classmates was notorious for holding their jackets while they beat us up. He went on to become a famous television executive. (Twenty-five years later, when I worked on a show under his supervision, he turned away when he reached me in a group waiting to shake his hand. I had his number, which did me no good.)

I became a particular target of the bullies because I compulsively talked back and was too fat to run away afterward. My weight has always been higher than my IQ.

I hated getting beaten up, hated having friends, especially the girls, be sorry for me, hated feeling my scabs harden and my insides shrivel, but it seemed preferable to giving in or sucking up or hiding. I don't think I was principled. I just couldn't help myself from sneering back at them when they kicked my bag or pushed me down or called me "Lippy" or "Lippo the Hippo." I couldn't stop myself from making some asinine retort and then trying ineffectually to defend myself. What a fag!

Though the school tended to separate us from the general student population, it didn't protect us. The principal of the school, Dr. Nussey, who taught Latin to the S.P. class and ran the schoolwide softball tournament, apparently believed in survival of the fittest. He would allow a little roughhouse as long as his own authority wasn't challenged. Boys will be boys.

Our S.P. homeroom teacher, Mrs. McDermott, made an effort to stop fights before we were hurt, but she couldn't be everywhere. The school enforcers, the beefy gym and shop teachers, would wait until the fight was nearly over, then peel the bullies off their victims and boot them down the street in a tough, humorous way that did nothing to condemn the ritual—in fact, probably reinforced it. The bullies loved the attention, the contact with bully teachers. They would posture while we slunk away.

The conventional wisdom in those days, dispensed by older friends and relatives, was that bullies would back down if you stood up to them, that they were basically cowards. This was not true. I think I sensed even then that fighting back was about finding out that the beating was bearable, that bullies couldn't kill you. Simply by standing up to them and surviving, you won a small victory that would give you the courage to keep challenging, to keep standing up, until they eventually left you alone and went after easier prey. Or, less likely but always possible, you could actually win.

Nowadays, when a bully may be packing a gun or a knife (or crouched in ambush behind a computer), the conventional wisdom is very different. Run, or return to school with an AK-47 and wipe out the cafeteria. I wrote a *Times* column suggesting that the arrogant, entitled behavior of high school athletes, encouraged by the adults who lived vicariously through their overhyped deeds, had created an everlasting divide between bullies and victims, often jocks and nerds.

The response was overwhelming, thoughtful, and sometimes emotional, mostly from middle-aged men who remembered high school with pain and in some cases guilt. There were hundreds of letters, calls, and e-mails. Two typical examples:

When I attended high school, I had so much built-up anger from being treated unfairly that, if I had access to guns or explosives, I would have been driven to do a similar thing to take revenge on the Italian and Irish white bastard jocks who dominated the school and made those 4 years miserable for me. After high school, I was not surprised to hear that a handful of these jocks had either died as a result of drunk driving and drug overdoses, or had spent a little time in jail for violence or drug possession. As for the dead ones, I would probably pee on their graves.

and

We really did get special attention both from the students, and from the teachers. We also did cruel things to other students. I have a 20th school anniversary this summer and plan on seeking forgiveness from the people I know I helped terrorize.

In the late 1940s and early '50s, the Halsey bullies, whom we called "hoods," affected outlaw garb such as dungarees, muscle T-shirts, and leather jackets, but in our striver neighborhood they weren't even petty criminals. They tended to be the better schoolyard athletes—bigger, stronger, quicker, more aggressive, more excited by the chance to intimidate. Those who went on to organized contact sports would be encouraged in those traits. That never changed.

Nor did the tone of language. In Halsey days, the killer word "fag" had less of a homosexual connotation than one of "sissy" or, worse, "girl." As we were taught to believe in the fifties, most women had no consequential professional futures; they might become teachers or even writers, but they would never get to do genuine men's work such as fly fighter planes, build bridges, kill bad guys, throw touchdowns. Fags wouldn't get that chance either.

That wasn't merely schoolyard talk. A book published in 1939, *You and Heredity*, by Amram Scheinfeld, had a chart that measured masculinity by your line of work. The top of the chart drummed with test pilots, engineers, explorers, pro athletes. On the bottom, clearly my future neighborhood, were clergymen, teachers, librarians, and writers.

By the time I found that chart, I knew I was going to be a writer because a writer could sit alone in a corner and control his universe, *create* his universe, by making up stories. In the stories I wrote in junior high school, skinny kids tended to die horribly. My dream was to publish a story in *Forest Trails*, Halsey's mimeographed literary magazine. The girl I adored from afar, Myriam, was the editor. She was brilliant and beautiful and had a French accent; I knew my only chance with girls like her would be as a star writer.

But writers, according to *You and Heredity*, were at the bottom of the masculinity chart.

I had found the book on one of the biweekly trips I took with Dad to the big Queens regional library. Dad and I, and later my sister, Gale, who is seven years younger than I, went to libraries the way other kids and their dads went to ball games. Dad never censored our choices, and he allowed us to check out as many books as we could carry. I'd been snooping in the Science section for a book with pictures of naked women and found instead that masculinity chart. I couldn't even discuss the chart with Dad because he was a schoolteacher. I didn't want to make him feel bad.

Now, of course, I wish I had. He could have taken it. I would have learned something. Maybe I was less concerned about his feelings than about appearing soft and weak to him. I saw Dad as a tough guy. He may have loved to read philosophy, but his career—from middle school English teacher through principal to director of the city's several dozen schools for troubled kids—had been in rough neighborhoods bristling with switchblades and zip guns. He usually worked several jobs at a time. That's how he managed to get us to an apartment in a comfortable, safe Queens neighborhood, afford a weekend house in upstate New York, and send me to Columbia University and my sister to the University of Wisconsin. My mother was a teacher and guidance counselor, but she subordinated her own career to his. For years she was a stay-at-home mom, which was conventional then, but she still chafed at the role. They had met in the early thirties as lab partners while taking master's degrees in psychology at Columbia. Both of them harbored literary ambitions. The house was crammed with books. They read voraciously and encouraged me to read and write.

For such a bookish boy, *You and Heredity* was a psychic land mine. It blew me sideways. Years later, from photos and eyewitness accounts, I figured out I was nowhere near as fat as I thought I was. But that book was there, and so were the bullies.

My worst tormentor, my regular bully, was Willie, who had staked me out in elementary school and followed me to Halsey. At P.S. 139, teachers had been alert to predatory kids, and because I lived near school I could waddle home while Willie was being detained for questioning and then bury my shame in peanut butter sandwiches, Hydrox cookies, Three Musketeers candy bars, and a glass of chocolate milk.

But in the laissez-faire atmosphere at Halsey, where Willie found support among other fag bag kickers, I didn't stand a chance. At least once a week, he found me and pushed me around. Nothing that I ever reported or complained about—at worst a bruise, a little blood, a pocket torn off a shirt—but plenty to feel bad about. Willie may have been a pathetic dork who had found a scapegoat for his unhappiness, but at the time, he was Grendel and I was no Beowulf. I was a fat kid trapped at the bottom of the masculinity chart.

It was a book, of course, that sprang me loose.

After I returned *You and Heredity*, I began trolling in sections of the library I had rarely visited. It was some weeks later in Travel that I was drawn to the blue cover of *The Royal Road to Romance*, by the adventure travel writer Richard Halliburton. The book, a best seller, was published in 1925, when Halliburton was twenty-five, a slim little Princeton grad, apparently gay (an authentic fag!), who disappeared at sea at thirty-nine.

In rereading Halliburton recently, I realized he could be accused of being an imperialist and Orientalist, condescending toward women and indigenous folk, not to mention an extreme tall-tale teller, but when I was twelve, when it mattered, his energy and enthusiasm lifted my spirit. This was no writer you could keep at the bottom of your masculinity chart. He climbed mountains, stowed away on freighters, hunted man-eating tigers. It was easy to imagine him swimming across crocodile-infested waters with his typewriter strapped to his back and a knife in his teeth. He'd carve up anything that tried to stop him. And then he'd write about it.

Even then, I didn't totally buy his stories, and eventually they seemed as spurious in their way as that masculinity chart. But all I knew in 1950 and all I needed to know was that his stories filled me with possibility.

When I finally returned *The Royal Road to Romance* several months later—I kept renewing it, and it often traveled in my fag bag—I swaggered past Science and flipped *You and Heredity* the bird. Just try to put Richard Halliburton at the bottom of your chart. He'll carve his way to the top. And I'll be right behind him.

Richard and Bobby are on their way, bullies. Watch out! Someday...

And then the day arrived.

It seemed no different from any other day. The S.P. class was coming out of school at three o'clock with the usual mixed feelings. School was over, which was supposed to be a liberation, but school was where most of us found an intellectual arena and a sanctuary from the less forgiving world of the street.

Outside Halsey, the hoods capered around us, kicking at bags, calling us names. My bully Willie found me and said something routinely stupid. As usual, my smart-aleck reply made the other hoods laugh. Willie pushed me. I stood my ground and sneered at him. Willie kicked my bag out of my hand.

And then—was it because Rose and Barbara, two girls I especially liked, were watching, because my hand really hurt this time, because Richard Halliburton had truly given me hope?—I snapped.

I hurled myself at Willie, just launched all that butterfat, double blubber, right into him. I was a rotund rocket of rage. We both went down, and, incredibly, I was on top. Had I known the rules of engagement of the after-school fight, I would have sat on his stomach and slapped him until he cried uncle or he would have thrown me off and beat me up yet again.

But how could I, who had never had a fair fight, know the rules? There were no rules in my mind, just survival and payback. All in or don't bother.

I jammed my fat knees down into his chest until his lungs were bursting for air. I grabbed fistfuls of his greasy hair and yanked until he began screaming, and then I began to bash his brains in. Literally. I bounced his skull on the cold gray sidewalk as if it were a pink rubber ball.

I smile as I write this.

What release, what joy, what an out-of-body experience!

I never heard Mrs. McDermott screaming "Robert! You'll hurt him!" because I was bellowing "I'm gonna kill you!" and my friends were cheering and Willie was crying and the hoods clapped. Then a shop teacher peeled me off and laughed as he put a steel-tipped toe in my rear. Dr. Nussey grabbed me and hustled me away. I thought he was trying not to smile.

I kept looking back over my shoulder. A kid was lying on the ground. Where was the bully? My fury had clouded the moment. It took days and the accounts of my friends before I pictured what had happened and a long time before I understood it. Of course, Willie never bothered me again. Nobody at Halsey or high school ever did. Sometimes even now, when I'm taking a beating, hard times, chemo, a death, when scabs harden and my insides shrivel, I think of Willie. His memory reminds me that I survived then, I can survive now.

That same year at Halsey, my short story "Planetary War" appeared in *Forest Trails*. I was a published writer! It's hard to say which was the more important defining event. Three years later, as an unfat high school junior, I screwed up the courage to ask Myriam, by now the editor of *Forest Leaves*, Forest Hills High School's glossy literary magazine, to a school play and pizza. It was my first date.

The relationship with Myriam didn't take, but my relationship with Willie has been sustaining. My bully lives forever in a little room in my mind, which I visit whenever I need to remember that every so often you have to go up against the Beast.

My Special Progress class is still in session, mostly through a Yahoo! group (I started a Facebook group but just can't seem to recruit too many of those old folks), and we get together at least once or twice a year for lunches and dinners in Manhattan. There have been reunions in Santa Fe, Washington, D.C., and London, hosted by classmates who live there, and someday we hope to meet in Rio de Janeiro or South Beach because one classmate, Teddy, lives in both places. Teddy, a dentist, left his wife and kids some years ago, came out of the closet, and ran off with a Brazilian heavy metal drummer whose band he manages. He's up for introducing his old and new lives. Some of us have stayed young.

So there are ample opportunities for me to interrogate witnesses about me.

Paul Stolley, M.D., draws a blank. He's a prominent epidemiologist and public health activist (Google him yourself, this is my book) but I remember Paul as the fourteen-year-old classmate who taught me to throw like a boy. I had just returned to Rego Park from a summer upstate, cutting lawns, during which I think I lost at least 40 pounds (I always jumped off the scale as the little black dagger headed toward 200), and Paul was the first person who spotted me in the schoolyard. In delight, he cried out, "Hey, fatty," a name he had never called me when it fit. I was thrilled. He threw me a ball. I threw it back. He shook his head and hurried over to demonstrate how to bring the ball behind my head before I let it go. That's all there was to not throwing like a girl, he said. Then I threw it like a boy, he smiled, and we played catch. It was the late start of my athletic career, such as it is.

Fifty-seven years later, in 2009, I recounted that story to Paul. He liked it but wondered if it was a self-defining myth. *Scientist.* Did he remember how fat I'd been? He shook his head. What about Willy? He shrugged. Didn't remember him.

The two girls who inspired my triumphant battle, both of whom I later briefly dated, Rose Ballenzweig and Barbara Rosenberg, are dead. In fact, it was at lunch after Rose's funeral in the spring of 2009, with the former Marcia Dollin, Anne Kanfer, and Doris Kameny, that I maneuvered a conversation about the addictive cupcakes from Shelley's, the bakery owned and run by Rose's family, to my belly and my bully.

The three women looked at me.

You weren't that fat, they said. You were bullied?

Willie, I said. But I can't remember his last name.

They looked blank. They didn't know his first name.

On the long drive home, I thought about that fight with Willie. Didn't everyone know about it? It was Hector and Achilles, Beowulf and Grendel's mother, Ali and Frazier.

I'm a reporter, I could find Willie. So I made some phone calls, sent some e-mails, Googled and Facebooked. No Willie.

So for now I'll just keep Willie in his little room in my mind until I need him again. I'm sure I will.

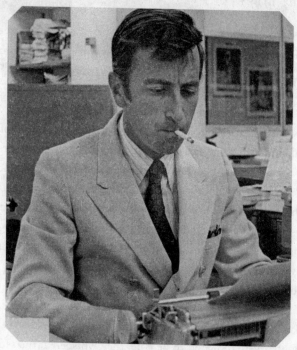

How could Gay, here at twenty-five, not be my idol? His ash will never fall. (Courtesy of Gay Talese)

TWO | The Piper

When I was twenty-five," wrote my idol Gay Talese of his early *New York Times* career, "I was chasing stray cats around Manhattan. . . . The year was 1957."

When I was nineteen, in 1957, I was chasing Gay Talese. I was a copyboy in the *Times* sports department, and Gay was a sports reporter whose feature stories were turning the so-called Old Gray Lady into Technicolor. He was showing the style that would make him the most influential of the so-called New Journalists of the sixties. He would soon write for *Esquire* what is considered the quintessential celebrity magazine article, "Frank Sinatra Has a Cold," and publish such best sellers as *The Kingdom and the Power*, about the *Times*, and *Honor Thy Father*, about a Mafia family.

You could learn from him, I thought; actually, I started out by slavishly imitating him, not only trying to write in his cadences but to observe as he did, being totally open to the half hidden and the unexpected, then stringing the precise details into elegant loops. I thought that his choice of subject—the forgotten, the ignored, the loser—was the closest a newspaperman could come to being John Steinbeck or Ernest Hemingway or Anton Chekhov, my youthful literary heroes. Gay used the grand sweep of fiction to string little facts to tell true short stories.

Not everyone felt that way. Some *Times* deskmen sneered that Gay had "piped" his stories—exaggerated if not fictionalized them. The quotes were too good to be true, they whispered, the settings too descriptive to be accurate. In the fading slang of the day, his stories had been puffed out of a dreamer's opium pipe. But they let him get away with it at the *Times* Sunday magazine and especially in sports, the only section where Mr., Mrs., and Miss were not required to be used on second reference (sports figures along with convicted felons were denied the respect of everyday honorifics). It was the right time to be in the *Times'* toy department.

And there I was in a job I mostly despised except for the stolen moments at Gay's desk. He listened to my complaints, read my stories, and encouraged me to use the slack periods in my late shifts to rummage in the newspaper's archival "morgue" for ideas, make long-distance calls on *Times* phones, and scope out "the sergeants and colonels who run this place."

He liked me, he told me in 2009, because I was "polite, smart, obviously brought up by educated parents." A former copyboy himself, Gay was always on the lookout, he said, for kids coming up. He identified me and Joe Lelyveld, the future editor of the paper, as "hot prospects."

Gay was remarkably generous with his time—he was never brusque, even on deadline—and with his advice, which I still use: keep all phone numbers (write them in pencil so you can change them easily); research your subject thoroughly; ask unusual questions, always including "Why is that?"; and rewrite, rewrite, rewrite. Then polish. And fight those bastard copyreaders (they weren't yet called "staff editors") for every word. Lelyveld recalls Gay's admonition to stay off page one, where the full weight of the *Times* stylebook could crush a lively story. A good writer, said Gay, will be discovered wherever he shows up in the paper.

Slim, handsome, friendly, impeccably be-suited by his New Jersey tailor father, Gay had been a *Times* copyboy after the University of Alabama (the only college he could get into and then with strings pulled by one of his father's customers). He had returned from the army to be a reporter in sports. He was simply too handsome, glamorous, and well dressed for the old grumblies and easy to dismiss as a "piper." New Jersey? Alabama? Despite a hierarchy of southern-born editors and City College (or no-college) reporters, the *Times* considered itself an Ivy League paper.

Gay often pulled night rewrite, and in those quiet hours he would expound: find a character through which to tell your tale with anecdotes, revealing quotes, and detail. I would stand at his desk as he leaned back in his chair, sipping at the paper container of cocoa I had brought him from a deli. He was very particular about that. "I don't want hot chocolate, Bob, that's powder and water, I want milk, and this is how you tell them it should be cooked." He wrote the same way, slowly, precisely, painfully. (He would say later that writing was like passing kidney stones.)

Fetching Gay's cocoa and the tutorials that followed were the highlights in a time of increasing frustration. I was a copyboy for almost two years, not an unusually long squirehood in those days, but I despised most of the cranky deskmen and their bullying. And I was tired. The first year I took graduate courses at Columbia in English lit. They were boring. The second year I went to Columbia's graduate school of journalism, which was lively enough, but writing standard who-what-where-when-why pieces on assignment for a bogus school newspaper seemed absurd; I already had an entry-level job at the world's greatest paper. As a student of the Talese School, I wrote leads that were often rejected by the J School teachers. I barely graduated. My final paper, about discrimination in broadcast journalism, was not considered newsy enough. It was also not very good. School was roughly nine to five, my job was seven to three. I also got married in there somewhere when two sets of parents applied the screws because Maria Glaser and I, both twenty-one, were living together, which was rare in those days. Maria was a part-time student at Columbia and worked in a doctor's office. The marriage lasted five years.

On Saturdays and Sundays before my copyboy shift, I covered sermons at $5 each for the Religion Desk, one way of getting into the paper. I became adept at making notes under my prayer shawl in Orthodox synagogues. Church sermons were easier to cover because priests and ministers would not only give me their texts in advance but discuss them afterward in the rectory over Scotch.

That first year, 1957, was a traumatic one in New York sports, and in sports departments. At season's end, the Dodgers and Giants moved to California, and though that made the pastime truly national, it upended the original order. New York suddenly had one major-league baseball team instead of three (fewer than Chicago!), and the sports section had a lot of vacant space for high school sports, fencing, harness racing. And feature stories. The rigid old sports editor, a former Latin teacher, was replaced by Jim Roach, the

Thoroughbred racing writer, a warm, lively, innovative editor who could calm cantankerous deskmen and ambitious reporters alike with his standard "Hey, we're trying to run the Fair Shake Athletic Club around here."

Even before his official appointment, Jim Roach was instrumental in sending Gay to Arizona to cover the Giants' first spring training as San Francisco's new team. Gay raised the mark for spring training coverage, wrapping the statistics and meaningless game detail inside feature stories. He found desperate rookies and sage old-timers ready to talk about their need for "security" in their lives and chronicled a new "gray-flannel-suit" generation that subscribed to *The Wall Street Journal* and wouldn't spike their mother even if she was rounding third with the winning run. Willie Mays, at twenty-six the "180-pound package of rare tenderloin," told Gay, "I'm changing from a kid to a man." This was all new. Gay was modern and funny without being snide. I'd rush into the wire room to get his incoming copy, then walk slowly back, reading it. He was the only *Times* sportswriter we ran to read with the same anticipation we had for Red Smith of the *New York Herald Tribune*.

One story Gay didn't write, but told me about on his return, was his amazement with his fellow scribes. A tall, messy sportswriter from the tabloid *Daily Mirror* would often show up drunk for games; a short, dapper sportswriter from the *Daily News*, his archrival, would write his story for him. What happened to competition? asked Gay. He would laugh and shake his head. Which story was better? How could you not write your best?

Even with Gay around, the nights at the *Times* were getting longer and I was more tired and frustrated. And then one night of snarling deskmen and lonely calls from Maria and no time to finish a feature story for a J School newspaper that no one would read, I brought Gay his cocoa and told him I was quitting.

"Why is that?" he asked. Just like an interview.

I spilled it out, and he sipped and nodded, no judgment. He said he understood but he thought it would be a mistake. I should stay. He told me that I had talent and would make it at the *Times*. I was exactly what the paper was looking for. But if I was determined to leave, he had a proposition.

He spoke very precisely. "Bob, I will give you five thousand dollars in exchange for ten percent of your earnings as a freelance writer for the next ten years."

I lost my breath. I was making $35 a week. He was offering me nearly three times my annual salary. He believed in me.

"You serious?"

"It's a good investment for me. You think about it."

Of course, it was all I thought about for days. I wasn't totally sure that he was serious (Maria didn't think he was), but he lifted my spirit as surely as Richard Halliburton had once done.

He gave me the confidence to soldier on. By the time I graduated from J School in 1959, I was a clerk, a step up from copyboy, handling standings and statistics. In the fall of that year, soon after Gay was transferred out of sports for a short-lived political beat that seemed almost disciplinary, I was promoted, at twenty-one, to reporter—knighthood.

I eventually became Gay's heir to jazzy features, sidebars to big stories, top assignments that required, as he characterized my work in *The Power and the Glory*, "a smooth literary touch." (That was all he wrote about me in all those hundreds of pages. I was hurt at the time.)

I'm always nervous before making the initial contact on a story. I keep telling myself that butterflies let me know I'm ready for something worth doing. But I couldn't understand why the thought of calling up Gay Talese made me so edgy. This was a courteous and generous man.

But you've hardly had anything to do with him in forty-odd years, Bobby, and he's important to you. You don't want to be rejected, fat boy.

Gay's very busy. I might catch him at a bad time.

So I sent him a letter and he called me as soon as he received it, inviting me right over, and there I was in his house on East Sixty-first Street. The last time I had been there was in 1964, after David Halberstam's Pulitzer Prize for his Vietnam coverage was announced. David, Gay, and I had take-out hamburgers before the party. I tried to get David, recently returned from Vietnam, to tell me what that country's infamous Dragon Lady, Madame Nhu, was really like, but he was interested in what I knew about the Yankees. Gay seemed delighted by the exchange.

Gay was basically unchanged: slim, handsome, glamorous in brown-and-tan shoes, brown slacks, a herringbone jacket over a brown suede vest, striped shirt, and orange tie. He wasn't even going anywhere. He was not dressed up, merely dressed.

He made me at ease immediately, had me sit on a worn brown leather couch. He sat in its twin, set perpendicular to mine. We faced each other sideways. He served sparkling water in wine glasses. In my haste to be on time (or was it an unconscious decision?) I had not worn my hearing aids. I strained, but it was fine. He spoke very clearly, exactingly, a man who wanted to be quoted accurately. Although he never used a tape recorder himself, I think he was disappointed that I wasn't recording.

I told him about this book, about the impact he had made on me. He nodded but looked slightly embarrassed at the praise. I filled the silence with something about how odd it seemed that as important as he had been to me, we'd barely seen each other over the years.

"You could have picked up the phone," he said. "Say, 'Hey, Gay, I'm in town, let's go to dinner.' I go out to dinner every fucking night."

"Yeah, right," I said. "You know the word 'intimidation'? Would you call up Jesus, 'Hey, Son of God, whacha doin' tonight?'"

He looked at me oddly. As soon as it had come out of my mouth, it sounded dumb. It did seem like a strange conversation for men in their seventies. Or was he thinking, Of course I'd call Jesus if I had the number?

I told him about going out for his cocoa. He didn't remember that. "Cocoa's a comfort drink," he said. "Something to put you to sleep. You know, this is like the difference between being a freshman and a senior. Freshmen always remember more than the seniors about what happened."

I sat there for several hours, becoming more and more comfortable as he chatted about himself. I had come with questions about me, but they faded in my fascination with him. Growing up the son of Italian immigrants in a WASPy town, sewing and delivering dry cleaning for his parents' shop, he said he had felt like an outsider. He might as well have been fat, I thought.

Before I left, he showed me his downstairs office, the bulging files, the endless lists, sticky notes everywhere, photos pinned to the walls. I worked that way, too. Had I caught it from him?

He told me to call when I was ready to come back and talk some more.

I would have to because I hadn't asked the Big Question. Had he been serious about giving me $5,000? Didn't I want to know? Burying the lead (or lede in journo jargon) is a journalistic misdemeanor, but not asking the question the lede will be based on is a felony.

Gay went off to Europe on a speaking engagement, so it was four weeks before we met again. I was wearing my hearing aids this time. We sat on the same perpendicular couches. He presented me with a copy of a letter I had sent him in 1973. So we had been in contact. I had needed to talk to him as my novel *Liberty Two* was inexorably disappearing into the literary sinkhole. He had been helpful and comforting. In the letter I thanked him and reminded him how that $5,000 proposal, now some fifteen years in the past, had swelled my "emotional bank account."

I read the letter while he answered a phone call. When he came back, we started talking about something that led to my laughingly saying "But you never went into therapy" and his surprised "For years, years, I was in therapy, I told them everything. But I would tell anyone anything. Any derelict on the street. Therapy wasn't worth it." Once, he said, he saw Jann Wenner, the founder of *Rolling Stone*, come out of a therapist's office, and the next week he read that Wenner had left his wife for a boyfriend. Gay said he thought he was spotting a new gay trend at the time, "Hey, I'm really on the ground floor of something here."

There was something surreal about the eight hours I spent with Gay that day and night. How could I have been so anxious about calling him up, this chatty, friendly narcissist? He needed people to talk to. He talked about his new book, a portrait of his fifty-year marriage to Nan, the beautiful and successful book publisher; it included at least one secondary "marriage," long absences, continuing friendships with women he often slept with. What about rumors of Nan having such relationships? He shrugged that away; she was much more private than he was.

Why was he writing this?

"I'm seventy-seven years old," he said, "and this is the only story I have left."

It took me a while to get to the Big Question. He did not remember the $5,000 proposal. He was making about $200 a week then. His highest salary at the *Times* was $315, although he always made extra money writing for magazines. He was a saver. He'd come out of the army with $10,000. He'd been an officer.

I pulled the conversation back to me. "Could it have happened?" I asked.

"It would not have been uncharacteristic." He leaned forward and peered at me. "Does that sound greedy to you, ten percent?"

"No, no. You know, I don't think you quite understand the impact it had on me, it was so inspiring. You need someone to believe in you so you can believe in yourself. It's a major lesson of my career." After a moment, I asked, "Is there any possibility you could have been kidding around?"

"Sure," he said.

My career had been piped.

Lippy and The Clipper at Yankees spring training, 1967. (Photograph by Jim Roach)

THREE | My Center Fielders (Part One)

On May 30, 1960, after a Memorial Day double-header at Yankee Stadium, some fans jumped out of the stands and raced across the outfield to surround Mickey Mantle. One of them punched Mantle in the jaw. It was shocking for the time. Recreational violence had not yet become commonplace in American sports.

The Yankees went off on a road trip on which Mantle was observed drinking his meals, which was not uncommon. But his jaw was swollen. The *Times'* regular Yankees beat writer would never have troubled the twenty-eight-year-old center fielder by actually asking him what had happened, so the following Friday night, after the Yankees returned to the Stadium, an expendable twenty-two-year-old was dispatched from night rewrite. I was thrilled with the assignment, the kind that Talese would have gotten had he still been in the sports department.

(Actually, two years earlier, almost to the day, Gay *had* gotten that same assignment. He'd been sent to the Stadium for Mantle's reaction to the fans who had been heckling him. They booed from the stands and squirted ink on his clothes if he didn't stop to sign autographs. Talese described Mantle as "smoldering" when asked if he minded the abuse. Talese wrote that Mantle had answered, "'If they bothered me I would not be where I am.' Then he turned away.")

Mickey and Yogi Berra were playing catch in front of the dugout when I politely introduced myself before the game. I'm pretty sure I was wearing a suit and tie that night, possibly a matching vest. I'm sure I called him Mr. Mantle when I asked if I might inquire about what had happened.

Mickey glanced over his shoulder and casually said . . . well, over the years, as this story became another one of my personal creation myths, I'd say, depending on the audience, "He made a rude and impossible suggestion," or, during the Bush II years, "He quoted Vice President Cheney to Senator Leahy," and sometimes I'd just flat-out quote him: "Why don't you go fuck yourself."

Now, I had heard such words before, but never from an American hero. I read the papers, I knew his story. The golden boy from the golden West had arrived as a teenager in New York in 1951 with muscles in places most people didn't have places and a country-fresh grin despite his damaged legs and a genetic black cloud: early fatal cancers ran through the males in his family. Another burden was Great Expectations: Mickey had been touted as the replacement for Joe DiMaggio if not Babe Ruth, and he had yet to come close except for his two Most Valuable Player award years, 1956 and 1957. Fans booed him now because he hadn't sustained the pace. Despite it all, according to the scribes, The Mick was a lovable gamer.

So I assumed I had asked the question incorrectly and rephrased it. Mickey signaled to Yogi, and they began throwing the ball an inch above my head. I was scared at first of being decapitated, then in awe of their control. They weren't going to hit me unless I failed to understand that the interview was over. I scuttled off.

I felt humiliated. What had I done wrong? How had I offended The Mick? Should I even be doing this work?

I waited until other reporters arrived to chat with Mantle, then lurked outside their circle and eavesdropped. They didn't bring up the punch directly, although someone asked how Mickey's jaw felt and he cheerfully told them he was eating lasagna now and expected to be biting into a steak soon. They all guffawed. No follow-up questions. In my story, I only alluded to his remark by writing that he had "grunted away" a question about the attack. I decided that he had reacted the way he had because he didn't know me and I had interviewed him too directly. My bad technique.

It was almost two years—in a Florida bar during the relaxed atmosphere of spring training—before I told the entire story to a more experienced reporter. He laughed. That's our Mickey, he said; we never write about him acting like a red ass because our editors know our readers don't want to read about it. And we don't want to lose access. Offend The Mick, and you're dead in the Yankees' locker room. You should see him spit at kids who want autographs. Welcome to the club. Don't let it get you down. Happens to all of us.

That should have made me feel better, but it only changed shame to anger. I didn't want to admit to myself that I had been bullied, that I was once again a junior high school victim, an S.P. fag. It was painful to realize that it was all too close to the feelings that women have when they are sexually harassed and made to feel that it was their fault, that they brought it on themselves.

I had arrived on the scene a naïf, unprotected by fandom or experience, and I think now that the Mantle episode loomed too large for too many years. Just get over it, Bobby. Had I adored him as a fan, I would have excused him—he was in pain, stressed out, just kidding. Had I been an insider, knowing that Mantle had his bullying moments, I would have stepped more carefully. I would also have known that there would be a lot more tense moments in my career.

Sportswriting isn't the oldest profession, although it is sometimes conducted that way. I like to imagine it began its modern era around the turn of the twentieth century, when Sheriff Bat Masterson, bored with shooting up Dodge, rode into New York City looking for action and became a sportswriter. He discovered that the pen is mightier than the pistol, especially when you promote such sporting events as boxing matches and horse races, then gamble on them, and then cover them for a newspaper.

By the time Bat died in 1921, at his *New York Morning Telegraph* desk while writing his column, Grantland Rice and the mythmakers of the Roaring Twenties had begun their conscious "godding up" of an American pantheon, the likes of Babe Ruth, Jack Dempsey, Bobby Jones, and Knute Rockne. Rice is best known for comparing the Notre Dame backfield of 1924 to the biblical Four Horsemen of the Apocalypse, also the title of a popular 1921 silent movie about World War I starring Rudolph Valentino.

In the vernacular of the time, Rice was a "Gee whiz" sportswriter, relentlessly positive, a booster, a jock sniffer. His contemporary W. O. McGeehan was the best known of the "Aw nuts" school, the rippers who snidely mocked the demigods, but in such a way as to make them seem important.

Those were the two main approaches to sportswriting when I showed up, although two spirited tabloid writers, Jimmy Cannon (the most socially conscious of his generation and a man who called sportswriters "the vaudevillians of journalism") and Dick Young were leading the way down from the Olympus of the press box to buttonhole athletes and coaches for quotes and explanations. Young was also running blind items in his gossipy New York *Daily News* columns that alluded to jock shenanigans, on and off the field.

But we were still in the shadow of the corrupt old Damon Runyon era. Brown envelopes with cash inside were still being handed out to sportswriters, along with free tickets and expensive Christmas presents. I was lucky to work for a paper that paid all my expenses; most other sportswriters got their travel and meal money from the teams or the promoters. An honest reportorial job could be considered an ungrateful act, to be repaid with loss of access.

There was emotional corruption as well. Players and reporters stayed at the same hotels on the road and traveled together, on trains and later on chartered planes. "Sports of the *Times*" columnist Arthur Daley referred to his newspaper colleagues as "lodge brothers," which was accurate. They were all male and white, and, with the exception of the few athletic and journalistic superstars, pretty much all the players and reporters were in the same struggling economic class. There was a community of interest. The fans were the rubes at the carnival.

For systemic criticism of sports, one would have to read a Communist, Lester "Red" Rodney, in the *Daily Worker*. Red Rodney, who died in 2009 at the age of ninety-eight, had been one of the most outspoken advocates of racial desegregation in major-league baseball. By the late fifties, he was gone in an internal Communist purge.

The professionalization of sportswriting didn't happen overnight (it's still in process, I hope), but my generation likes to point to an incident that began the expulsion of player and scribe from their sweet, sweaty Eden.

The crab apple of knowledge seems to have been Leonard Shecter's report in the *New York Post* that Yankees coach Ralph Houk and pitcher Ryne Duren had scuffled on the train coming back from winning the 1958 American League pennant. Such family squabbles or drunkenness or screwing around were never reported. Shecter, like the other reporters, tacitly agreed to turn a blind eye at first. He was young and happy to be on the beat; he had yet to become a beacon of hard-nosed honesty, the curmudgeonly scourge of entitled jocks. But when a rival tabloid reporter ran an item about the Yankees siccing private detectives on carousing players, Shecter was under pressure to come up with something as good or better. He told his editors what he knew about the Houk-Duren fight. Duren, probably drunk, had gotten rowdy. Houk, while subduing him, had accidentally cut him over the eye with his World Series ring. The *Post* editors blew the story into a torrid melee. There was a front-page headline as well as a back-page piece without a byline.

"With one dispatch," wrote Alan Schwarz in the *Times*, fifty years later, "Shecter had violated a sacred code that had existed in the 100 years of newspaper coverage of baseball."

Actually, sacred codes were being broken all over SportsWorld by then. The Giants and the Dodgers had jilted a city, and black players were emerging as stars in baseball, football, and basketball. Soviet bloc teams, often chemically enhanced, were dominating many Olympic sports. The concept of amateurism—playing for the love of the game—was under siege. And television was pushing its snouty eye everywhere, giving athletes the direct access to their fans that broke the pencil press.

The shaky trust between player and scribe—and among scribes—was shattered just in time for me. I don't think I would have functioned well in the old clubby atmosphere. Former fat boys never do. We're too suspicious, too used to watching from the sidelines. By the time I got my first major assignment, a certain wariness had set in and the climate was more businesslike. It was nowhere near as adversarial as it is today, but athletes were careful until they knew you, and writers kept score of which athletes other writers were talking to. Writers tended to move in packs, as on class trips, and get nervous if someone was missing.

Shecter was in St. Petersburg, Florida, for the first spring training of the New York Mets, and so was another of the new breed of sportswriter, Stan Isaacs, the sunny, funny, slyly subversive columnist from *Long Island Newsday*. They befriended me. Among the older writers were Milton Gross of the *New York Post*, the first of the press box–shrink columnists, and the fiery Dick Young of the *Daily News*, whose "Clubhouse Confidential" column, with its radioactive combination of sexual innuendo, right-wing demagoguery, and hard-core baseball knowledge became a must-read for players, as well as fans and other writers. Also there was the most important sports journalist of my era, Howard Cosell, a tall, dorky radio reporter who once made room for himself at a press conference by slamming his tape recorder into me. Who knew it would be the beginning of a beautiful friendship?

Among the greatest innovations of this group was actually interviewing ballplayers and doing real reporting. They were all generously helpful to me as a twenty-four-year-old newcomer. Some were good guys, some understood that I was no threat. Yet.

I was still too busy competing with Talese.

Gay's spring training pieces were my yardstick. Though I never came close to his easy breezy style, writing against my memory of his work was better for me than running with the pack. It was great fun, looking for stories the other reporters had missed (or, more accurately, dismissed). I even thought I had a major scoop once. The Mets had declared the hotel pool off limits to players. The official explanation was that swimming strained baseball muscles. But I heard that several guests had complained about Negro players being in the water with them. I cornered the Mets' manager, Casey Stengel, a man whose face I had variously described as "creased as a pleated skirt" and "carved from imperfect Mount Rushmore stone." (Worse yet, I described his walk as that of an "arthritic chimpanzee.") Stengel was seventy-one, the same age I am as I write this (walking like an arthritic chimpanzee), but he seemed truly ancient. He was bitter at having been recently fired from the Yankees after twelve glorious seasons that had included appearances in ten World Series. I phrased my question about the pool fairly directly. I was two years past my Mantle moment, an army veteran now, thicker-skinned, narrower-eyed.

"Thass right, pool's off limits," he snapped. "And I told 'em they couldn't fuck either. All season. Now print that."

Hanging around Stengel, on the field, in the clubhouse, at the Colonial Inn bar until closing time, was entertaining and an endless source of copy (Casey told rookies, "Get yourself in shape now, you'll be able to drink during the season") and of stories illuminating baseball history—he had played in the time of Babe Ruth, and he had managed Joe DiMaggio (whom he called "The Dago"). I also got to understand the news pack through Stengel.

Columnists and baseball writers from newspapers outside New York (and the likes of Daley of the *Times*) would sweep into the Mets' camp and plug into Stengel's never-ending monologue. If you stayed long enough, the references would be clear, the story he was telling would make sense, and sometimes the insights would be brilliant. But fifteen minutes of "so this here feller on second base, let me tell you he was not as horseapple as he was in Kankakee, which was amazing for a left-handed dentist which I did not get to be" was enough to anchor a column about "Stengelese," the private language of an eccentric who might well be losing his marbles. It was a lot easier than logging time and listening. Stengel was probably a baseball genius in his game tactics and use of players. You could get a graduate seminar on the game at his elbow at the bar.

You had to stay alert, though, because Stengel amused himself at the expense of second-rate ballplayers and the reporters. That spring training he trotted out his two worst rookies and announced that they were the hopes of the franchise, which we all wrote. There were no stories a few weeks later when they disappeared from the roster forever. They never appeared anywhere else.

Without fanfare, Stengel was also capable of enormous patience and acts of kindness toward old people and the disabled. When I described several such incidents, an experienced reporter suggested that I had been duped, that Stengel had let the blind kid touch his face, that he had taken time with the nervous dad and his surly son just to impress me, a liberal milksop. When I said, "If that's true, then you should write he's a manipulative virtuoso, instead of your usual Stengelese bullshit." He shrugged. "People like to read he's a nutty old fart."

That spring training was a wonderful experience and the first time I could measure myself against other reporters on the same story. The most important lesson was that most of them were lazy. If I worked hard, I could compete with these guys. Stay a little longer, make a few more calls. I thought I did okay at spring training, the office seemed happy, and Lou Effrat, the *Times'* old Brooklyn Dodgers reporter who believed I had usurped his rightful assignment, gave me a left-handed compliment: "Everybody's talking about your writing, kid, too bad you don't know what the fuck you're writing about." (That's always been the rap on me, and sometimes it's true. I prefer Jimmy Cannon's testimonial the first time we met: "Kid, your stuff sticks out like a sailor's joint on a Saturday night.")

After spring training, I covered baseball now and then, writing World Series sidebars and sometimes traveling with the Yankees or the Mets to spell the regular writers, but by 1964 Muhammad Ali was my beat. I didn't go back to spring training until 1967, this time with the Yankees. The big story was Mantle in twilight. His legs were shot. The Yankees were trying to make him a first baseman.

Seven years from my Mantle Moment, without pleasure or sympathy, I watched him struggle at first base. He wasn't looking for compassion: he was just a guy trying to hang on way past his prime because there was nowhere else he wanted to be, certainly not home with his wife and kids. He was a shadow of The Mick, but no one was booing or squirting ink. Everything had changed in 1961, when Mantle, closing in on Babe Ruth's record sixty-home-run season, was sidelined and weakened by an abscess caused by an injection administered by a "Dr. Feelgood" whose license was revoked a few years later. Roger Maris, no fan favorite, pulled past Mickey to break the record and win the hostility of the crowd.

In 1967, Maris was on the championship-bound St. Louis Cardinals and the Yankees were headed for ninth place under manager Ralph Houk, the former Marine major who had decked Ryne Duren in 1958 and changed the course of sportswriting. Houk welcomed me by inviting me into his office and asking if I was "a ripper or a booster." When I stammered something about just trying to be a fair-minded reporter, he cocked an eyebrow and said, "We're all in this together."

I took that as a threat and a kind of welcome challenge. My star was rising at the paper; my Ali coverage had been a triumph, I'd spent six weeks covering sports in Europe, a similar spin through the Soviet Union was scheduled for that summer, and I knew I was being groomed to be the third man after John Kieran and Daley ever to write "Sports of the *Times*" regularly. I was full of myself, and no pin-striped bully was going to push me around. Not Houk, not Mantle, no Yankee could intimidate this hotshot word slinger.

Well, there was one Yankee.

Joe DiMaggio was in camp. He had been brought down for public relations purposes, but he was elusive and we were told to leave him alone except for staged group meetings lest we alarm him into thinking we would ask about his former wife Marilyn Monroe;

this was less than five years after her death, and she was still a tabloid topic as the rumored lover of both John and Robert Kennedy.

The Clipper had been in center field the first time I ever went to the Stadium. I had pestered Dad into taking me. I'd listened to a few Yankees games at night in bed, and in the molasses tones of Mel Allen I'd seen Joe D's whipping bat, his easy grace over the large, lush greensward.

Dad took me to a game in a dutiful way. He never showed emotion, but I could tell he was not impressed. He had seen Babe Ruth. This was Mantle's rookie year, 1951, and DiMaggio's final season. I was not so impressed either. He was no longer "drifting," as the broadcasters described it, under fly balls. He was chugging after them, stiff-legged. I was also underwhelmed by the Stadium itself, less grand than I had imagined. But such disappointments were minor. Dad and I at a ball game, like other fathers and sons! Maybe the library trips weren't enough. In any case, DiMaggio was now linked in my mind with Dad, and so his star shone for me even after he retired, married Marilyn, lost her, then handled her funeral with such class. A fresh rose on her grave, every day, forever! He remained a distant luminary in SportsWorld.

We finally ran into each other—literally—one gray, chilly day in Fort Lauderdale that spring training. I was studying a roster as I hurried along a plank walkway over wet ground that led from the Yankees' locker room out to the field. DiMaggio's head was down to avoid eye contact as he strode toward me. We collided. Face-to-face with me, DiMaggio froze. With his long, melancholy face, the deer-in-the-headlights cliché seemed appropriate.

After an embarrassingly long time, I finally blurted, "Not baseball weather."

He blinked, took a breath, and looked up. "That's an outfielder's sky."

And then, as if he were Michelangelo describing the ceiling of the Sistine Chapel, he talked about the roof of his world, about the danger of losing balls in the clouds as easily as in the sun, about smog and shadows and smoke, about the line of the ball, rising or looping, about the spin. I was mesmerized. I took no notes. I barely breathed, afraid to break the spell. I suddenly understood (but maybe I inserted the revelation later) that he hadn't just "drifted" after all, that he was a scholar, that he had prepared for every kind of sky, patch of blue, burst of sun. He always knew where he was going to meet the ball.

He paused only once, to notice I was shivering. "Rook!" he roared at a young pitcher sprinting by. It was Stan Bahnsen, a prize prospect who would be the American League's Rookie of the Year the next season. "Get this man a jacket." Bahnsen stripped off his warm-up jacket and gave it to me. DiMaggio helped me put it on.

We might be talking still, but a Yankees PR official made a big show of rescuing DiMaggio from what he assumed was a media ambush. DiMaggio seemed reluctant to leave. The PR man said DiMaggio was late for an appointment. It sounded like a lie, but DiMaggio was too much the gentleman to show the man up. He asked my name. He said, "Good-bye, Lippy," and gravely shook my hand.

Lippy. All through childhood and adolescence I had battled that hated nickname. Now it was an honorific.

The Mantle at First experiment failed, and he retired the next year. He referred to the next five years as a kind of death; he felt excluded and forgotten. And when he was remembered, it was not always with reverence. In 1970, *Ball Four*, the locker-room-wall-shattering valentine to baseball that former Yankees pitcher Jim Bouton wrote with Len Shecter, portrayed Mantle as a lovable teammate, a hard drinker, and somewhat adolescent; he led Yankees on "beaver-shooting" expeditions to hotel roofs to spy on women undressing. Bouton didn't spare himself as a cutup and carouser (although, as one of the most intelligent and politically sophisticated major leaguers, he demonstrated against South African apartheid and for American civil rights). Bouton was attacked by the baseball establishment (which included sportswriters such as Dick Young) for betraying the sanctity of the locker room. Sportswriters felt burned; here they had prostituted their calling by writing claptrap in exchange for access, and they had been scooped by a bona fide insider. Bouton, who loved Mantle, was hurt when told incorrectly that The Mick was angry. It was many years before that was reconciled.

In 1974, Mantle was inducted into the Hall of Fame, with the attention and memorabilia bonanza that comes with official sainthood, and he was hot again. I was three years gone from the *Times* by then, in a New Jersey basement happily writing fiction, and I didn't pay much attention. I was not keeping up with sports; I thought I was through with journalism. I certainly had no idea that I wasn't through with Mickey or Joe, that we would meet again in a few years. I hadn't yet learned the lesson that as you grow and change, you keep rewriting your best stories.

In the middle of the night after his gig, in a hotel room, Greg and I taped the book.
(Photograph by Marjorie Rubin Lipsyte)

FOUR | *Nigger*, the Book

Following my hero, Gay Talese, I began writing nonsports pieces for magazines, somehow specializing in cop stories. This was in 1963, a year after the Mets' first spring training and a year before Cassius Clay beat Sonny Liston for the heavyweight title. I wasn't committed to sportswriting yet, and I didn't want to be pigeonholed for life. I hadn't yet figured out that sports led me to everything and everything led me back to sports.

My favorite piece, for the *Times* Sunday magazine, was about two narcotics detectives who disguised themselves as bums, old ladies, hippies, to bust heroin dealers. Hanging with the cops was exhilarating. Now, these were authentic men! They had guns! We swaggered through the streets, daring the bad guys to make their moves!

The magazine article attracted book offers. The cops told me to go ahead and make myself a deal but leave them the movie rights because there was a huge case they were wrapping up that would make us all rich and famous. I signed a contract for a nonfiction book about the central characters in one of their big drug cases. It was less about them than about NarcoWorld, including the dealers and the buyers, but they were key characters. I got my first advance, $1,500, one-third of it up front. I felt like a real writer.

I kept hanging with them, but as time went on I began liking the older, alpha cop, Eddie Egan, less and less. He was a self-absorbed jock who had had pro baseball dreams. He was hard and violent. I thought his partner, Sonny Grosso, had a soul, but I wasn't sure Eddie had one. One day Eddie and I went up to Harlem on a case (people thought I was a cop by this time, or maybe an assistant DA), and he kicked in an apartment door and started slapping a young white woman who cowered on her bed clutching a mixed-race baby. He stopped when he remembered I was there. Later, he said to me, "I hate it when white women fuck niggers."

I sensed that as I dug deeper into the story, there would be more incidents like that one. There was no way I could write about these guys as heroes and no way I could write the truth so long as they had some say over the final product. I hadn't promised them veto power, but I had promised them a look at the manuscript. I wanted to write this book, a nonsports book, but I returned the advance. I was glad I had a day job.

A few weeks later, the book editor called back. He was looking for a writer to collaborate with Dick Gregory on his autobiography. Gregory was already under contract but hadn't clicked with any of the writers who had been sent to meet with him. I wasn't that interested in ghosting a book, but I was interested in meeting Gregory, the first black comedian to make it in the major white clubs. He was earning $5,000 a week! While much of his act was standard stand-up about dumb cousins and vicious mothers-in-law, his racial rim shots ("'Leven months I sat in at a restaurant, then they integrated and didn't even have what I wanted") were repeated everywhere as social commentary if not uncomfortable truths ("We won't go to war in the Congo 'cause we're afraid our soldiers will bring back war brides"). At thirty, he was hailed as the Jackie Robinson of topical comedy, a Will Rogers for the Atomic Age.

So on the evening of September 16, 1963, I walked into a New York City hotel suite, where I was politely told by Gregory's wife, Lillian, that he was in the bedroom and could not be disturbed.

I knocked and without waiting for an answer barged in. I introduced myself to a pudgy man in underwear curled into a fetal position on his bed. I sat down and asked him why he was crying.

He slowly rolled over and looked up. "Don't you read the papers?"

"Sure," I said. "I work for one."

"Didn't you read about the four little girls who were murdered yesterday in a Birmingham church?"

"It was terrible," I said. "Now, about this book thing . . ."

But he had rolled onto his back and was talking to the ceiling. "How can the white man be so evil to kill four little girls who weren't even demonstrating for their civil rights?"

He talked for hours, deep into the night, about the racial cancer destroying the nation and how most of the blame was on people who looked like me. You people stunt the lives of children and break up families, he said, you have the power to wound the innocent simply by calling them "nigger." I took some notes because that's what I did, but I mostly wondered what I was doing there. This man was not the cool, slangy hipster I had seen on nightclub stages, the Chris Rock–Dave Chappelle–Bill Cosby of his time whose humorous, rats-to-riches autobiography I was supposed to write.

The man on the bed, alternately blubbering and ranting about the Birmingham bombing, was not funny or particularly insightful, I thought at first, just angry. I resented his making me the stand-in for all hateful white men. But something kept me there, and the more I listened the more I was engaged. As disturbing as it was, it began to make sense. I wondered if we could find a common ground. I began to wonder how I would feel right now if I were black. I'd never had a black friend. The only black person I knew was my parents' cleaning lady. Gregory was taking me somewhere I had never been. I was open, and he must have sensed it. When I finally got up to leave, he asked me to come back the next day so we could start writing the book.

It went badly. Greg was sometimes an hour or two late for an interview session, and when I complained, he'd say, "I can tell you been waitin', baby, you sound colored." He always called me "baby." He didn't remember my name.

I began to envy the collaborators he had rejected. Once Greg and I started tape-recording, it got even worse, endless, unusable diatribes against white America. He had strong arguments and solid facts, but this was deadly speechifying, hardly the human stuff of autobiography.

I took it for about two weeks of sporadic sessions before or after his nightclub appearances and my *Times* assignments. One day, I waited three hours for him with a prepared monologue. I told him that I didn't need this jive job badly enough to put up with an irresponsible, selfish fool trying to hang me up in reverse prejudice. In fact, I declared pompously, the only thing I didn't have against him was his color.

I stood up, said good-bye, and marched out of his hotel room to the elevator. He followed me and got in. On the way down he said, "Bob Lipsyte, right?"

"Too late," I said.

He said he was going to have a sandwich at the hotel coffee shop. Would I join him?

While we ate, he kept repeating my name. When we finished, he said, "Let's go back up. I think we're ready to write a book. A real book, one they're not expecting."

We went back up. The book that emerged was basically my editing of taped hours of emotional storytelling that my wife-to-be, Marjorie, transcribed when she got home from her *Times* job in the music department. She typed and cried, later laughed, along with Greg crying and laughing as he lay on his hotel bed like a patient in therapy. His stories were raw and unsentimental. The most poignant scenes for Margie and me were of little Richard sitting with his mom, who was dressed and rouged, waiting for Greg's dad, Big Pres, to make a rare cameo in their lives. It always ended with Big Pres beating both of them for asking him to stay.

It was a thrilling, intense education in race, politics, comedy. Being with Greg in those tumultuous years of 1963 and 1964 informed the rest of my career, most immediately my coverage of Cassius Clay/Muhammad Ali. We never stopped talking, mostly about civil rights and Vietnam as Americans went south in voter registration drives and to Asia to fight an illegitimate war triggered by the phony Gulf of Tonkin incident. Medgar Evers and President Kennedy were murdered, and the Reverend Martin Luther King, Jr., received the Nobel Peace Prize. Black ghettos blew up into violence during "the long, hot summer" of 1964. By the end of that year, the conservative white Berkeley campus had erupted into riots during the Free Speech movement that eventually led to the university lifting a ban on student activism.

We also talked sports. Greg had gone to Southern Illinois University on a track scholarship. One of the first stories he told me about himself once we were past the diatribes was how he had become an activist. I didn't believe it.

In 1951, his junior year in high school, Greg told me, he had set a St. Louis schoolboy track record for the mile. When it didn't appear in the annual city yearbook the following September, he complained to his coach, who explained that only records set by white boys were listed. Greg was outraged, and he ditched school the next day to go to City Hall to protest to the mayor. It also happened to be the day that thousands of other African-American schoolkids were marching on City Hall to protest overcrowded conditions in their segregated schools. Greg was quickly recognized as a sports star. It was assumed he was there to protest with them, and he was appointed a marshal and asked to run up and down the line of march, maintaining order and morale. He was interviewed by newspapers and local TV. By the time they got to City Hall, Greg was talking about overcrowded conditions. When he got home, his mother was in tears. Someone on TV had called him a Communist. He told me it was the beginning of his political awakening.

It sounded like one of those celebrity creation myths. But when I checked out the story in the *St. Louis Post-Dispatch*, I was surprised. Dates, quotes, everything matched what Greg had told me. I began thinking about my own racism. Why had I thought his story was piped? And I began to trust him. Even in his hyperbole there would always be a core of truth.

Once we got cooking, we taped mostly early in the morning in New York or Chicago or San Francisco after Greg had appeared at a club. It would be a long and wonderful night that began with Greg ambling onstage, climbing on his stool, lighting a cigarette, and asking the nearest white waiter for a Scotch and soda. When the drink arrived, Greg would shake his head and say, "Damn, Governor Barnett should see this." The audience would laugh and then applaud the subtle compliment he had paid them and their city, so far advanced beyond segregationist Ross Barnett's Mississippi. I thought many of them felt that the money they were spending in the club was somehow a contribution to "the cause." And in some ways it was; the audience never knew that Greg stipulated in his contracts that the nightclub had to hire some black waiters, at least during his engagement.

We'd go out to eat after the gig, at least half-a-dozen people, to whatever joint was still open, and Greg would order for everyone, much too much food. He would taste everything, almost delicately, savoring bites, obviously feeling comforted by the abundance. He had been hungry as a kid, and he remembered eating the silky sand that blew through St. Louis in the summertime.

Just before Christmas 1963, after a late show at Mister Kelly's in Chicago, I got the idea for the name for our book, although I didn't know it right away. (The approved working title at the time was "Callous on My Soul," which I hated.) We were eating at Mammy's Pancake House, an all-night luncheonette on Rush Street, where Greg had ordered three kinds of pancakes—chocolate, Dutch apple, and sausage—roasted barbecue, scrambled eggs, and a breakfast steak when he suddenly said, "Someday I'm going to open up my own restaurant, call it 'Nigger,' just one table, five waiters, and an orchestra, the royal treatment to anybody who has the guts to come in. And every white man in the South will be giving me free publicity."

And then we went back to his hotel room to tape. In those eerie hours before dawn, he would lie on his bed and reach back to Richard Claxton Gregory, one of six kids, a welfare case born on Columbus Day 1932, who fantasized that school closed every year in honor of his birthday.

He often talked about his "monster," his term for the ego, ambition, drive, and survival skills that had outwitted bigger boys with humor, kept him running track until he was out of the ghetto, pushed him to polish his comedy act at parties and black honky-tonks until January 13, 1961, when the Chicago Playboy Club called him to replace the popular double-talk comic Professor Irwin Corey, who was sick. When Greg arrived, the manager was blocking the stage door. He was panicked at the number of southern convention-eers in the house. Maybe another night. But the monster refused to be canceled. The manager sighed and opened the door.

Greg had a plan. He started by making fun of himself.

"They asked me to buy a lifetime membership in the NAACP, but I told them I buy a week at a time. Hell of a thing to buy a lifetime membership, then wake up one morning and find out the country's been integrated."

Now he had them, and he could say anything he wanted as long as he stayed away from sex.

"Last time I was down South, I walked into this restaurant, and this white waitress came up to me and said, 'We don't serve colored people here.'

"I said, 'That's all right, I don't eat colored people. Bring me a whole fried chicken.'

"About then these three cousins come in, you know the ones I mean, Klu, Kluck, and Klan, and they say, 'Boy, we're giving you fair warning. Anything you do to that chicken, we're going to do to you.' So I put down my knife and fork, and I picked up that chicken and I kissed it."

Sometime early in that first Playboy show a heckler in the back yelled, "Nigger!" Greg said, "Say that again, please. My contract calls for fifty dollars every time that word is used."

That fifty-minute show lasted almost two hours because the crowd wouldn't let him leave the stage. When he finally did, he got a standing ovation. Hugh Hefner showed up for the second show that night, and when it was over he signed Greg to a three-year deal.

The monster that had led him through the stage door would never concede defeat or admit it had been tricked. It also worked in smaller, more subtle ways.

The assistant pastor of a black church in Harlem, a theatrical white man who called himself "a public relations man for God," had invited Greg to speak one Sunday morning at a service for young prison inmates. Greg accepted immediately. But when he and I arrived at the large, ornate church, it was filled with hundreds of well-fed, well-dressed parishioners. He'd been tricked into showing up for the fat cats.

Greg asked, "Where are the prisoners?"

The assistant pastor smiled. "Their services are conducted much, much too early for an entertainer with your hours."

Greg stalked out of the church. "You can tell them the incense made me sick."

The assistant pastor, sweat bubbling on his pale, fat face, blocked Greg at the bottom of the steps. He sank to his knees.

"They saw you, the pastor is such a tyrant, I'll be in such trouble," he babbled, wringing his hands. "I plead with you in the name of God."

I felt embarrassed for the minister and began looking for a cab. I assumed that Greg, furious at being conned, would let the fat fool grovel, then stomp away.

"Get up," I heard Greg say in a flat, hard voice. "I'll go in."

We sat in a back pew and watched an elaborate service conducted by ministers in flowing robes. Greg was very still, a smile tugging the corners of his mouth. I wondered what he was plotting. When his time came, he strolled down the aisle to the pulpit, stiff-legged, almost swaggering. A gunfighter's walk.

He looked down at the congregation and told them how the middle-class Negro churchgoer was a hypocrite for avoiding the civil rights struggle.

"You sing the hymn 'Were you there when they crucified the Lord?' Well, a crucifixion is going on right now in America. Were you there? That's what your grandchildren are going to ask. What are you going to tell them? That you were just standing around?"

After twenty minutes, he stopped abruptly and walked out of the church. He was grinning when I caught up with him on the street. "Man, if I had been mentally prepared I would have knocked those people into the aisles, no preacher in America could have followed me." He began to laugh and slap his leg. That was the monster in action.

Once we decided on the title, *Nigger*, he held his ground against the publishing house. I loved his dedication: "Dear Momma— Wherever you are, if you ever hear the word 'nigger' again, remember they are advertising my book."

The book has been in print for more than forty-five years, and although the reviews were mostly good to great, the title didn't help sales. Most blacks and fair-minded whites hated the title and found it hard to ask for the book by name. The whites who liked the title weren't about to buy a black man's book. In retrospect, I think it was a mistake, destructive defiance on both our parts. These days, it's even harder to mention the title. I find myself talking about a book that I am very proud to have helped write as "Dick Gregory's autobiography."

By the time *Nigger* came out in 1964, Greg's entertainment career was in a downward spiral. The nightclub stage wasn't big enough for him anymore. He was integrating jails, schools, restaurants. Club owners and TV producers were unwilling to book a performer who might show up late or not at all because he had decided at the last minute that flying south to a civil rights demonstration was more important than making white liberals laugh. Civil rights leaders have said that Greg's appearances at demonstrations—which invariably brought a Huntley-Brinkley NBC news crew—not only advanced the cause but persuaded most hard-core segregationists to leave their guns at home.

Playboy called him the Scarlet Pimpernel of the civil rights movement, and the writer Thomas Morgan called him the Lone Ranger, but too many commentators suggested that he was merely demonstrating for publicity, he wasn't sincere. When he ran for mayor of Chicago, journalists wondered if he were a serious candidate. They weren't interested if he was merely trying to get attention for issues such as welfare, housing, jobs, hunger, health care, and police brutality.

I enjoyed campaigning with him, especially when a street hustler would sidle up and ask what he could do to help. Greg would laugh and say, "Really be something else if the rumor got out that Mayor Daley's precinct captains were paying $20 a vote this year, then, when they come around with the usual $2, folks be so mad they run him out of town."

In 1968, Greg ran for president. I voted for him, of course, and when my friends upbraided me as if it were my fault that Richard Nixon had beat Hubert Humphrey, I'd quote Greg: "Look, brother, you got two girls and one is a full-time prostitute and the other is a weekend prostitute. If you choose the lesser of two evils and marry the weekend prostitute, you're only fooling yourself if you don't think you're marrying a whore."

I don't believe that now, and I wonder if I believed it then or was merely so delighted to be able to vote for a person who had eaten in my house. The lesser of two evils is still evil, that's true, but isn't less evil better than more evil?

The year after Greg didn't win the presidency, a book I hadn't written about the narcotics detectives Egan and Grosso came out. It was called *The French Connection*. The Academy Award–winning movie followed three years later, in 1971, the year I left the *Times* and about the time Greg left the nightclub stand-up circuit. We didn't see much of each other for the next few years. We kept up through late-night phone calls. He faded from media view except when he made an outrageous claim, suggesting in 1981 that the seventeen black children murdered in Atlanta had been part of "fiendish" government medical experiments. His antiabortion stand infuriated Margie and troubled me.

He began fasting in civil rights demonstrations and lost more than 60 pounds. It became the flip side of his obsession with food. He started running again, in marathons. He hawked a diet powder on the New Age circuit. He helped the boxer Riddick Bowe trim his weight on a kelp diet and win the heavyweight championship.

We had a wonderful reunion in 1990 when he came on my WNET public affairs TV show, *The Eleventh Hour*. It was vintage Greg. He talked about rich women who get prescription drugs when their husbands cheat on them and poor women who go out and get crack. "Both of them are drugged out so they don't have to deal with their problems from an ethical standpoint, from a spiritual standpoint."

He talked about black folks needing to change their priorities. "Michael Jackson comes to town, I buy my child a forty-dollar ticket and give him twenty dollars to buy a silly glove. I never gave that child twenty dollars to join the NAACP."

It was a reaffirmation of my old admiration for him. Greg has said that there have been only three comic geniuses in America: Mark Twain, Lenny Bruce, and Richard Pryor. Pryor credited Greg with opening the door for him. I wonder if Greg would have gotten into that league had he stayed primarily in stand-up comedy, especially after late-night TV shows opened up for black comics. But Greg followed his monster. Civil rights activism made him a hero but a dangerous commodity. His forays into the New Age nutritional circuit, which I never fully understood, seemed more calling than commercial opportunism, but they diminished his mainstream reputation as a social commentator.

In the spring of 2009, when I saw an ad for a rare appearance at Manhattan's comedy club Caroline's, I was torn. I desperately wanted to see him, but I was afraid of being disappointed, of having my memory smudged. I decided to show up unannounced. I'd catch him afterward. Maybe.

It was a ten o'clock weeknight show, and the crowd was predominantly middle-aged, mostly white, lots of jeans, sweatshirts, and running shoes. Tourists. They were old enough to agree with the MC who called him "the legendary comedian." My nervousness that he wouldn't be funny, that he would be out of touch, evaporated quickly.

"I'm suing Bernie Madoff. That's right. A civil rights suit. He didn't rip off any black people."

He was onstage for an hour and a half, sitting down, punctuating his rap with broad winks, pauses, head and eye rolls. I recognized a lot of the 1964 riffs that people talked about.

"If Jesus had been electrocuted, we'd be wearing little chairs around our necks—how do you make the sign of the chair?"

And my favorite of the night: "Biggest loss of the Obama presidency is for black entertainers and athletes. Sports and entertainment used to be the only tickets out. We're not better athletes and dancers, just twenty-two million parents making their kids practice."

Afterward, happy and proud, I decided not to try to fight through the crowd outside his dressing room. I wanted to keep the high, think about the past flowing into the present, how our subjects choose us, and how lucky we are when they choose wisely. Greg had taken me through a door into another world and changed me.

I remembered how thrilling and exhausting it was hanging with Greg in the sixties, always on the run to a cab to a train to a plane, ending up in an unscheduled city a stop ahead of our clothes, marching in a demonstration, sitting in on a Supreme Court hearing (where a black janitor let us in a side door and slipped Greg some papers), whispering in a restaurant bathroom with the water running to foil listening devices. Years later when I got my FBI file through the Freedom of Information Act, I wondered if some of the redacted pages were about Greg. Joe Louis, Jim Brown, civil rights leaders, writers, politicians, gangsters, blues singers paraded through his dressing room. He took me on visits to Malcolm X and Harry Belafonte.

Once I took him along to visit Muhammad Ali, who covered the phone and asked Greg what advice he should give to some Muslim ministers calling from Africa.

"Tell them to look to the east and pray," said Greg.

Ali uncovered the phone and said, "Look to the east and pray to . . ."

"No," snapped Greg. "They know who to pray to."

The morning after Clay won the title. That pale face above a tie, in the lower right corner, is mine. (UPI Photo/Corbis)

FIVE | The Onliest (Part One)

Muhammad Ali was my first Big Story. He put my name on page one. He made me a columnist. He was also the single most important sporting lens through which I learned about politics, religion, race, and hero worship. I've written far more about him than any other subject, and in watching him change and grow for almost fifty years I've watched myself.

Loving Muhammad Ali has been easy. It's grasping what he stands for at any given moment that's been hard.

Our journey began as sheer joy. The first time I ever saw him, I was standing with the Beatles.

That was February 18, 1964, when his name was Cassius Clay. He was twenty-two years old. I was twenty-six. The *Times* was so sure that Gaseous Cassius, which was one of his early derogatory dubs, would be knocked out early in his heavyweight title fight against the champion, Sonny Liston, that instead of sending the regular boxing writer, Joe Nichols, down to Miami Beach, the paper sent a feature writer whose time was less valuable. I was thrilled with the assignment, another Talese-type adventure.

My instructions were cold: as soon as I landed, I was to drive my rental car from the arena to the nearest hospital, mapping the quickest route. The paper didn't want me to waste any deadline time following Clay to intensive care.

After my mapping expedition, I drove to the seedy old Fifth Street Gym (in what is now trendy South Beach) to watch Clay's daily training session for the first time. He hadn't arrived yet, but the gym was packed with tourists and sportswriters—Clay had been on the cover of *Time* for his coffee house doggerel readings ("This is the story about a man / with iron fists and a beautiful tan") and his ability to predict the round in which his carefully chosen opponents would fall. He had not yet earned the right to challenge the champion, but boxing needed a box-office draw against the unbeatable monster Liston. Clay was considered a necessary sacrifice. It was hoped that enough people would pay to see the Louisville Lip buttoned for good.

As I climbed the splintery stairs, there was a hubbub behind me. Four little guys around my age in matching white terry-cloth cabana jackets were being herded up. Someone said it was that hot new British rock group on their first American tour.

I was annoyed. Bad enough this disgrace to poetry was sullying boxing, now these noisy mop tops were trying to cash in on the sweet science. (In preparation for the assignment, I had read and reread A. J. Liebling's *The Sweet Science* and carried my annotated copy with me. It would be some time before I began to figure out why so many of the boxing trainers and cornermen who seemed all but mute to me were masters of aphorism for him. Liebling was a superb writer.)

A British photographer traveling with the Beatles had tried to pose them with Sonny Liston, but the champ had refused—"Not with them sissies," he was supposed to have said—and now they were settling for a photo op with the challenger.

At the top of the stairs, when the Beatles discovered that Clay had not yet arrived, John Lennon said, "Let's get the fuck out of here." But two huge security guards blocked their way and crowded them into an empty dressing room. I allowed myself to be pushed in with them, figuring to get a few funny quotes. Had I understood who those four little guys were, I might have been too shy to become, briefly, the fifth Beatle. But then I was also clueless about Clay.

The Beatles were cranky in that damp dressing room, stomping and cursing. I introduced myself, rather importantly, I'm afraid, and they mimicked me. John shook my hand gravely, saying he was Ringo, and introduced me to Paul, who he said was John. I asked for their predictions. They said that Liston would destroy Clay, that silly little overhyped wanker. Then they ignored me to snarl among themselves again. Silly little overhyped wankers, I thought.

Suddenly the locker room door burst open, and Cassius Clay filled the doorway. The Beatles and I gasped. He was so much larger than he looked in pictures. He was beautiful. He seemed to glow. He was laughing.

"Hello there, Beatles!" he roared. "We oughta do some road shows together, we'll get rich."

The Beatles got it right away. They followed Clay out to the boxing ring like kindergarten kids. You would have thought they'd met before and choreographed their routine. They bounced into the ring, capered, dropped down to pray that Clay would stop hitting them. He picked up Ringo, the bittiest Beatle. Then they lined up so Clay could knock them all out with one punch. They fell like dominoes, then jumped up to form a pyramid to get at Clay's jaw. The five of them began laughing so hard their impromptu frolics collapsed. That photo op is a classic. (Check YouTube; you might even see me.)

After the Fab Four left, Clay jumped rope, shadowboxed, and sparred as his court jester, Drew Bundini Brown, hollered, "Float like a butterfly, sting like a bee, rumble, young man, rumble!" Afterward, stretched out on a dressing room table for his rubdown, Clay pretended to fall asleep as reporters asked him what he was going to do after he lost. Finally, a crabby old reporter from Boston said, "This whole act is a con job, isn't it?" and Clay pretended to wake up and he said, "I'm making all this money, the popcorn man making money and the beer man, and you got something to write about. Your papers let you come down to Miami Beach, where it's warm." The Boston reporter shut up.

I think that was the moment when I began to wish this kid wasn't going to get his head knocked off, that somehow he would beat Liston and become champion or at least survive and keep boxing. He would have been such a joy to cover, I thought. Too bad he's got no chance. Too bad he's only passing through, a firefly fad like those Beatles. We could all have had a blast.

My reverie of regret was interrupted by Cassius, poking me. He put his head close to mine and whispered that he had noticed me coming out of the locker room with the four visitors. "Who were those little sissies?" he asked.

The weeklong buildup to that fight was intense and clamorous, a feverish, hilarious, nutty series of encounters with down-and-out old boxers, sleazy hustlers, hookers, gamblers, and the likes of Benjamin "Evil Eye" Finkle ("I'm the number one hex man of the sporting world," he told me). My notes read like ideas for a picaresque novel. While the week was a twilight reminder of the

Damon Runyon days, it was also a foreshadowing of the more politicized days to come. Clay's mentor Malcolm X, then a Black Muslim minister and white America's designated bogeyman, was floating around the edges of the scene. His presence made plausible the rumor that Clay was waiting until after the fight to announce his membership in the Lost-Found Nation of Islam, a mysterious sect somehow conflated in the mainstream media mind with the Mau Mau, the Kenyan insurgents of the fifties who had terrified the British Empire.

I kept an eye out for Malcolm that week in Miami but never saw him. He fascinated me. The summer before, I'd been assigned to yet another Talesian turn, a sidebar to the second Floyd Patterson–Sonny Liston fight. This usually meant a chat with Patterson's wife or former manager or some old juvies from his neighborhood. I didn't want to do that. I'm not sure if it was my political nature kicking in or if I was trying to create my own style, but I headed out to Brooklyn, where a thousand blacks and whites were protesting racial bias in the construction industry. I asked the demonstrators what they thought about the upcoming fight. A black lawyer said, "They'll always give us opportunities to act like animals." That was not quite good enough to justify my angle on the feature.

Then I spotted Malcolm, whom I recognized from newspaper photos. Dick Gregory thought highly of him. Tall, handsome, cold-eyed, the former Malcolm Little, a robber, drug dealer, and pimp who had found Islam and radical politics in prison, was standing across the street smirking at the demonstrators. I rushed over and asked him what he thought the fight signified. He said, "That's a stupid question," and his bodyguard, three black-suited members of the Fruit of Islam, the paramilitary wing of the Nation of Islam, shoved me into the gutter. As I went down, I yelled, "The only stupid question is an unanswered question!"

Malcolm smiled and nodded. The Fruit picked me up. I introduced myself. He said, "I'm pleased to see that the two best men in the sport are black. But they'll be exploited, of course, and the promoters will get all the bread. They'll let a Negro excel if it's going to make money for them."

That sidebar was a turning point for me. It gave me courage to find my own signature. The *Times* ran the story without discussion. Jim Roach liked it. Grumblies on the desk began treating me better. That story may have led to my being sent to Miami Beach six months later.

That week of his first title fight, Clay dazzled with charm and braggadocio. The sportswriters of my generation were delighted with a subject who reflected our happening times of hippies, pop art, psychedelics, free love, rock and roll. We bemoaned his imminent demise at the hands of the baleful ex-con Liston, whose most searching remark about Clay, written in red in my notebook, was "He's a fag, I'm a man."

The older sportswriters—Red Smith, Jimmy Cannon, Dick Young, Arthur Daley—clustered in Liston's camp. That widened the generation gap in the media and made Clay even more the young writers' fighter. The old writers derided Clay's unorthodox boxing style (he leaned away from punches rather than letting them "slip" over his shoulders). They seemed offended by his trash talk, "Liston's a big ugly bear" and "I am the greatest" (which sounded to me like a public version of the ghetto insult games called "dozens" or "joning" or "selling wolf tickets" that I'd heard in my travels with Greg). The old writers also resented the casual way he treated them, his cheery disrespect for their importance. Their ideal was Joe Louis, the seemingly humble Brown Bomber of the thirties who had carefully concealed his penchant for white movie actresses and rarely said more than "I do my talkin' in the ring." Poor Joe, crushed by his double life, was already on his way to cocaine addiction and dementia. He had been the most powerful athletic symbol of his time, for black

Americans in a time of inequality, for all Americans in a time of war. I knew this intellectually, but it was years before I understood how important he had been, how shabbily he had been treated.

An older reporter who had befriended me kept dragging me over to Liston's camp to mingle with his crowd and with Louis, who was part of the champ's entourage. When I finally asked the older reporter, Barney Nagler, why he was wasting his time with this shambling, addled old man, his eyes got misty. "You don't understand. He was so beautiful."

(Some twenty-four years later, at the party after Mike Tyson beat Larry Holmes, I dragged a young reporter I had befriended over to meet Ali, who was already a bit unsteady. The young reporter asked me why I was wasting my time with this old guy when I could be talking to Tyson. I had a flashback, and it was all I could do not to say, "You don't understand. He was so beautiful.")

The fight, of course, was my professional dream come true. The first inkling that the prohibitive 7-to-1 odds against Clay might be a mistake came when the fighters met in the middle of the ring. Clay was *bigger* than Liston. Round by round, I kept losing my breath. Except for the moments when he was apparently blinded by some chemical from Liston's gloves, Clay totally dominated the fight. It could happen, I thought. Clay danced around Liston, he jabbed, he slugged, he mocked the brute. I began thinking of a lede. Then Liston sat down on his stool and wouldn't get up, and it was over. Clay capered on the ring apron, yelling at the press, "Eat your words!"

And then it was my turn, minutes to deadline, banging out a paragraph on my little Olivetti, ripping out the page, handing it to the telegrapher at my side, banging on. I loved the rush of writing under the gun. I'd never say it was better than sex, but it was in the same ballpark.

The front-page, above-the-fold story I filed began, "Incredibly, the loud-mouthed, bragging, insulting youngster had been telling the truth all along. Cassius Clay won the world heavyweight title tonight when a bleeding Sonny Liston, his left shoulder injured, was unable to answer the bell for the seventh round."

I don't remember what I did with the rest of that night, but I don't think I slept. I still have the scrawled notes of my future-story file: Muslims, Malcolm, Clay's early life in Louisville, Liston's reputed mob connections, whither boxing?, a new model of sports hero. I wanted to hang on to this story.

It got even better the next morning at Clay's press conference. He was subdued and polite, and after he said that he would give Liston a rematch and fight all contenders, he said, "I'm through talking. All I have to be is a nice, clean gentleman."

The older reporters liked that. They smiled and nodded at one another. It had all been a put-on after all. They shifted a little nervously, though, when he added, "I'm sorry for Liston. You people put too much load on him, you built him up too big, and now he has such a long way to fall."

At that, most reporters, certainly the older ones, left to file their stories: all was right with the world, Clay was a nice kid if a little full of himself. Some would write that he had gotten lucky, a few that the fight might have been fixed so Liston would get an even bigger payday next time.

My cohort lingered, unsatisfied. We asked about Malcolm and about the Muslims' nationalism and their espousal of racial separation.

"Listen," said Clay. "In the jungle the lions are with lions and the tigers with tigers and the redbirds stay with redbirds and bluebirds with bluebirds. That's human nature, too, to be with your own kind. I don't want to go where I'm not wanted."

Most of us were integrationists, supporters of Freedom Rides, sit-ins, voter registration drives. We looked at one another. Is he kidding?

Someone asked, "So are you a card-carrying Muslim?"

Clay sounded annoyed. "I go to Black Muslim meetings, and

what do I see? I see that there's no smoking and no drinking and no fornicating and their women wear dresses down to the floor. And then I come out on the street, and you tell me I shouldn't go in there. Well, there must be something in there if you don't want me to go in there."

"What about your responsibility as champion to the youth?"

He quickly replied, "I don't have to be what you want me to be, I'm free to be who I want."

That sounded like an athletic declaration of independence to me. Maybe my heart didn't quite leap, but it bounced a little. This was going to be a big story, and it was going to be around for a while, and I was going to ride it to the buzzer.

Back in New York, it was obvious that I had made my bones. I was anointed the new boxing writer, which meant the Clay beat was mine. I got a raise. In the next few weeks I scored a series of exclusive interviews: with the newly named Muhammad Ali; with the Muslim leader Elijah Muhammad at his Chicago home while pregnant young "secretaries" padded about; and with Malcolm, recently split from the Muslims, in the back room of a Harlem bookstore. He was witty, wise, intellectually stimulating. Likable. Greg arranged that meeting. When Malcolm told me that my coverage of Ali had been the fairest, I was so pleased I made the mistake of telling the sports editor, who cracked wryly, "That's just great, we'll put it up on the trucks."

It was the headiest of times, chasing Ali and finishing *Nigger*, which came out that year. My Ali coverage gave me confidence that hard, dogged work would allow me to compete successfully with the top sportswriters. The book gave me confidence that I wasn't confined to sportswriting, that I had choices. There were offers from other places: a column in the *Herald Tribune*, writing lifestyle stories for *Newsweek*. But I loved the *Times*, and the paper loved me back, more raises and more freedom to make my own assignments, more freedom to find my own style. I was twenty-six, and I thought this would last forever.

With that measure of autonomy and the *Times'* willingness to let me travel, the Ali story was a magic carpet, although the ride was not always smooth. There were surreally delicious moments: strolling the beach in Key West with the sensuous Sonji Roi, Ali's first wife, as she told me how sweet he had been and how the Muslims had stolen his mind and broken up their marriage; loitering in his Stockholm hotel room while Swedish reporters berated him for his apparent bias against white women. Why wouldn't he go out with them? Ali tried his redbirds-bluebirds riff, then gave up, bewildered. They were mad because he *wasn't* screwing white women?

There were weird moments. When I tried to explain to him the *Times'* policy of referring to him as Clay instead of Ali because he hadn't changed his name legally, Ali patted my head and said, "You just the white power structure's little brother." That's what should have gone up on the trucks.

And there were ugly moments. Ali and I quarreled after I questioned him about the 1965 assassination of Malcolm X, after he had publicly broken with the Muslims and was on his way to becoming a charismatic international spokesman for peace and understanding. I've always thought that somewhere up the road, Malcolm and the Reverend Martin Luther King, Jr., who was assassinated three years later, would have joined hands and created a powerful moral authority.

Ali made himself unavailable for a while after Malcolm's murder, claiming death threats against himself. I hadn't expected Ali to leave the Nation of Islam when Malcolm did, soon after that first Liston fight. Malcolm was disillusioned by the Nation's religious rigidity, its reactionary politics, and its leader's hypocrisy—those "secretaries" were pregnant by him. Ali was still in thrall to the Honorable Elijah, and by pointedly saying that anyone who turned away from Elijah deserved death, he seemed to be almost offering his preapproval of Malcolm's execution. When I finally got the chance to bring that up to Ali, he brushed it aside, then got annoyed. Malcolm got what he deserved, he said. We went back and forth angrily until someone intervened. (Years later, I forgave him but never forgot my own feelings about his betrayal. It became a bone of contention between me and Ali's fourth wife, Lonnie. She wanted me to stop writing about it.)

This was the first major low point in the cycles of my relationship with Ali. The magical youth was getting tiresome with his dogmatic religionism on one hand and his cunning asides on the other, his sotto voce "I don't believe all the stuff I say," and, most disconcerting, the continual dismissal of compliments with the throwaway line "I'm just another nigger trying to get bigger," which I could never get into the paper of record.

The two fights of 1965 were dissatisfying—the first-round "phantom punch" that knocked out Liston in Maine and the cruel tormenting of Floyd Patterson, who had insisted on calling him Cassius Clay in a defense of Christianity and America. Ali shouted, "No contest, get me a contender!" as he carried Patterson for twelve rounds. He could have knocked him out, but he chose to pick him apart with painful blows.

It was a repulsively fascinating fight, but I had to struggle to keep my mind on it. There was a more compelling story line buzzing through my head.

Two nights earlier, I had taken an old boxing manager to dinner. He was rheumy and garrulous and very old, I thought then, although later I figured out he was only fifty-seven, though thirty immeasurable years older than I was at the time. Constantine "Cus" D'Amato, who had managed and trained Floyd Patterson, among others, to championships, was on the skids and going through a depressed period. He had been brought to Las Vegas with "walking-around money" to dress up the fight promotion and regale reporters like me.

He told me about an old gym he had once owned in a rough section of lower Manhattan. The gym was on the third floor, and late at night Cus would sit at the top of two shadowy, twisting flights of stairs with a gun and a German shepherd, listening for footsteps. What he dreamed of hearing was the hesitant yet resolute steps of a kid climbing up those stairs alone, driven by the desperation of his life on the street to fight his fear of the dark stairs and the unknown at the top, a kid who wanted to fight because he wanted to be somebody.

A kid like that, who used his fear as fuel, said Cus, would have a chance to become a contender. I wondered, what kind of kid would dare to come up those steps, what would be going on in his life, what would he find at the top?

The plot formed on the flight home: a black high school dropout, his life a dead end, the local gang on his back, climbs those stairs because he needs to learn to fight. At the top, he learns to live. When I got back to the *Times* office, as if preordained, there was a letter from an editor at Harper & Row Publishers, Ferdinand Monjo. He wondered if I had ever thought of writing a book "with boxing as its milieu." I called Mr. Monjo right up and began to babble, Yes, I said, I've been thinking about a book with two flights of stairs and a young black hero. I'd call it *The Contender*. Mr. Monjo said, "Go right ahead, dear boy."

I knew nothing about young adult literature then. This was just my novel, "with boxing as its milieu." It was linear, it had a seventeen-year-old protagonist, and there was no sex.

The Contender was a great success when it came out in 1967 and has been in print ever since. The times were right for the book. Government money was available, there was a desperate need for books with minority protagonists, and, perhaps most important, there was a generation of librarians and teachers dedicated to getting realistic fiction into the hands of boys. That's been a mission of mine, too.

· · ·

I had just started writing *The Contender* when Ali made his great leap into the cauldron of global politics. I was there to do a feature story on his training for an upcoming fight when it happened.

On February 17, 1966, we were sitting outside his little rented bungalow in Miami, ogling schoolgirls on their way home. On television—although not on his television—Senate hearings raged over the war in Vietnam. Sharp political lines were being drawn. A nation was pulling apart even as I was writing down Ali's best pickup line, "Hey, little girl in the high school sweater, you not gonna pass me by today."

The phone rang inside the house, and his cook came out. A reporter was calling. When Ali came back, he was fuming. His draft board in Louisville—which had originally classified him as unfit for service, perhaps as a gift to the local pillars of white society who had sponsored Cassius Clay back then—had just reclassified him 1A, ready for combat. His first response was "Why me?"

He began to rant. After embarrassing him with a classification that implied he was too dumb or nutty for the army, how could they suddenly reclassify him without another test? Friends and bodyguards from the Nation of Islam showed up to stoke his mounting fear and fury. He would be called up right away, they said, sent to the front lines, cracker sergeants would drop live grenades down his pants.

Ali became more upset. He was the heavyweight champ. Why didn't the draft board call up some poor boys? Think of how many guns and bombs his taxes paid for. This was hardly the response of the pacifist he would claim to be, but it was real. How much of the antiwar movement was principle, and how much was fear of getting hurt or killed or even of merely having your life interrupted?

Television news trucks pulled up. Interviewers sensed his anger and provoked him further.

"Do you know where Vietnam is?"

"Sure," he mumbled, but he didn't sound sure.

"Where?"

Ali shrugged. (In 1966, I only dimly knew where Vietnam was.) This went on for hours, questions about war, about going off to kill Viet Cong. It was dusk when a newcomer with a mike asked the question for the hundredth time.

"Well, what do you think about the Viet Cong?"

Exhausted, exasperated, scared, Ali blurted the sound bite that would help define the sixties, a headline sentence that made him simultaneously hated and beloved. He said, "I ain't got nothing against them Viet Cong."

That was the original line. He would repeat it, and it would eventually become "I ain't got no quarrel with them Viet Cong."

Everybody in the world except me led with that as if it had been a prepared statement. I heard it as a provoked response. It didn't seem like the key to the story, which I thought was his selfish rant about being drafted. Was I out of touch with the world, too deep into the story? What I thought was a nonstory was only one of the biggest of the decade. It sold a lot of papers.

It got bigger. On April 28, 1967, he refused to step forward and be drafted into the army. Within minutes, it seemed, boxing commissions withdrew their recognition of him as champion and refused to license him to fight in their cities or states. Once indicted and released on bail, he was not allowed to leave the country. For the next three and a half years, prime time for a twenty-five-year-old boxer, he was unable to ply his trade.

Boxing commissions are appointed by politicians, so it was easy to ascribe their actions to patronage or patriotism, but there was another likely reason: the former owners of Ali's contract, the Louisville pillars, had been supplanted by a new company led by Black Muslims. The commissions were concerned that those folks would be a lot harder to deal with than the traditional New York and Las Vegas types who ran American boxing, many of them decadent millionaires and front men for the Mafia.

That year, Ali took a seventeen-year-old Muslim bride as his second wife and slipped off the media screen. I didn't have time to miss him. I was anointed a columnist in September 1967, sharing the "Sports of the *Times*" space with Arthur Daley. I had a sense of power and responsibility.

I kept tabs on Ali in his exile, but I was writing mostly in the mainstream currents: the Olympics, the human rights movement briefly coming to sports, Billie Jean King and women's tennis, and an amazing year and a half in which New York's Mets, Jets, and Knicks all won championships. Tom Seaver! Joe Namath! Bill Bradley!

I wrote more columns about Bradley than anyone other than Ali. He was the anti-Ali, a Princeton- and Oxford-educated, politically aware, white Christian banker's son who had served in the military (a brief air force reserve stint). He avoided the media and selflessly played a team sport. The Knicks' rise, dragging the NBA up with them, occurred during Ali's exile from the ring and my first hitch as columnist.

Much of the media attention was on Bradley's *whiteness*, and how his presence in a sport whose aura was urban schoolyard, black, and drug-ridden helped sell it to a cool New York crowd. That 1969–70 Knicks team image (two whites: the patrician Bradley and the working-class Dave DeBusschere; three diverse blacks: the flashy hipster Walt Frazier, the mysterious intellectual Dick Barnett, and the stoic captain, Willis Reed) was a model for a postracial America. It was clever pop sociology and great marketing but missed what terrific basketball they played together and how crucial Bradley's fierce and heady contribution was. Sometimes I thought Bradley's *jockness* did not get its due. He wanted to win, demanded to win.

Meanwhile, Ali was out growing up, mostly without me. Early on, he had lost the crowd on college campuses with jokey slurs against marijuana and mixed-race couples. He learned from the experience, listened to the questions, asked questions, and eventually became a rousing Black Is Beautiful and antiwar speaker.

I was delighted when he returned to boxing in 1970. My Big Story was moving into a great new chapter, I thought, as I settled into my ringside seat at Madison Square Garden on March 8, 1971, for the so-called Fight of the Century against Joe Frazier.

I have a copy of the next day's front-page *Daily News* photo, Ali on his back, eyes closed, mouth open; Frazier standing over him, fists cocked; and Lipsyte shouting into a telephone, face contorted. I keep trying to imagine my thoughts. Was I surprised? Was I sad? Was I already thinking that the Big Story was over, that Ali would now be just an "opponent," a sacrificial lamb for champions and kids coming up?

My job that night had been to keep the desk apprised of the progress of the fight so it could update the story when necessary. Within a few rounds, my clipped capsules of the action became a blow-by-blow account and I was patched through to every speakerphone in the Times Building. I was broadcasting. And even though the official decision was unanimously for Frazier and most boxing writers thought Frazier had won, everyone who listened to my account was led to believe that Ali was winning, even after he got up from his knockdown, unsteady, face swollen.

I think it was that blindly biased private broadcast as much as feeling burned out by the column that dictated my own next great chapter. I was losing it as a fair-minded, clear-eyed observer. I'd crossed over, become a fan. And this time Ali was certainly all finished. My Big Story was over. I quit the paper six months later. I was thirty-three.

I stayed in touch with Cus D'Amato, who moved to a friend's house in upstate New York. He would eventually open a gym there.

One day in 1979, a former boxer who had once trained with Cus and now was a counselor at a nearby juvenile correctional facility, showed up with a problem, thirteen years old and 200 pounds, who had beaten up every kid in the reform school and started pounding on the guards. Could the old boxing manager meet him, talk to him, maybe even train him—try to channel all that fury into boxing instead of beating up people?

Cus said no, but the counselor was insistent, and finally Cus said, Okay, bring him around, but no promises. Something magical happened between the old white Italian and the black teenager. Eventually, Cus taught him to fight, inflamed him with his philosophies of fear and violence, and legally adopted him.

When I knew Mike Tyson in those days, he seemed like a sensitive kid. He was also an unstoppable young slugger. It was a great story. A classic. Unfortunately, a classic like *Frankenstein*. Cus apparently never finished his creation, and when he died, a year before Tyson became, at twenty, the youngest ever to win the heavyweight championship, the monster began to spin out of control. Over the years, interviewing Tyson the champion, the ex-champion, the convicted rapist, grieving father, junkie, lost soul, now struggling entertainer and family man, I would always see the teenager who had climbed up his own shadowy, twisting flights of stairs.

Howard Cosell at fifty-seven, in 1975. He was at the top of his game and happy to tell you how good he was. (Getty Images)

SIX | Uncle Howard

oward Cosell once said to me, "Bobbin, you have a face for radio and a voice for print." This, coming from a horse-faced man with a bad toupee whose nasal voice was the most irritating on the airwaves, was nothing less than inspirational. The opinionated loudmouth was one of the main reasons that ABC was no longer the Almost Broadcasting Company, why *Monday Night Football* was the blockbuster hit of prime time, why a white sports audience came to understand Muhammad Ali's persecution. One year, in the same poll, he was voted both the best-liked and most-hated sportscaster.

I had no such ambivalence. I loved Howard Cosell. He was encouraging to me, personally and by example; he used his radio and television pulpit to become the most important commentator on sports-related news in the country. Sure, he hustled sports—football, boxing, baseball briefly, the Olympics, and some made-for-TV early reality games—but he also delivered thundering jeremiads against greed, exploitation, racism, and the spurious use of tax dollars and eminent domain to build stadiums that would enrich the owners with whom he loved to mingle.

I took his credo—"You can't always be popular and right at the same time"—as a moral lesson and sometimes as a shelter when I was attacked for being a contrarian. In those days, it was rare for someone on TV or radio to stand up to public opinion. Cosell stood up. He was often called controversial because he wasn't bland. His attacks—on his radio shows, on his excellent, short-lived TV magazine, *SportsBeat*, and in interviews with anyone who would listen—against the news media's pandering to illegal sports gambling, the inconsistencies of drug testing, and the brutality of boxing were unusual for his times.

Cosell's sudden refusal in 1982, after the brave but untalented Tex Cobb lost a one-sided bout to heavyweight champion Larry Holmes, to broadcast any more professional fights was considered a grandstand play. What took him so long? asked his critics; the hypocrite made a fortune at ringside with Ali and so many other boxers. It *was* late. But among those who demanded reform when the overmatched Duk Koo Kim died after a fight with the lightweight champion, Ray Mancini—which was only days before the

Holmes-Cobb mismatch—Cosell was the only one willing to sacrifice a job, which he did, helping push through reforms. Cosell's play-by-plays and color commentary were entertaining and informative but not irreplaceable. What was irreplaceable, as he knew, was his presence, which gave a kind of moral seal of approval to the increasingly corrupt sport.

I once wrote that he was "a living mixed metaphor . . . symbol, know-it-all uncle, stern coach, comic relief. He was even a dichotomy: Who else could lure us into the SportsWorld tent with promises of jockomamie delights, then, once inside, berate us for wasting our time at such foolish entertainments?"

He often told me how annoyed he was at the dichotomy line, but I think he liked the idea of someone taking him so seriously. Cosell criticism usually came down to variations of Jimmy Cannon's lame put-down: "Cosell put on a toupee and changed his name [from Cohen] to tell it like it is."

He could blunt criticism with his own self-assessment: "Arrogant, pompous, obnoxious, vain, cruel, verbose, a showoff. I have been called all of these. Of course, I am." The twist, of course, was that he reveled in being able to get away with bad behavior. He modulated it with an exaggerated charm around tycoons, sports stars, and famous entertainers, as well as hot dog vendors and kids on the street, especially if there was an audience.

Cosell recognized the transcendent importance of baseball's first modern-era black ballplayer, Jackie Robinson—the word he used was "unconquerable"—and long before anyone knew what Howard was talking about, he dubbed O. J. Simpson "that little lost boy." If Cosell seemed a bit fulsome in his praise of Green Bay Packers Coach Vince Lombardi and harsh in his condemnation of baseball gambler Pete Rose, it was because he was, at heart, a True Believer. "I believe in all the clichés," he said. "I am a sports fan."

He was a True Believer in America. A Brooklyn Jew, a lawyer, an army officer in World War II, of course he would believe in the country's promise to all of fairness, constitutionality, meritocracy, order. In that sense, I was a True Believer, too. We saw that in each other. And he was an accidental sportscaster.

As a Manhattan lawyer, he was representing the Little League of New York when ABC radio asked him to host, for free, a Little League show. After three years, in 1956, he decided to become a full-time broadcaster and proposed a weekly show. He was giving up the law, so he wanted to be paid. He was told to get a sponsor. He did. That interview and opinion show, *Speaking of Sports*, and later *Speaking of Everything*, were ABC mainstays, intelligent, contentious, unafraid. He did pre- and postgame TV shows. He produced and voiced such groundbreaking documentaries as *Grambling College: 100 Yards to Glory*, which brought national attention to the historically black Grambling College and its legendary football coach, Eddie Robinson.

I met Cosell in 1962, at the Mets first spring training camp, when he whacked me with the thirty-pound Nagra tape recorder slung over his shoulder. This pushy stork—a radio reporter, yet, then the lowest on the lodge brother pecking order—was merely trying to get closer to the subject of a news conference.

It was a few spring trainings later that I saw him at a hotel poolside, ostentatiously annoying an attractive middle-aged woman and her two cute teenage daughters. As I came closer, he brayed, "There he is, Bob-bee Lip-syte of *The New York Times*, destined for stardom." I froze, embarrassed. The woman he was hitting on said, in a husky contralto, "Now just shut up, Howard, can't you see you are embarrassing the boy." And he shut up. He sat back with a sheepish grin, and he looked very happy. The woman was Emmy, his wife and keeper.

Through the next thirty years, Howard became my colleague, my friend, briefly my employer, and a loud booster of my career—

which did not endear me to other sportswriters and sportscasters, most of whom he treated with vicious, almost pathological contempt.

I liked the idea that Howard made so many in the sports media so crazy. His celebrity—he was often better known than his sports star subjects, who seemed delighted by his attention—gave him great access. His insistence that he was "telling it like it is" made it seem as though everyone else was fudging and piping, which was often true. But his sarcastic contempt for most other sports journalists often came from jealousy or paranoia. He didn't understand that most of the younger ones just wanted to sit at his feet. So he kicked them.

The first time Bob Costas met Cosell was at the 1983 World Series as both were entering the Baltimore ballpark. "I know who you are," brayed Cosell, "the child who rhapsodizes over the infield fly rule. You'll have a great career."

I later asked Costas if he had been offended or flattered. He thought about that. Sort of both, he said. Who else but Cosell could so neatly recognize your existence and then sarcastically dismiss it?

"I wanted to be his friend," Costas told me.

That never happened. Ten years later, when Cosell was out of television and ill, Costas called him. "I told him that I had admired him and that I and my generation just wanted to be friends with him but that he had pushed us away.

"There was a pause, and then he said, 'Maybe you're right, maybe you're right. We'll talk again.' We never did."

It was Howard's relationship with Muhammad Ali that was both the high-water mark of his career and the target of journalistic resentment. It was even the subject of one of the best books of the Ali oeuvre, *Sound and Fury: Two Powerful Lives, One Fateful Friendship*, by Dave Kindred, a rigorous reporter and a phrasemaker with insight. "Before Ali," he wrote, "sports was a slow dance. After, it was rock and roll. Before Cosell, sports on television was a reverential production. After, it was circus."

I particularly liked Kindred's recounting of the late-night flight in which Ali read to me at high volume his lecture on friendship. "'Whenever the thought of self-interest creeps in that means destruction of friendship. It can never develop into a real friendship, it can only develop into a business relationship. It will last as long as the business relationship lasts. Like me and Cosell. I lose, he goes to somebody else.'"

Cosell never went to somebody else with such intensity, because, as for me, there was never another subject that deserved it. And for Cosell, no other subject for which he would be the willing straight man. Ali was the star, and Cosell, to remain a journalist, had to keep some distance. Cosell gave airtime to Ali's religious, political, and social opinions when they were under attack by the government and the mainstream media, but he never endorsed them. He defended Ali's right to have his opinions. It was a standard that I tried to emulate, although in my arrogance back then I wouldn't have allowed that anyone else was my model.

At the end of his career in 1992, during a celebration of him at the Museum of Television & Radio in New York, Cosell was asked if there was anyone to whom he could "pass the torch." He cleared his throat and glared, and coldly said he didn't think there was anyone in broadcasting who could cover the range of topics he had covered with similar intelligence or morality.

Sitting there that night, I totally agreed. There was no one with his range of knowledge, his biblical old prophet's rage, his insider information. But I also had to laugh. This was from someone who loved playing himself on sitcoms, who had hosted "Battle of the Network Stars" where the likes of Captain Kirk (William Shatner) and Wonder Woman (Lynda Carter) competed in goofy athletic events. Of course, he did storm off the set of Woody Allen's *Everything You*

Always Wanted to Know About Sex* (*but Were Afraid to Ask)—when he found out he was cast as a sperm. But it was probably because he was only one of many.

I could find the dichotomy endearing, but many fans and media could not. And they never forgave him for patronizing and later ridiculing his teammate in the *Monday Night Football* booth, Frank Gifford, who as a New York Giant in the fifties and sixties was the beau ideal of jock manhood, handsome, brave, pleasant, bright enough. Gifford was beatified by a former University of Southern California classmate, Frederick Exley, in the critically acclaimed *A Fan's Notes: A Fictional Memoir*, which fixed Frank in the literary imagination. As advertising found sports, Frank became a Madison Avenue favorite. Frank was not a talented broadcaster and certainly no journalist. Howard must have resented Frank's looks and athletic credentials, the unfairness of his coasting through the world while Howard was always, as he said, "on the precipice of professional peril every day of my career."

Which was true. Howard could be in trouble for slurring his words on a broadcast (he said flu, they said drunk) or calling a black football player "a little monkey" (Cosell, a stalwart antiracist, often called quick little players of any race "monkeys"), while Frank, sweet-natured and cooperative, managed to be forgiven by the media for an incident in which a woman successfully lured him to an assignation to get photos and a story for a tabloid newspaper.

By the end of 1975, the high drama of the Muhammad Ali saga was winding down. Ali had regained the heavyweight championship in "The Rumble in the Jungle," in which he outlasted George Foreman in Zaire, and he had completed the Joe Frazier Trilogy with "The Thrilla in Manila," which he won as both men took terrible punishment. But Howard was still at the top of his game, and his turns on *Monday Night Football* were clearly not enough for him. If he couldn't be a senator, he thought, why couldn't he take that personality, that celebrity, that incisive intellect, that penetrating wit into the wider world of entertainment?

Well, he couldn't, and the proof was a variety show called *Saturday Night Live with Howard Cosell*. In his best joke, the head writer, Walter Kempley, wrote, "This show is so bad not only is no one watching, they are going next door to turn off their neighbor's set."

Before the show made its debut, while I was waiting for my supposed valedictory to the lodge brother biz, *SportsWorld: An American Dreamland*, to be published, Howard asked if I would be interested in working on it. I had no TV experience as yet, didn't consider myself a particularly funny writer, and wasn't plugged into the entertainment scene. But Howard didn't think those were problems, and we batted around the idea that I would be the show's "journalist in residence." I would make sure the scripts didn't fawn over guests too obviously, and I would scout for stories that Howard could break on air. I jokingly suggested that one such story would be getting the fugitive heiress Patty Hearst, who had been kidnapped in 1974 by the Symbionese Liberation Army, a ragtag group of criminals and radicals she had then apparently joined, to surrender to Howard live on stage. His eyes lit up. More than a year after the kidnapping, Patty was still a Big Story. Then he asked me how I would introduce the show's first booked act, a Beatles wannabe Brit band called the Bay City Rollers. I said, "Are they the hope or the hype?" Next thing I knew, I was offered twice as much weekly salary as I had ever earned.

I hated the job, hated it more than being a copyboy in the sports department. I had very little to do and few friends because most of the staff assumed that I had been hired by Howard to spy on them, which was probably true. Howard took me to lunch a few times a week and tried to pump me, but I knew nothing. He mostly wanted to know what the staff thought of him.

There were some very talented people on that show, including

Kempley, who had written for David Frost, Johnny Carson, and Jack Paar. He dreamed of writing novels and considered his TV and Hollywood work "pillaging." I was the number three writer on a two-man team and would sit in the writers' room with Kempley and David Axlerod, laughing myself breathless at their old jokes, repartee, and skit ideas, few of which got on air.

They were further frustrated because the show's recurring comedic actors, the Prime Time Players, insisted on writing most of their own material. They were unknown youngsters named Christopher Guest, Brian Doyle-Murray, and Bill Murray. Their best stuff didn't get on, either. To make matters even worse, the show's executive producer, the imperial Roone Arledge, routinely called on Saturday mornings to impose a new idea for that night's show, sometimes based on something one of his kids had told him. The Eagles are hot, Dad. Book 'em!

And Howard was no Mr. Tell-It-Like-It-Is here. He kissed up to John Wayne, sang "Anything You Can Do" with Barbara Walters, and showed little of his arrogance, feistiness, or wit among the non-jock celebrities he fawned over.

I wanted to quit, but the amazing $1,150 per week was my pillaging.

I did try to generate some work for myself on the show. I put out feelers about Patty Hearst and got the sense that having her surrender live to Howard was unlikely but also not impossible. There were people out there, some of whom I knew . . . (about which more later).

I wrote a recurring skit for the Prime Time Players in which Howard and "the boys," as we called them, sat in a *Monday Night Football*–like booth reviewing the nonsports events of the week as sportscasters might. But the edginess of the parody was blunted by Howard's new timidity, and the boys got bored. Soon after our show was blissfully put out of its misery, they joined the Not Ready for Prime Time Players on the rightful *Saturday Night Live*.

But before we got canceled, I got mad at Howard for the first and only time.

Time Warner had announced plans to produce a blockbuster Superman movie. It was holding auditions for the Man of Steel. I wrote a skit in which Howard wins the title role, dons the Superman suit, and brings on stage Jerry Siegel and Joe Shuster, who as teenagers in Cleveland created the comic hero but never shared in the bonanza. They were old men now and down on their luck. In my skit, while Howard, Siegel, and Shuster were onstage, the real head of Time Warner walks on to give each of the Superman creators $10,000 a year for life.

A Time Warner executive brusquely dismissed my idea over the phone ("You have to be fucking joking, *Howard Cosell?*"), but I decided to press on, if only to embarrass Time Warner. With the help of Mickey Kelley, a young researcher who would become Bill Murray's first wife, I had Siegel and Shuster flown to New York with their families and put up in a good hotel. Since I was considered Howard's spy, no one on the staff challenged my orders.

At the Saturday-morning rehearsal, Cosell and Emmy, who was never far from his side, decided that the two men were "too unattractive" to be onstage with Howard. Besides, if Time Warner wouldn't cooperate, why make it look bad? My entire segment was canceled. I was furious. I threw a tantrum. How could anyone be too unattractive to be onstage with this horse-faced creep with a bad toupee? And what did Howard Cosell stand for if not righting old wrongs? I told Howard that if Siegel and Shuster did not appear, not only was I quitting, but I would be writing about it. In some weird way I think Howard enjoyed my outburst, like the Halsey Junior High principal Dr. Nussey trying not to smile after I beat up my bully Willie. Except that Howard was both the bully and the principal here.

We compromised: Siegel and Shuster would sit in the first row during the live telecast, and Howard would walk down from the stage to chat with them on camera.

That worked out fine, live on Saturday night, and on Monday morning we got a request from the National Cartoonists Society for the phone numbers of Siegel and Shuster. The Society was going to threaten to strike if Superman's original creators did not get a piece of the action. Eventually—and I want to believe Mickey and I had a part in this—Siegel and Shuster each got $20,000 a year for life.

The show went off the air after eighteen weeks. I went off on a book tour for *SportsWorld*. People along the way asked me about Cosell almost as much as they asked me about Ali. Soon after I returned, Howard and I were coming back from a lunch when we passed a bookstore selling *SportsWorld*. He suggested I go inside, announce myself, and offer to autograph copies. I shrank at the thought. I was too shy.

He grabbed my arm, pulled me into the store, and bellowed, "I am standing here with Bob-bee Lip-syte, the greatest sportswriter of . . . our . . . time. If you buy his new book, *SportsWorld*, I will autograph it."

We sold a pile.

In 1985, Howard published his third and best memoir, *I Never Played the Game*, written with my old friend Peter Bonventre. His critiques, particularly of *Monday Night Football*, were more than the network suits could bear. And, in truth, ABC didn't need him anymore. Roone Arledge had won. ABC was one of the big three networks. Cosell was fired. He began to fade away.

In 1990, Emmy, who had been under treatment for lung cancer, died of a heart attack. The fight went out of Howard. The next summer, already in failing health, he had a cancerous lump removed from his chest. When I called after the surgery, he said, "Leave me alone, Bobbin, I just want to die." I called the next day, and he said, "I told you, leave me alone."

I decided to skip a day. I was busy, working on a documentary about him for ESPN, and I found out that the new management at ABC had refused to release his videotapes for our production. When I called Howard, after he told me yet again to leave him alone, that he wanted to die, I thought I might get his blood moving by telling him about the refusal. There was a brief pause, and then he roared, "That man is *dead!*"

Cosell was back.

It is probably unnecessary to add that he made some calls and we got the videotapes.

Dave Kindred thinks I talk about Cosell as if he were a crazy favorite uncle, and that is certainly part of the story, maybe more than I think. There were those lunches when I couldn't match iced teas to his martinis (his so-called silver bullets), when he would lean back and say, "Bobbin . . . ," the start of a monologue in which he would rail against his enemies, bemoan the world's misunderstanding of his genius, and excuse my naiveté. He talked lovingly, sometimes mawkishly, about his wife, his daughters, his grandchildren, but sooner or later he would come back to rail against the fools he refused to suffer, the worst of the "jockocracy," the ex-athletes on the air. (I gave him that term after hearing it from the feminist activist Flo Kennedy. Howard gave me credit the first few times, and then it was his.)

But his own naiveté might have been his flaw, his grandson Jared Cohane told me. Now a lawyer in Hartford, Connecticut, Jared spent summers with his beloved "Poppa" in his Hamptons summerhouse, absorbing his work ethic. Only the broadcaster Keith Olbermann, whom he worked with at ESPN, came at all close to Cosell in intelligence and insecurity, according to Jared.

"From a distance now, I think there was a certain naiveté," said Jared in 2009, "in that Poppa never saw the possibility of repercussions in the things that he said. And when there was a negative response, he immediately said that people were out to get him. You just can't be controversial and thin-skinned.

"And he never got the team concept. He didn't grasp that he was part of a team with people he worked with, that it wasn't right to criticize them the way he did in his books."

I found myself defending Cosell to his grandson. "I think he always saw himself as an outsider, a Jew, an English major in the jockocracy, a kind of Lone Ranger. He didn't feel like part of the team. He was on his own. It was probably his strength and his weakness." After I said it, I wondered how much of it applied to me, too. Maybe that was what we saw in each other.

The last time I saw Howard was on March 25, 1993, his seventy-fifth birthday. He was already drifting away. I gave him a teddy bear in a baseball uniform and what turned out to be a goodbye kiss. I also wrote about it in my *Times* column, which infuriated his daughters, perhaps rightly, because they were such fierce curators of his legend. They couldn't bear their father being portrayed as weak and vulnerable, as less than Howard Cosell. (Over the years, Jill and Hilary both told me I had "no idea how hard it is to be Howard Cosell's daughter.")

I'm still not sure if I crossed some boundary between the personal and the professional. They didn't invite me to his memorial service, although I went anyway. After all, I had spoken at Emmy's memorial service, at Howard's invitation. Jared remembered that.

When I told Jared that Howard would be rediscovered, especially since no one has replaced him, he said, "Maybe you're right. Listen to this."

He pulled up a bookmarked interview on his computer. A few days earlier, on November 3, 2009, the Pittsburgh Steelers' head coach had talked about his upcoming game against Denver. "If you like challenges," said Mike Tomlin, who at thirty-seven was exactly Jared's age, "this one has just about everything you're looking for.

You've got a great team in their venue, it's *Monday Night Football*, it's going to be awesome, and all we need is Howard Cosell."

I'd second that but extend the need beyond Monday nights. What would Howard be saying now about pro football, a violent sport that has lost its moral compass? Players' salaries are limited by an owner-imposed cap, there are no guaranteed contracts and no long-term responsibilities for players' health, even as we're finding out how dangerous the game is to the brain, the heart, and the joints. I like to imagine Howard rising in his version of a biblical old prophet's rage, telling it like it is, right if not popular.

Althea Gibson winning Wimbledon in 1957. Fifteen years later, she would be my tennis pro. (Associated Press)

SEVEN | My Muscle Molls

The only woman in the *Times* sports department when I arrived in 1957 was Maureen Orcutt, a big, jolly, fifty-year-old backslapper who seemed to have a vaguely secretarial function. Now and then, she went off to cover women's sports, mostly golf. Her stories tended to be short and dull. I liked her but agreed with the copydesk consensus that didn't take her seriously as a journalist, which after all was a man's job, especially at the *Times*. Fresh from Columbia, another boys' town, I carried an attitude toward women that has evolved slowly over the past half century, through four marriages, a social earthquake, and lessons learned from the struggle of female athletes for a place in the arena.

It was years before I learned Maureen's backstory, mostly because I wasn't interested. She was part of the sports department furniture as far as I was concerned, fun to banter with but no threat, and no one, I thought, who could teach me anything. Maybe that was the first story I missed at the *Times*. Maureen was a *Mayflower* descendant, the daughter of a former *Times* editor. She'd been married for two years in her late twenties. She'd won sixty-five major golf tournaments. She had been the runner-up for the U.S. amateur title in 1927 and 1936. And she had beaten Babe Didrikson!

Now, I knew who Babe Didrikson was because Paul Gallico's *Farewell to Sport* was a favorite book. Gallico, a New York *Daily News* columnist, was an influential sportswriter of the twenties and thirties who pioneered participatory journalism long before the bestselling stunts of George Plimpton. Gallico even lasted two minutes with a heavyweight boxing champ, the Manassa Mauler himself, Jack Dempsey. Gallico then went on to become a prolific fiction writer (*The Snow Goose, The Poseidon Adventure*). No wonder he was an early role model of mine. I tended to believe his bullshit.

In his chapter on women athletes, titled "Farewell to Muscle Molls, Too," Gallico wrote that Babe had become the greatest female athlete of her time (from the early thirties to the early fifties), perhaps of all time, in basketball, baseball, track and field, and golf "simply because she would not or could not compete with women at their own best game—man-snatching. It was an escape, a compensation. She would beat them at everything else they tried to do."

Can't get a date, so you become an all-time sports legend. Sounds right. This, I learned much later, was a classic Jock Culture reaction to getting your ass whipped. Gallico was a former college athlete (Columbia, no less) and vain about his jockness. During a golf match, his colleague Grantland Rice had mischievously talked Gallico into a foot race with Didrikson. Naturally, the Olympic gold medalist had left the scribe for dead. After that race, Gallico began writing about Babe's Adam's apple. If a woman beats you, she can't really be a woman. Probably a dyke.

I wish I had figured out that lesbian-branding scam a lot earlier, because in some ways it was the flip side of calling boys who didn't fit easily into Jock Culture "fags." Women athletes as good as or better than average male athletes were obviously as queer as were males who weren't good at all or who refused to give it up for Coach. I was a sportswriter covering those *Tea and Sympathy* coaches who left Kotex pads in boys' lockers before I realized it was more about control than homophobia, and it did keep straight boys in line. For gay male athletes, it frequently meant giving up football and baseball for cross-country or dropping out altogether. For women athletes, many of whom *were* lesbians (throughout the twentieth century, sports was often a safe harbor), it meant staying in the closet and/or looking "feminine." Babe Didrikson married, started wearing makeup, and even seemed to grow her bosoms, which sportswriters noted approvingly, as if she had done it for them. The rumors of her lesbianism, which may have been true, dropped away. Maureen Orcutt came to the office nicely dressed and coiffed, but she was built for football and acted like one of the boys.

We covered few women's sports events at the *Times* then, except in Olympic years; the Cold War with the Soviet bloc was measured in medals as well as missiles, and women's medals counted as much as men's. Thus, right after the willowy sprinter Wilma Rudolph won three gold medals in track and field at the 1960 Rome Olympics, she was brought to the *Times* office to be interviewed by the rookie on rewrite, me. She was a real story; an African-American polio survivor and one of the most beautiful women in the world. She had gently brushed off Cassius Clay when he had hit on her in the Olympic Village. Now she was in town for a medal from the mayor, some banquets, and an appearance at the children's ward of a local hospital. Classy lady, as we said then. Worth six hundred of our precious words that began, "The speediest woman in the world ambled through New York yesterday, using up the seconds she had saved in the Olympics."

Cute. Most of the rest of my story concentrated on her aching feet and how hard it was to get up in the morning. Would I have treated Ralph Boston, who had won the Olympic broad jump and was also in town, as breezily? Ignorance is no excuse, but it didn't hurt in those days to write in the bubble of clever, especially when you had no context, no sense of history. There are plenty of absorbing books now on women's mighty efforts to get leagues of their own; if there were books then, I didn't know about them.

Four years later, Althea Gibson was delivered to my desk for an interview. She had recently become the first African American on the women's pro golf tour. Golf was a new sport for the barrier-breaking tennis champion. I'm sure I treated her respectfully (I was still a polite boy in those days), but I knew only the bones of her life, not the flesh and blood. What it must have taken—and taken out of her—to become the first black woman to make it in the white country club world of amateur tennis! She was reviled, shunned, patronized, and then exhibited like a prize horse when she became a box-office draw. I understood this intellectually but had no idea of all the women, not to mention black women, who had struggled before her. Althea won Wimbledon forty-three years before Venus Williams became only the second African-American woman to win it. I wonder how much our covering Althea as an anomaly, a sister from another planet, added to SportsWorld's ingrained sexism and racism.

Althea was nowhere near as nice as Wilma Rudolph nor as easy an interview, but by then I was a cajoler of quotes and the story was fine, the sort of faux-Talese fast feature that was my signature in the days when I could write, "In her bland, round face and in her cool measured words still lurk the drives of a little girl who fought like a boy through the streets of Harlem and a lanky young woman who slammed her way to amateur and professional tennis supremacy." (It would be a few years more before I got a taste of those slams, some coming right at me.)

And then I met Billie Jean King.

As with Ali, it takes an effort to rewind, to feel again that tingle, breathe the stir in the air when you are first meeting someone who not only radiates such joy and possibility but includes you in her aura. In 1968, I wrote, "Billie Jean is a delight, perhaps the best woman tennis player in the world, certainly the most human. She throws off vibrations on the court, and when she nets an easy return and punishes herself with a sharp slap on the face, the stands rock gently with laughter.... Her muscular thighs make her seem chunky, although she is slim, and from the grandstand her face seems snubby instead of perky."

Does a whiff of condescension, sexism, rise off the page? Sorry. But Bobbin was in love. I was besotted by Billie Jean's looks, her charm, her skill, and her attitude. She was also great copy—ten minutes with her, and my notebook was fat—which has always affected my feelings.

There was more. I was thirty, a columnist, married to my second wife, Marjorie Rubin, who had started as a secretary in the *Times* music department, written a number of well-received features and reviews, and worked her way up to a demanding but unsatisfying job as an editor/writer in the women's ghetto of the family/style department. She'd quit because she didn't think she could handle both the job and our relationship, which was conventional wisdom then; her editor, the trailblazing, unmarried Charlotte Curtis, agreed.

Our second child, Sam, had just been born (the first had died at birth). Professionally, I was confident, gaining attention as a different voice in the sports pages; adjectives such as "irreverent" and "iconoclastic" were used to describe me, as well as "uninformed," "self-consciously liberal," and "commiekikefag." The changes in sports, especially the increasing distance between reporter and subject, were working to my advantage as an outsider, a critic of the status quo.

But personally, I was struggling to figure out my role, at least my posture, in the changing dynamic between men and women. What did the "liberated" woman want? Liberation from the likes of me? Did I want to be a liberated man? In SportsWorld, that seemed faggy.

And here was Billie Jean, this dazzlingly smart, accomplished, daring woman, who not only was great copy but seemed to have some answers. Once she complained to me with a certain wonder that "almost every day for the last four years someone comes up to me and says, 'Hey, when are you going to have children?' I say, 'I'm not ready yet.' They say, 'Why aren't you at home?' I say, 'Why don't you go ask Rod Laver why he isn't at home.'

"They say, 'Oh, but Rod Laver's the breadwinner.'"

At that point, those blue eyes flashed, just thinking about the top male tennis player. "Well, that's not the point at all. I love to play tennis. My husband understands this. But people don't. If I was a ballet dancer or an actress people wouldn't pester me to retire right away to have kids. I'm twenty-six, I've got time, but they don't seem to understand how I could find such great satisfaction in improving, in putting it together for a good match. I'm winning. When you've made the right moves for the right shot at the right time, it's a very aesthetic feeling."

Hearing those words in 1968, writing them into my notebook, reading them in my column the next day, began a pattern of thinking about men and women that zigzagged through the next forty years. There was no question that Billie Jean was a jock, as invested in her talent, as fierce in her ambition, as serious in her preparation as any man. So why couldn't we treat her like one instead of as a delightful or—in the case of the tight-assed tennis establishment—a pesky aberration? Most of the press liked Billie Jean for her accessibility and provocative quotes yet still regarded her as a second-class (read: nonmale) athlete. Was it because sports was considered an exclusive crucible for men, a place to get strong and tough, to prepare for competition in business, politics, war, academia? Was the presence of challenging women intimidating? Had Gallico been right to feel threatened?

Such thoughts seem quaint and simple-minded now, but when Margie and I married in 1966 there was no question whose career would take precedence. In fact, we even came up with an equation in which professional decisions and the personal choices that supported them would be made on a 70–30 basis. That would include where we lived and how we spent our money and time. At least 70 percent of the attention and effort would go into my career. The leftover was hers. I accepted the equation; well into the seventies, for example, I took for granted that Margie would keep the kids quiet whenever I wanted to work, including evenings and Sundays. As the decade lurched on, however, she was no longer taking that for granted. She wanted the time and space to write, too. The women's movement claimed that as her right. The percentages were shifting. For a while, we worked that out with more babysitters. But that meant I had to generate more money for more quiet. I resented that in a vague, passive-aggressive way but was proud that I could generate the money. I tolerated the situation, thinking myself if not liberated at least liberal.

. . .

In 1972, during the tennis boom, a large indoor club opened near my suburban New Jersey town, Closter. The marquee teaching pro was . . . Althea Gibson! I was writing a thriller for which I had gotten an advance big enough to support the family for a year or so. It seemed the right time to finally learn how to properly play this writerly game. My Columbia freshman tennis numerals had been awarded as a gift in return for cutting oranges for the varsity after my backhand was exposed.

I didn't mention our previous meeting to Althea when I showed up for my first lesson, and she didn't make the connection, looking at her clipboard and saying, "It's four P.M. Tuesday, so you must be Bob." Then she began barking at me, criticizing my nonwhite shorts and polo shirt, my unshaven face, and my slowness to "housekeep" the court of vagrant balls. She was not a good instructor of fundamentals (probably because I was just too fundamental), but she was demanding and inspiring, and she made me run, concentrate, think ahead, practice, shave, and dress better. By spring we were playing mock games, and every so often, after she'd had a big business lunch, I would score a point. She would scowl, and I could see that old competitive monster rise. On the next point, she would try to drive me off the court with a thunderous serve or hit me with her return. At forty-five, she still had the heat. It dawned on me that, after my mother, she was the first female power figure in my life. I had never had a woman boss or coach, or even an important woman teacher after sixth grade.

I still lost early in the club's B-level tournament.

A year later, Billie Jean became the worldwide symbol of the challenging and threatening woman in what was arguably the most socially significant yet silliest tennis match of all time, the so-called Battle of the Sexes at the Houston Astrodome, live on network TV with Howard Cosell himself at the mic.

Billie Jean, twenty-nine years old, the best female player in the world, had trained ferociously for what she believed would be her most important match. Her opponent was Bobby Riggs, a fifty-five-year-old hustler whose life up to then had been the prelude to his biggest con. He had already beaten a top-ranked woman, Margaret Court, who had not prepared well enough and had been easily psyched out. That was seen as a setback to the second wave of feminism, led by Betty Friedan and Gloria Steinem, among many others, and to Title IX, the 1972 law barring discrimination by sex in federally funded educational activities. Billie Jean *had* to win. The movement needed a warrior.

Billie Jean was carried into the arena by half-naked male "slaves" and Riggs by a "harem" of underdressed young women. I thought the hoopla and the match were absurd, yet I held my breath for her—and for myself. I had a stake in the outcome. I had come to believe in equality for women, not only because it was fair and because I had a sister, wife, and daughter whose dreams I wanted fulfilled, but because I thought it was good for men like me; if women had equal professional opportunities, the men in their lives would have more of a chance to fulfill *their* dreams instead of spending all their energy making money to support a family. It seemed pragmatic. For me, it would mean more time to take chances writing fiction, a big book, going for the killing. Two years gone from the *Times* and from daily sportswriting, I was a scrabbling freelancer. It was easy to see Billie Jean playing for me as well as for Margie.

More than anyone else, Billie Jean made it clear to me that the women's movement wasn't just for women. In her push for equality in tennis, she revealed the way male tennis players were controlled through the draconian rules of "amateurism." (Hard to believe now how players were forbidden to accept money beyond the under-the-table payoffs from promoters and sponsors that kept them in a kind of serfdom.) She was as responsible as anyone for "open" tennis, in which professionals and amateurs could compete together, and then for the honest professionalization of the game for everyone.

This made male sportswriters uneasy. Gender was very important. We were complicit in keeping women out of press boxes, much less locker rooms. When women sportswriters began showing up, male sportswriters were less welcoming than male athletes. Women diminished the prestige of our tree house, the men-only access we gloated over to friends and neighbors. Equal access reminded us that in Jock Culture most of us were treated like girls, lesser species to be bought, used, toyed with, dismissed by most athletes, officials, and owners. We could get back at them by refusing our services or spreading nasty tales, but boys were the ones with power.

In 1973, when Billie Jean beat Riggs, Margie and I were both writing from home and making an attempt to share housekeeping and child care. We were trying to edge toward 50–50. I was trying to become more than a *theoretical* feminist. I took my turn shopping, cleaning, getting up in the middle of the night to feed a baby, later taking the two kids to and from school. As long as I acted like a committed participant, not someone *helping out* Margie, it worked. Of course, I slipped now and then, and sometimes I needed to go out on a magazine or newspaper assignment to bring in some fresh cash. I came to like the sharing, especially the closer relationship with the kids. Billie Jean's "liberated" relationship with her husband was a supportive model.

What I didn't know at the time, despite the standard Jock Culture rumors of Billie Jean's lesbianism, was that her seemingly modern marriage—which included being "open" to experimentation—was one of traditional convenience. Billie Jean and her husband, Larry King, whom she often described as the "better feminist," were in more of a business relationship than a marriage. They slept with other people, in both cases women. It didn't all come to light until 1981, when Billie Jean was sued—in a sense blackmailed—by a former lover and the story erupted in open court. (She had also been on a 1972 *Ms.* magazine list of prominent women who had had abortions; Billie Jean claimed she thought she was merely signing a petition in support of choice. Eventually she admitted to the abortion, which enhanced her feminist cred and for a while checked the lesbian rumors.)

I was disappointed, not about her lesbianism but about the false example of a successful modern marriage. She had told us that Larry and she were not only on the same page politically but mutually supportive. He was cool with her as the major breadwinner and himself as the man behind the woman. And they still had dynamite sex! Meanwhile, so many of our friends—like Margie and me—were struggling with the new demands in male-female relationships. We thought that if the most famous woman in the world (at least in my world) was able to juggle career and marriage, maybe we could, too. Hey, what are role models for?

In retrospect, the big lie seems less hypocritical than poignant. She was terrified, she told me later, at the prospect of coming out to her conservative southern California blue-collar parents. And she had no professional choice. The conventional wisdom, probably true, was that even a hint of lesbianism would scare off fans and corporate sponsors. Billie Jean's coming out would have wrecked the nascent women's pro tennis tour of the seventies. That tour was precarious enough; the only sponsor willing to take a chance on it was Big Tobacco, eager to expand the women's market for cigarettes.

As time went on, I needed to compartmentalize my negative feelings about her Virginia Slims ("You've come a long way, baby") tour. It was crucial to the growth of women's tennis and a boost to all women's sports. Yet was it complicitous in the spike in teenage female smoking and later in women's increased incidence of lung cancer? If so, was it worth it? How can you make that equation, even assuming the lives saved and enhanced by women's sports?

By the time of her forced coming out in 1981, Billie Jean had been supplanted as tennis queen by Chris Evert and then Martina Navratilova, so it had little impact on the game. Her parents embraced her. But the major endorsement deals she and Larry had begun to line up fell away, and she needed to continue playing past her prime. No telling what she might have accomplished as an entrepreneur with money and time.

Nevertheless, I believe that Billie Jean was the most important sports figure of the twentieth century. Not only was she the symbolic leader of a movement representing half the world's athletes and potential athletes, she had also been a leader of the revolution that had overthrown the most oppressive concept in sports, amateurism, a dictatorship in which sports officials, well-paid executives if not wealthy aristocrats, controlled unpaid athletes. Early on, the control came through class—only athletes rich enough to support their training and travels could compete in tennis, golf, and Olympic sports. Later, as working-class kids like Billie Jean rose, the control came through doling out money surreptitiously. By cracking open tennis to professionals, Billie Jean helped create a climate of player power that would sweep through all sports, eventually leading to free agency in baseball.

Billie Jean and Muhammad Ali were the mom and pop of the so-called Athletic Revolution of the 1960s and '70s, even though neither of them was political or intellectual in the way of the academic commandos of that movement. But leaders such as Jack Scott, Richard Lapchick, and Harry Edwards, among others, found models for courage and action in the superstars' principled stands.

Billie Jean was a populist visionary. I admired her concept of World Team Tennis, which would not only make the game more accessible to spectators but bridge the gap between player and fan. She created a league in which top pros played on traveling teams in small venues and afterward gave clinics to local players. They helped create community-based recreational coed teams of all age groups, much like bowling leagues. It's a terrific program that still exists, although nowhere near what I think it might have been had Billie Jean not lost so much influence, money, and momentum in the wake of her palimony trial.

For all my scholarship in women's jock studies, I failed my first important exam. In 1988, my seventeen-year-old daughter, Susannah, was playing high school field hockey, a beneficiary of the Title IX surge in women's sports. I was a fan on the sidelines, thrilled to watch Susannah racing downfield, red-faced and roaring, "Get outta my way!" She was an all-state forward. Sports was our tenuous connection. Her mother and I had just separated, our marriage a casualty, in some ways, of the changing rules. With Sam away at college and Susannah a very independent high school senior, 50–50 wasn't hard in the day-to-day running of a household. Now the problem was our emotional balance.

Margie was writing and editing at a local feminist newspaper. I thought I was being enthusiastic and supportive, while she thought I was being patronizing and pedantic. Maybe I just missed print journalism. She also thought my interest in her fiction was a form of pressure. In 1980, she had published a roman à clef about the *Times*, *Hot Type*, which I liked, but a chauvinistic review in the *Los Angeles Times* and disappointing sales had depressed her. She kept starting and discarding new novels. I wanted her to work harder. And make some money.

In the late eighties, *The Washington Post Magazine* offered us a weekly column about the contemporary minefield of middle-class, middle-aged male-female relationships. My friend Jay Lovinger was the editor, and serious money was involved. I was wildly excited. Margie turned it down. Since I was a TV correspondent then, the heavy lifting would be hers, she said. Less time for her work. What work? I might have shouted. I didn't know how to deal with my anger and disappointment, the last straw in a pile of discontents, and eventually I left the house.

So we would stand on the sidelines of Susannah's games, barely talking. But my discomfort was quickly swept away in the pride of my daughter's team and the pleasure of watching her play. I was a fan! I loved those games. Too bad they were so fraught. Susannah was playing field hockey because the Northern Valley Regional High School at Demarest had no soccer team for girls, the sport she had played passionately for years in a local recreation league. Susannah and her friends had complained. They had been upset and talked about a petition, but there was no strong organizing support beyond their group. They had given up, found other sports, or stopped playing sports. We didn't talk about it much at the time. The split-up in the family absorbed most of our attention.

Susannah still loves soccer and plays when she can. It still upsets her to think about not playing high school soccer. When we recently talked about it, she said she found it ironic that I could have been writing about Babe Didrikson, Althea Gibson, and Billie Jean King in the eighties and not have been at all involved in the gender inequity right in front of me. When Susannah and her friends asked the school for a soccer team, they were told that they already had field hockey; they couldn't have a second fall field sport.

They could have used a sportswriter, a male TV sportswriter at that, to remind school officials that the boys had both soccer and football in the fall. Title IX, anyone? The law was sixteen years old then and still not being rigorously enforced. In retrospect, I feel ashamed. And stupid. What a chance to put into practice all that abstract reporting, that pose of liberated macho, make a fuss, challenge the school, create a soccer team. Be useful.

In 2009, I interviewed Billie Jean for a weekly PBS show I was hosting, *LIFE (Part 2)*, about aging and renewal. She had just written a book, *Pressure Is a Privilege*, in which she offered a new spin on the 1973 Battle of the Sexes. Now it was the Battle of the Ages, and the late Bobby Riggs was her current role model for successful aging, for never giving up. Her victory, she said, had come about because she respected what he had done in the past. He wasn't just a fifty-five-year-old hustler to her, he was someone who had won the singles, doubles, and mixed doubles at Wimbledon in 1939 and so must never be taken for granted. Respect history and your elders. That's why she had prepared so hard.

I thought that was good (certainly good for the show), but Billie Jean has always had a second serve that can surprise you. She also said that she had come to a number of new thoughts through long-term talk therapy. For example, she understood how sports competition can be used as an escape from everyday life, as a way of putting off all the issues that need eventually to be addressed. You don't have to face your fears when you can focus on the next match. Once she stopped playing regularly, she said, she found herself substituting binge eating for the addiction of competitive matches.

It was a fascinating insight, but we didn't have a chance to develop it. Next time, we promised. Billie Jean has always been a mind in motion, one of the smartest athletes I've known, and I left with unanswered questions. How many athletes find in sports an avoidance of responsibility and stay in sports to defer adulthood? We easily understand the adrenaline rush of competition; what about the narcotic of dissociation from everyday life?

Covering sports, particularly on deadline, can offer a similar rush, and during the absorption of chasing a story it's easy to justify not fulfilling the obligations of a relationship, of a family. Maybe I'll get to the next Thanksgiving with the in-laws, the next school play or teacher meeting, the next meltdown, drug scare, college application. Can't make this one, I've got to file my story.

The first family of the Athletic Revolution. Left to right: Bill Walton, William Kunstler, Micki McGee, and Jack Scott. (Courtesy of Barton Silverman)

EIGHT | Jock Liberation

J ust as the feminists were going to make my life as a man easier, the Athletic Revolutionaries of the 1960s and '70s were going to bridge the gap between the jocks and the "pukes"—the label a Columbia University crew coach had slapped on anyone in 1968 who wasn't on his boat, which included hippies, pot smokers, antiwar demonstrators, bearded weirdos, guitar players, and, yes, English majors. (When the coach, Bill Stowe, used that word in an interview, he looked at me with a cheerful condescension that made clear which side of the gap I was on.) In hindsight, I don't think any of the Revolutionaries could have bridged that gap because they were jocks—enlightened but still entitled, ambitious, focused, driven, able to dissociate from everything but the path to the goal. Compared to them, even while ruthlessly plunging ahead on a story, I feel woolly, distractible, sometimes handicapped by the lack of certainty that nothing matters except winning. Sort of puke-ish, I am.

Maybe I was attracted by their certainty that sports was important and was being perverted by the establishment. That reinforced my own growing sense that professional and big-time college sports were merely an extension of the reigning power structure, those pale, male, straight preppies who made money and made war. They were jocks. They were big bullies.

Thus the story that most interested me when I became a columnist in 1967 and could pick most of my own assignments was the growing resentment among athletes, particularly black college football players, at their exploitation by authoritarian coaches who dictated their lives on and off the field. A player could lose his scholarship for growing an Afro or a mustache in defiance of rules, for dating a white woman, for just acting uppity. Meanwhile, he was subject to "stacking," a practice in which black players were forced into nonleadership positions (many black high school quarterbacks, for example, were turned into running backs and defensive backs in college) and to playing while hurt, risking their careers, even permanent injury, in the interests of their coaches' game plans.

The players' discontent was supported by the revolutionary campus climate. Big-time college sports (basically football and basketball), though traditionally shady enterprises, had yet to become the corrupt conglomerates they are now. So-called student-athletes were not yet living, eating, and studying in jock quarters, isolated from student-students. So they could pick up the antiwar, antiracist, antiestablishment excitement while strolling from their dorms to their classrooms (so many foxy chicks handing out leaflets, chanting!), and they were stung by the reproof of their classmates—

"Dumb jock, can't you see how the oppressive patriarchy is fucking you over?" Few athletes joined the demonstrations and risked being cut from the team, but they began to catch the spirit as it applied to them—they *were* being fucked over. "And look what the pigs did to Muhammad Ali!"

With its political, racial, and social justice aspects, that story—which would also lead me into a corner of the biggest tabloid tale of the time, the Patty Hearst kidnapping—seemed like a natural progression from covering Ali, now in his period of exile from the ring. I checked in on him intermittently as I got to know the leaders of the so-called Athletic Revolution, mostly bright academics whose sensibilities were much closer to mine than were those of the hard-core coaches I usually interviewed. I liked the Revolutionaries. Some became friends as well as subjects, which was unusual for me, and troubling. What would happen if I came up with negative information about them? Would I betray my friendship or my professionalism? I had always been contemptuous of reporters whose cozy relationships with their subjects included advising and protecting them. I hated the idea of becoming any subject's "bobo," or toady, even if I agreed with him. I felt I needed to be careful not to get too friendly, to lose professional perspective. In retrospect it seems quaint and righteous, even a little paranoid. But I also understood the journalistic symbiosis (or Faustian bargain): I was one of their few major media outlets, and they gave me the chance to write about issues that interested me.

The most enduring of the Athletic Revolutionaries was Richard Lapchick, accurately referred to these days as the "social conscience of sports" (his annual racial report cards have been critical in keeping the media sensitive to biased hiring practices, especially in college sports). The son of a famous player and coach who helped integrate pro basketball, Rich, a close friend, has connected academia, the media, and corporations to college and pro teams in progressive programs combating sexism, racism, homophobia. His reformist missions are international.

One of the most visible of the Revolutionaries was Harry Edwards, whose Olympic Project for Human Rights led to the world-stopping black power salute by his San Jose State students, Tommie Smith and John Carlos, on the medal podium at the 1968 Mexico City Games. Eventually an important sports sociologist at Berkeley and adviser to pro teams, Big Harry (six foot eight, 300 pounds, a former basketball player and track star) was a stunningly eloquent speaker, quick thinker, and intimidating presence. In private, he was warm and funny; I enjoyed hanging with him and treasure his advice, even if I can't follow it: buy waterfront.

Probably the most polarizing was Jack Scott, scornfully dubbed "the guru of jock liberation" by the soon-to-be-disgraced vice president, Spiro T. Agnew. Still, it was an accurate moniker. Scott wanted to teach athletes to take control of their bodies and their games. He believed in discipline, hard work, fair play, civil rights, and equal athletic opportunities for women. Like Cosell, he was a true believer in the meritocracy of sports. Scott could admire the idealism of the Olympic movement, while despising the racism and hypocrisy of someone like Avery Brundage, the Nazi sympathizer who headed first the U.S. and then the International Olympic Committees.

Scott was farsighted, a hustler, and one of the most outrageous name-droppers I've met ("Fidel Castro turned me on to margaritas," he once told me while drinking one). Scott fascinated me because I liked and distrusted him at the same time. He kept me guessing, on guard, a good thing.

The first time I saw Scott, a tall, lean twenty-seven-year-old, he was standing at the front of a University of California classroom wearing red running shoes, a baseball cap, and gym shorts, which in 1970, even in Berkeley, was not considered appropriate academic garb. He brought several hundred undergraduates to startled order by blowing a whistle.

He did that, he later explained to them, because "Three hundred yards from here, men who are also supposed to be teachers act and dress like this all the time, curse their students, and impose arbitrary rules about hair, clothes, social life, and no one thinks twice about it."

Scott could be more outrageous than that, at various times describing coaches as "soulless" reactionaries or implying that many lusted for their players. It got him publicity but tended to distract from his message, which was basic democracy—sports was for the players, not the coaches, officials, and owners, and everyone, regardless of age or gender or size or disability, should have cheap, easy access to participation—but was interpreted as socialism by a lot of people back in those Commie-haunted times.

Scott was no ivory-tower theoretician, no liberal philosopher who had grown up relegated to the sidelines. He had been a hard-hitting high school football player called "Chief" and a college track star. For better and worse, he brought those same jock drives to win, to be celebrated, to kiss the cup, from the field to the revolution. In some ways it may have undone him; it certainly led him to become involved with Patty Hearst, the fugitive heiress who was implicated in robbery and murder.

Scott had only about five years as a besieged and beloved guru. He wrote the seminal *Athletics for Athletes* and *The Athletic Revolution*, noisy, contentious books that outlined his philosophy, which he was able to put into practice as athletic director at the liberal Oberlin College. He created a prototypical Title IX program, gave athletes a voice in the selection of their coaches, and, four years after Tommie Smith's Olympic gesture, hired Smith as track coach. But Scott was soon fired along with the progressive president who had hired him.

Scott helped prepare for publication several countercultural sports books, including Dave Meggyesy's *Out of Their League*, the memoir of a blue-collar stud's political awakening as he played big-time college and pro football. It is justifiably one of *Sports Illustrated's* best sports books of all time. He and Meggyesy, who remains a friend of mine, fell out during the process, which was not atypical of Scott's relationships with athletes he tried to mentor.

Though I agreed with most of Scott's views on repression and exploitation in sports, I didn't share his worship of athletes. He once told me that the violence at the 1969 free Rolling Stones concert at the Altamont Speedway in northern California as well as at other rock concerts at that time would never have occurred if more athletes had been present. "What bullshit," I said. "What about all the jocks on campuses who beat up fellow students?" "You're right," he said unconvincingly and tried to move on.

But I couldn't stop. What about that überjock Avery Brundage, Scott's ideological opposite in sports? Brundage, the Olympic dictator, had himself been a former standout young athlete (he had lost to Jim Thorpe in track events at the 1912 Olympics). But the restrictions he imposed on athletes' freedom to earn income had led to the nickname "Slavery Avery." For Brundage, it was always about the games, not the gamers. His determination that "the Games must go on" no matter what else was happening included downplaying Hitler's treatment of German Jews before the 1936 Berlin Games. In one of its most trivial yet cautionary manifestations, the prelude to the Holocaust included barring Jewish athletes from the German team, which violated the Olympic charter. (Brundage's anti-Semitism and pro-Nazi sentiments are well documented and were probably helped along by German contracts at his Chicago-based construction company.)

Brundage's personality and power exemplified what Scott was up against. Running Smith and Carlos out of Mexico after their mild, silent gesture was obviously Brundage's idea of affirming his grip. After a couple of interviews, I came to despise that arrogant sleaze, even before I knew about his Nazi connections and his relentless philandering, never attractive attributes in the righteous. The integrity of his amateur principles was a sham, too, always bendable when the Games were in danger of being superseded by other sports spectaculars or there simply was money to be made; see the nationalism, commercialism, and corruption (cities paid off Olympic officials to grant them rights to stage the Games) that marked the late twentieth century. By 1992, the basketball players were no longer amateurs and acted accordingly. When the U.S. Dream Team—including such stars as Charles Barkley, Larry Bird, and Magic Johnson—went to collect their gold medals, Michael Jordan actually wrapped himself in the American flag. He was a Nike endorser and didn't want to be seen on the podium in the uniform that Reebok had paid the U.S. Olympic Committee for the players to wear. I remember being overwhelmed by the symbolism. Or was it satire?

Brundage died in 1975, a few weeks before I flew to Portland, Oregon, on a *Times* magazine assignment to profile the relationship between Jack Scott and his housemate Bill Walton, the vegetarian Grateful Deadhead who had led UCLA to two national basketball championships and now was an NBA star with the Trail Blazers. Although Walton did not want to be interviewed at length by me (it wasn't personal, he assured me, it was the crass consumerism and counterrevolutionary nature of the *Times*), Scott convinced him that I was a fair and sympathetic major media outlet by showing him a copy of *Nigger*. Walton had recently demonstrated with Dick Gregory and César Chávez, the Mexican-American farmworkers' union leader.

So I spent most of a week living with Walton, Scott, and their womenfolk, Susie and Micki. I puzzled over Scott's relationship with Walton. In the course of a day the thirty-two-year-old Scott could be the twenty-three-year-old Walton's political tutor, editor, athletic trainer, bobo, sidekick, and mooch, a posse of one. The "Big Red-Head," as Walton was called, seemed kind of goofy and did not have all that much interesting to say. He was mostly busy rehabbing his bad legs and eating—he was almost seven feet tall, and it took a heap of veggies to fill his protein needs. I often pitched in, scraping and chopping in the kitchen. Since I was eating, too, it didn't seem to be violating any *Times*ian rules of objectivity and distance.

It soon became clear that Scott was far more interesting than Walton, even more interesting than their relationship. This was in the waning days of an athletic revolution that was turning out to be less of a rebellion than a temporary mood change. The big shoe companies were buying up athletes, coaches, college teams, and professional leagues. TV money flowed. Jocks were beginning to get rich. The Vietnam War was over. African-American athletes were beginning to dominate pro sports, and they could wear their hair any way they wanted and screw indiscriminately. What was there to demonstrate against?

A man of his times, Scott had moved on, into the violent belly of radical politics.

He had recently emerged from six weeks underground to face charges of harboring and transporting Patty Hearst and surviving members of the Symbionese Liberation Army after a bloody shootout in Los Angeles. The SLA was a ragtag group of radicals and criminals, a violent, cultish gang that had kidnapped Hearst, then a nineteen-year-old college student, from her Berkeley home in 1974, a year and a half earlier. It had offered to release her first in exchange for several imprisoned members, then for a multimillion-dollar Bay Area food distribution program. It was a sensational story, made more so as the SLA robbed, murdered, and released tapes of Patty espousing their revolutionary line under the nom de guerre Tania. She was seen in a bank security video brandishing a rifle and barking commands at the robbery victims. The pundits debated whether she was a true revolutionary or a brainwashed subject of the Stockholm syndrome, in which captors become emotionally attached to their captors.

Scott, who had connections in the Bay Area radical community, was seized by the opportunity to get a piece of the action, as a journalist or a deal broker. He would tell me coyly that whatever he had done was "to save lives."

In Portland that week, he had been evasive, although he had dropped enough hints to lead me to believe he had indeed been involved in Patty's escape from L.A. after the shoot-out. I wasn't alone in that belief. Scott's older brother, Walter, stayed in the house for a few days, adding a frisson of danger. Walter, friendly yet sniper-eyed, was recuperating from nasty wounds on his body, suffered, he said, when a grenade had been thrown into his Phnom Penh hotel room; he had been one of several hundred civilian gunmen flown in to provide security for the U.S. Embassy's withdrawal from Cambodia. Walter, whose story of being a government assassin we had no trouble believing, told me he thought he had been targeted by leftists who were concerned he would rat out his kid brother. Which he probably did. Later, he told the FBI that Jack and Patty had been lovers while on the lam.

Maybe he even did it that week. Short-haired men in suits and ties were watching the house in cars across the street, and they followed us on trips to the gym and the vegetable markets. Once, when I was in the house alone, they rang the bell and showed me FBI credentials. I told them who I was and started asking them questions. They backed away; I figured they didn't want to be in my story.

After a few days, my notebook was fat, and Scott thought we deserved some R & R. On an unusually lovely summer day, we drove to his favorite pool in Eagle Creek, a fast-moving, gin-clear stream that sliced through a lush green thicket. We scrambled down a steep bank, stripped, and dived into shockingly cold water. After a while, we climbed onto flat rocks and dried in the sun. Scott said that after working so hard on the story (I let pass the implication that we were *partners* in my assignment), this was our time to relax and commune with nature. And what could be more natural than *yerba buena?*

So I found myself lying naked on a large flat rock above a rushing stream, baked by a noonday sun and the fat joint I was sharing with the subject of my story, similarly unclad and supine. My notebook and pen were out of reach. Off in the bushes, in their suits and ties, the FBI watched. I could imagine the silly smile on my face, but I knew I was also thinking, What the fuck am I doing here?

I'd been conditioned since nineteen to believe that for "a gentleman from the *Times*," objectivity extended to a detached deportment. Chopping vegetables was bad enough, but doing dope? With a subject, yet? That had to be even worse than dressing badly while representing the paper. Even stoned and naked on that rock, I knew I was too comfortable to be doing my job properly, that I should be beside myself, at a remove, as controlled by boundaries as any shrink or lawyer. I should be spying from a distance like the feds.

I was mildly surprised at not being struck dead by the Jehovah of Journalism and that my piece was accepted and published (although my account of getting stoned with Scott didn't make it into that counterrevolutionary magazine). I *had* gotten too friendly with Scott, who became the main focus of the piece—I spent more space on his subsequent legal issues than on his relationship with Walton. Yet all that access led to a story that did not totally please Scott, especially my suppositions that his political activities came out of the same driving ambition that had made him a stand-out athlete.

I never wrote about the last time Jack and I talked on that trip, in a men's room at the Portland airport as I was leaving. He turned on a water tap to foil any FBI listening devices, lowered his voice, and asked if we could talk strictly off the record. I said that would be dangerous if something came up that immediately affected my story. He promised it wouldn't, and I was intrigued enough to agree.

He said he was in a position to supply me with enough information about Patty Hearst, her kidnapping, her time with the SLA, her fugitive life, to make a best-selling book. We could figure out later the financial terms of what would surely be a million-dollar-plus advance, but basically I would split it with a famous left-wing lawyer, possibly William Kunstler, who would use his share to pay Jack and to defend me when the FBI wanted to know where I had gotten my information. Obviously, I would have to be ready to go to jail to protect my source.

I asked Jack how much time I had to think about it. He said he needed an answer before we left the men's room. I washed my hands, peed, washed my hands again. Finally, I said yes. With one proviso: I had to meet Patty.

Jack's eyes got hot. "You don't trust me?"

"Think of it as due diligence," I said. "I'm ready to go to jail on your word. I just want to meet Patty."

We went back and forth a few times. I asked him if he had harbored and transported her. He repeated the line that whatever he had done was to save lives. I said that wasn't good enough now. He said, "You don't trust me," and stormed out of the men's room.

He was right, of course. I didn't trust him. Ultimately, I don't completely trust anyone I write about. Our interests are different: mine to find what I can consider truthful as well as readable, theirs to be presented in the best light. But there always seemed an undercurrent of hustling with Scott, even if it seemed to be mostly for the right causes. That undercurrent made me uneasy. I am always alert to being conned. As Dick Gregory would say, "Too hip to be happy."

By the time Scott died in 2000, at fifty-seven, of the throat cancer he'd been battling for years, I had been through the first recurrence of a testicular cancer originally diagnosed in 1978 and had written a book about it. I admired the focused, jock way he dealt with his disease. He had long ago forgiven me for rejecting his book deal and told me the rest of the Patty Hearst story: with herohood and that book contract in mind, Scott and his parents had driven Hearst cross-country from California and hidden her in New York and Pennsylvania. Two of his close friends, Phil Shinnick, an Olympic long jumper and university professor of social psychology, and Jay Weiner, a promising young journalist, had also guided fugitive members of the Symbionese Liberation Army. They eventually went to jail. But Scott, the guru, the mastermind, did not.

To this day, that remains a mystery to me, as it does to Weiner, who became a successful journalist in Minneapolis, and to Shinnick, who emerged from his ruined academic career to become a practitioner of acupuncture and other complementary treatments in Manhattan. Both have remained friends of mine.

When Scott died, I expressed my wonderment in a column: Had Scott cut a deal to escape prosecution?

I had gotten hold of an FBI interview with Scott just before he died in which he claimed that while he was helping Hearst elude the police in 1974, she told him she had arranged her own kidnapping. She'd wanted to break off her engagement with the man she was living with in Berkeley, but she hadn't wanted to give her parents the satisfaction of having been right about Mr. Wrong. So she asked her local dope dealer to make a connection with the Symbionese Liberation Army, which could snatch her and make the guy look like a wimp in the process. Was it true? Did Scott make up that story? Shinnick thinks so.

Could Scott have been close enough to the Hearst barony to have it put a lid on his prosecution in return for not revealing that Patty had lied about her abduction? The twenty-two months she served for her adventures (a thirty-five-year sentence was commuted by President Jimmy Carter, and she was pardoned by President Bill Clinton) was a fraction of the time she would have served had the judge and jury believed she was not a victim at the start.

Scott's wife, Micki, was apparently angry enough at my speculations to disinvite me to Scott's memorial. I regretted missing the chance to say good-bye with that old revolutionary crowd, see what they were all up to. But I understood that in the end, the journalist stands alone. Or should.

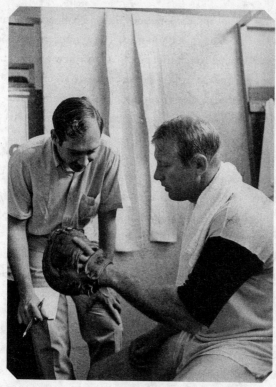

I'm not sure whether I am teaching Mickey how to use his new first-baseman's mitt or if he's giving me the finger. (Courtesy of Barton Silverman)

NINE | My Center Fielders (Part Two)

Mickey Mantle was banned from baseball in 1983, which brought him back into my life. He had taken a public relations job with an Atlantic City casino hotel, which the Major League Baseball commissioner thought put him too close to the evils of gambling. It seemed like an overly pious ruling, but

Mantle was philosophical—nobody in baseball was offering him $100,000 a year to hang out and grin. The producers of *CBS Sunday Morning with Charles Kuralt* thought that their new on-camera essayist, me, would find Mantle a perfect subject among my soft-core sports pieces—rodeo clowns, linebackers returning after cancer, Iowa girl basketball players, legless gymnasts. Mantle in his very off season.

The most difficult part of the transition to TV for me was learning to trust producers, editors, and crews enough to be truly collaborative, to share the creation and direction of a story. I was used to hunting and gathering by myself, writing in a bubble, then fighting editors over words they wanted to change. In TV, the collaboration extends to the subjects; a cranky, uncooperative subject might still make a good newspaper story but rarely good television. And at *Sunday Morning*, especially in the more featurey sections such as music, art, Americana, and sports, we picked mostly people we liked, with whom we wanted to share time. People who delighted us, maybe even were worth our admiration.

I was up for The Mick. It had been twenty-three years since he and Yogi had tried to part my hair, and I had come to realize that the shame I'd felt that night at Yankee Stadium and the anger later had been misdirected. Mickey was Mickey. The sports media that had godded him up were the guilty parties. I had covered plenty of heroes in those twenty-three years, even come to admire a few, such as Muhammad Ali, Billie Jean King, Malcolm X, and Dick Gregory. But I knew they were all humanly flawed and that totally embracing or rejecting a hero was silly.

I still didn't grasp the worship of Mantle beyond his amazing natural abilities, but I was long past making him the demon in my dreams. I felt a little sorry for him—he had squandered his talents. But I was open to Mantle. Or so I thought.

. . .

So on a chilly day in early May 1983, I followed him around a New Jersey golf course on a joke-a-stroke corporate outing. He drank his way from hole to hole, offering ribald bonhomie to thrilled businessmen. Mantle was mellow by the time we sat down in a deserted clubhouse bar for a long on-camera interview.

He continued to drink as we talked. He seemed determined to knock down some old myths: he said his legs had never been as bad as the sportswriters had made them out to be, nor had he lived in fear of an early death. In fact, he said, grinning slyly, he rarely ever gave it a thought unless some reporter brought it up. "Now I'll probably have a hard time sleeping tonight."

I asked him if he had any regrets.

"My only regret is that I didn't take better care of myself like Willie Mays and Stan Musial and Hank Aaron. I think I could have played a lot longer."

I asked him if taking care of himself included drinking less.

His cool blue eyes flicked over my face, narrowed. His voice changed to a growl. "Let's close this off. Haven't you got enough?"

I felt myself stiffening, and my voice seemed to be coming from a great distance, perhaps all the way from 1960 while a ball whipped over my head.

"Are you in a hurry," I snapped, "or is all this bothering you?"

That let some of the air out of Mantle. He seemed momentarily confused. "Well, I'm not in a hurry." His voice softened again. "We've been doing this for thirty minutes . . ."

My voice softened, too. I explained that people were more concerned about their health these days, and given that athletes are role models, what he had to say on the subject could be useful. It sounded lame to me as I said it, but it gave both of us room.

He said, "From, say, 1960 to 1968, when I retired, my wife and kids didn't come to New York with me. I stayed in a hotel, and from the time the game was over till the next day there wasn't very much for me to do, you know, except I would go out to eat and I would start drinking."

It sounded packaged. I wanted more from Mantle, some inner glimpse. Sometimes you have to give to get. So while the cameraman changed tapes, I told Mantle about our first meeting in 1960. I told him that a lot of newspapermen thought his rudeness was a result of his stress and pain, but that I didn't know that at the time and his casual curse words had rocked my boat and informed the rest of my career.

He listened carefully, flashed that Oklahoma Kid grin, and lifted his drink. "I remember that well, Bob. It always bothered me. That's why I started drinking."

That was the moment when I finally started liking that sarcastic country slickster. For the first time, I understood his appeal, why middle-aged men cried when he showed up at their surprise birthday parties (for a reported $10,000) and why Bob Costas and Billy Crystal revered him. Mickey was truly cool and funny in that smart-ass, deflecting style of the locker room, also the police station, the barracks, the trading floor. No wonder he attracted man crushes. He was the quintessential jock with both easy charm and the neuroses that hinted of vulnerability. The wounded warrior. Why had I never gotten that before? Had I seen only the bully? How much else had I missed along the way?

The interview got a lot better after that. I ordered a drink. I asked him if he still thought about baseball.

"I dream about it. Every night, almost."

"What kind of dream?"

"Well, first of all I take a cab to the ballpark, and I'm in my uniform and I've got a bat. And I get there and the game's going on and I hear them say, 'Mickey Mantle batting, number seven, Mickey Mantle.'

"But I'm not in the ballpark, and the gates are closed. There's a hole that I can crawl under, and halfway through the hole I get stuck and I can still hear the guy saying, 'Now batting, number seven, Mickey Mantle.'"

He paused to sip his drink, and I didn't dare breathe. This is great, I thought, I can see it on TV, a breakthrough in understanding The Mick, Freud at bat, and he's giving it exclusively to me. The 1983 payoff for the 1960 brush-off.

"And I can see Casey and Billy, Whitey, Hank Bauer, all the guys are looking around, like, where's he at? And I'm stuck in the hole and they can't hear me . . . and then I wake up. And I usually can't get back to sleep."

I started winding it down then, even though Mickey seemed to have gotten a second wind. Now I wanted to end it, get back to New York, screen the tapes, show off this great stuff, new, fresh, a never-before-seen side of The Mick.

Driving back, I wondered if Mickey would have his dream tonight. And I wondered what had been on his mind that night back in 1960. Had he been hung over, distracted, lonely, already burdened by regrets? Had he felt stuck in a hole? Had I been too young to have had compassion for him then, starstruck, just not empathetic enough?

That Sunday, I found the same dream in a fine, long *Washington Post* feature story by Jane Leavy, who had even gotten a second dream, a classic *falling* dream involving a pole vault.

Oh, Mickey, I thought, you got me again. But this time I laughed.

(In 2010, Jane published *The Last Boy*, a masterful, sympathetic biography that portrayed Mantle as a hero, victim, and jerk.)

Even as Mickey made his comeback into the public consciousness (he had actually never been that far out of it as adoring baby boomers made him one of their benchmarks and flocked to his Manhattan restaurant, opened in 1988), DiMaggio lost some of his luster. His fans never forgave him for his Mr. Coffee commercials; what right did he have to commodify our iconography? Rumors leaked out about his abusive treatment of Marilyn. His dignity and aloofness were rein-terpreted as antisocial behavior. I thought the revisionism was unfair.

In 1985, I wrote a piece for *People* about our spring training encounter in 1967. I sent it to him and asked if he would sit for a *Sunday Morning* interview. He never answered my letter, but when I chatted with him in spring training that year, he said he had read the piece and remembered our meeting but didn't want to be inter-viewed just yet. But if I showed up at the Yankees' locker room at 10 A.M. on Old-Timers' Day that summer, he would make himself available. Over the next few months, I was unable to confirm the date; he and his representatives never called back.

But I believed he would remember and be there. This was Joe D! He meant what he said! Reluctantly, *Sunday Morning* let me take a producer and a crew on what was considered an outside chance. We arrived at 10:05 A.M.

The Clipper was waiting for us in the locker room, tapping his foot. "Where've you been, Lippy? I've been here an hour."

We set up in the Yankees' dugout, but the public address system was blaring music and announcements, drowning our audio. This had happened before at the Stadium. There was no recourse. No interview. We explained this to DiMaggio, who lifted an eyebrow, then summoned a Yankees PR man to bring him a telephone. Was he calling George Steinbrenner? A moment later the PA was turned off. Who else but the great DiMaggio could silence the Stadium?

It was a long interview, and I can read my sweat in the transcript. He was cooperative, even chatty, but he wouldn't or couldn't go too deep. His insights into baseball, his fellow players, New York in the thirties and forties, when he had owned the night, were sweet. He remembered Fifth Avenue at 3 A.M. in the winter filled with swells coming from El Morocco and other nightclubs. "New York was always New Year's Eve," he said. He remembered the great black dancer Bill "Bojangles" Robinson doing a soft shoe on the dugout roof during a game.

He could be precise about individual games, even at-bats and catches, and about his various injuries and ailments, including ulcers. He'd "loved" playing and poured into it all his energy and emotion. But it hadn't been easy; he'd always had "a knot" in his stomach because he was so shy and tense. He indicated that those were the feelings that dominated his life—it was only now that the knot was unraveling—but that was as far as we got emotionally.

He had little to say about contemporary baseball. His wonderment at the Simon & Garfunkel song "Mrs. Robinson" seemed sad; at first he had thought it might be an insult, but later he had been flattered when Paul Simon explained that the line "Where have you gone, Joe DiMaggio?" was a tribute to his iconic stature. Simon had had the grace not to add (as he did in interviews) that Mick-ey Mantle didn't have the right number of syllables.

DiMaggio kept coming back to his shyness, the dominant emotion of his life. I reminded him that Mantle had said that when they played together in 1951, "you needed an appointment to talk to DiMaggio."

He shook his head. "Now, there was a really shy person. I was looking at myself when I first saw him."

His loneliness and his decency were touching. He seemed never to have had a real relationship with a woman. His public dates were mostly party girls his gofers herded toward him. And oddly for a man from a big Italian family, he socialized mostly with hustlers.

Was all this true, was it just in my mind? I thought a lot about my warm and irrational feelings toward DiMaggio. Am I one of those fans I disdain, who want our heroes in soft focus, a reflection of our hopes and dreams? You're such a thinker, Lippy.

I got high marks for the DiMaggio piece from my CBS colleagues. But I kept thinking that either I had missed the vein or still waters sometimes run shallow. I didn't like either thought.

· · ·

Mickey Mantle died in 1995 at sixty-three, overwhelmed by cancer from a liver that had been removed and replaced only months before. The controversy—had he been bumped to the head of the line, and how could a patient with such advanced disease even be considered for a transplant?—was muted by admiration for Mantle's gallantry, his call for organ donations, and his candor about his alcohol abuse and his destructive history as a husband and father. At the time I wrote, "Just before he died, Mickey Mantle gave us a reason to love him. He was willing to use himself as an almost anti–role model in a very heroic way."

But in the same column I also compared the male boomers' adoration of Mantle to the way Mike Tyson, the former heavyweight boxing champion, had become a symbol to alienated black youth. At about the same time Mantle died, Tyson had begun a series of comeback fights after three years in prison for rape.

There was a flood of mail attacking me for linking Mantle and Tyson and for mentioning the controversy over Mantle's quick liver transplant. "You are a wart" was one of the kinder messages. Others brought up a column I had written a month earlier urging the Baltimore shortstop Cal Ripken, Jr., if he "has any class," to take a day off before he broke Lou Gehrig's record of 2,130 consecutive baseball games. That was not even an original idea; several years earlier, the Hall of Fame third baseman Mike Schmidt had suggested that if Ripken were truly "decent," he would tie Gehrig's record, then sit out one game. No shame in sharing the record with a man who'd had to quit because he was dying. Ripken, as good as he was, benefited from a 1995 conservative need to gild a so-called lunch pail hero who gratefully came to work every day. I thought he was lucky not to get sick, be replaced by someone younger and cheaper, or see his place of business moved out of town.

I didn't think I was being contrarian about all this, but I understood how out of tune I must have sounded after I read Bob Costas's eulogy for Mantle in a Dallas church packed with old Yankees.

Costas said he was representing "the millions of baseball-loving kids who grew up in the fifties and sixties and for whom Mickey Mantle was baseball. And more than that, he was a presence in our lives—a fragile hero to whom we had an emotional attachment so strong and lasting that it defied logic. Mickey often said he didn't understand it, this enduring connection and affection—the men now in their forties and fifties, otherwise perfectly sensible, who went dry in the mouth and stammered like schoolboys in the presence of Mickey Mantle."

Costas lovingly mentioned Mantle's flaws and regrets and ended with this: "I just hope God has a place for him where he can run again. Where he can play practical jokes on his teammates and smile that boyish smile, 'cause God knows, no one's perfect. And God knows there's something special about heroes."

In those days I talked incessantly about Mantle with my best friend, Roger Sims, who was on dialysis waiting for a kidney transplant. Roger was my age, formerly an air force pilot in Vietnam, a TV news producer, and a passionate Yankees fan. He was very conflicted. He loved Mickey, he wanted Mickey to live, he could say logically that Mickey's transplant, even if immoral, could do great good for the cause of organ donations.

But even Roger thought Mickey didn't deserve to be jumped to the head of the line, not with the spreading cancer he had. And Roger felt the same way about himself; at fifty-seven, with serious diabetes and heart disease, Roger wasn't sure *he* deserved a new kidney, certainly not when there were younger, healthier, "worthier" people who needed them. He was six years younger than Mantle.

But even Roger got teary at the part in Bob Costas's euology where Mickey was up in Heaven, running.

Costas invited me to dinner soon after Mantle's death. We had gotten to know each other during the shooting of *Heroes of the Game*, a six-hour documentary I wrote for Turner Broadcasting on the

American Century through the lives of transcendent sports figures. On the show, Costas talked about Mantle, among other subjects, and I was struck by his intelligence, clarity, and basic decency. I had always admired his broadcasting skills and thought he was better than the games he called—he seemed ready to be a late-night host.

But our dinner was not comfortable. Speaking carefully in full sentences and paragraphs, Costas suggested that I might be happier—certainly my readers would be happier—if I tried less to be provocative and more to be open-hearted. He said he sensed my humanity but thought I was suppressing it, moving past the boundaries of skepticism into cynicism, not finding pleasure in the games or the goodness in even flawed athletes. I was flattered that he had taken the time to mentor me—he was fourteen years younger—but irritated by his presumption. We did not speak again for fourteen years, but I recalled the meeting vividly whenever I saw him on TV. I wondered if he could have been right. Should there only have been paeans to Mantle right after his death? Why? Didn't journalism dictate a full, fair portrait, wonders and warts both? And was Costas a journalist, moving so easily from solid interviewing to fandom to the broadcasting of events for which his network paid?

DiMaggio died in 1999, at eighty-four, from lung cancer. He had been a chain smoker. There were some elegiac memories of him drifting under fly balls, but his time had passed. A year later came another nail in the coffin of his image, Richard Ben Cramer's *Joe DiMaggio: The Hero's Life*, one of the most absorbing and readable sports biographies in recent memory, as well as the most credibly demystifying and, ultimately, the most disagreeable. Cramer managed to diminish DiMaggio into a greedy, petty pig. It was hard to argue against his research, and his interpretation was his to make. I thought the book was provocative and mean-spirited, without humanity. I began to make the connection to Costas's feelings about me.

Until he died in 2004, my friend Roger never tired of talking about the Yankees, current and old. He thought Costas was a great broadcaster, if a little precious. He thought Costas was presumptuous to lecture me and I was pathetic to take it seriously. Roger's bass voice would get very rumbly and he'd retell a Vietnam story, usually about strafing bicyclists who might have been armed. It was his way of telling me to be less introspective, to stay tough. Between the Mekong Delta and Yankee Stadium we pulled him through many bad nights. He'd call at 3 A.M. out of his mind with pain, and we'd go through the breathing exercises I'd learned in yoga. That would bring him down to a low moan, and he'd ask to hear my Mickey and Joe stories for the hundredth time. Roger always laughed when Mickey told me to go fuck myself and when Joe D called me Lippy. Then he'd fall asleep.

Gerard Papa, Keeper of the Flames and maybe "the good man" in this book.
(Jose Lopez/The New York Times)

TEN | The Saint Wore Black Leather

For all my hard line on sports heroes, I think I was looking for—at least willing to find—someone I could admire who did something of real value to justify my own version of godding up. Especially on television, it's hard not to be promoting the subject of your story. The trick becomes picking the subject.

That's why, for three decades, I have had some version of the following conversation with Gerard Papa. This particular time, we were sitting in the kitchen of the Bensonhurst, Brooklyn, house he shared with his mother when Papa suddenly said, "The only time Christ ever got hostile, expressed any kind of wrath, it was for the religious leaders of his day. The 'whited sepulchers,' He called them." Papa took a breath and laughed a little bark of punctuation he uses to signal irony. "The Catholic Church taught me all this stuff."

The year was 1997, and he was preparing to battle the bishops in State Supreme Court.

"So the bishops are evil," I said.

"I am not saying they are evil men, I say they are doing evil." He gave me the baleful look he calls his ghetto stare. "You understand what I'm saying? How long do you know me?"

"Fifteen years, Gerard." I gave him my own version of a baleful look. "So you're Jesus in this story."

"C'mon, Bob, I'm not comparing myself to Jesus. Any more than the kids on my team compare themselves to Michael Jordan. But you got to strive toward an ideal."

"You're the good man in this story?"

"I am not perfect," said Papa. "No one is. But . . . yes."

I probably snickered then, but, yes, Papa is the good man in this story. Maybe the good man in this book.

The conversation usually begins—in his house, my house, a gym, a schoolyard, a courtroom, a restaurant, walking the Coney Island boardwalk, or riding in his car—with the Flames, the name of a basketball team Papa founded in 1974 that eventually became an interracial youth organization that has served more than fifteen thousand kids. The conversation quickly broadens into discussions of good and evil and then on to Jesus as a role model. Papa insists that despite my Facebook declaration of being a "lapsed atheist"— my way of saying that even denying the existence of God is too religious for me—I am one of the most spiritual people he knows.

I don't snicker at that. Four years before I met Papa, I had a conversion of sorts.

In August 1978, I was diagnosed with testicular cancer and began a two-year campaign against that bully. I needed to see the disease in that way to keep up my fighting spirit. There were two operations and a river of chemotherapy, which had just ended when my wife, Margie, was diagnosed with breast cancer. Those intense years in the country of illness topped off what I think of as my post-*Times* emotional growth spurt. Now I was a grown-up. The fourteen years at the *Times*, which began when I was a teenager, were in an environment that was as structured and sheltered for me as college or the army had been. My identity consisted of being a "*Times*-man" (Dad particularly liked to call me that). Rules and goals were clear. My last name was Of the New York Times. After I left in 1971, for the next ten years as a freelance writer, I was on my own in every way, especially financially, as the sole support of a wife and two little kids in the fast-changing social environment of the seventies. But in losing the protection of the *Times*, I also shed that arrogant entitlement of importance, that assumption of knowing better. I was more professionally vulnerable without the *Times*, and illness added an understanding of physical vulnerability. I like to think I gained a greater empathy for other people and an openness to their lives and experiences. I hope I became a better listener, a better reporter. Though none of that made me a religious man, I think it unlocked the possibility of sometimes thinking in more spiritual ways. I was ready for Papa.

After leaving the *Times*, I had been mostly in the basement of a Closter, New Jersey, split-level, mostly writing fiction, including screenplays and four young adult novels. There were a few brief forays out for magazine pieces, about Ali, Jack Scott, and pro football coach George Allen's relationship with Richard Nixon, and one big foray into tabloid newsprint. Around Christmastime 1976, Margie and I met the author and journalistic legend Pete Hamill and his new date, Jacqueline Kennedy Onassis, at a Harlem writers' benefit. Pete, friendly and expansive, mentioned that he and Jimmy Breslin would be writing columns about the city for the *Daily News*. Wouldn't it be great if I joined Murray Kempton as a city columnist at the *New York Post?* I mumbled that it would be great, and when Pete suggested I give the new owner, Rupert Murdoch, a call, I responded with a helpless shrug.

Jackie O., that amazing face smudged with pencil lead (she had just come from her job as a book editor), turned to Pete and in her wispy voice said, "You'll make the call for Bob, won't you, Pete?"

"Of course," said Pete, shooting his cuffs.

He did. A few weeks later, Murdoch, briskly friendly, was asking me, "How would you improve this paper?"

Unintimidated because I didn't need the job and because I didn't yet know who he was, I pontificated, "For starters, I'd hire more women, blacks, Latinos, gays in the newsroom so the city can be properly covered."

He regarded me coolly. "Hmm, yes," he said, "but instead I'm hiring a liberal like you."

I lasted seven months. Since that included the summer that David Berkowitz, the confessed serial killer of six who called himself the Son of Sam, dominated *Post* headlines, it was a fevered time. Like every other reporter, I was hunting for Sam. Such stories were fine with Murdoch. What got me into trouble was scrutinizing Mayor Ed Koch or Israeli-American politics or writing about marching with gay and women's right demonstrators. Also, wearing the wrong shoes. Apparently Murdoch—or one of his overreactive henchmen—had spotted the beige Italian soft suedes I liked, and word came down that "the Boss wants you to lose those poofter boots." Aussie homophobic bully! So I wore them every day. My column, supposed to run on page two, began drifting toward the back of the paper. Sometimes it was edited into incomprehensibility. I must have been whining around town because Dave Marash, then a news anchor on WCBS-TV Channel 2, told me I could quit the *Post* live on his eleven o'clock show. Murray Kempton, with whom I shared an office (that courtly, erudite, and disciplined man would come in to write his column carrying one bag of potato chips and one bottle of beer), advised me to concentrate on crime until things cooled down for me. He had some Mafia sources he could share.

Finally, after a column of mine (about Mayor Koch's androgynous persona) was killed, I called Marash. Just before I went to his studio that night, I wrote a letter of resignation and went upstairs to Murdoch's darkened offices to leave it on his secretary's desk. As I felt my way in, a figure rose unsteadily from the floor. It was Steve Dunleavy, the *Post*'s Aussie tabloid ace, sleeping off another mythic drunk. He said, "Don't do anything rash, mate." Then he collapsed.

It was a slow news night, and I led Marash's show. More people saw me that night on TV than had ever read me at the *Post*. It occurred to me that there might be something in this new medium.

But first, another little fling with print, an offer from the Times Publishing Company to write a book about the Son of Sam. They would even provide David Berkowitz. I was slipped into Kings County Hospital, where he was being held for psychiatric evaluation. Money must have changed hands, because a guard gave me a white coat to wear and ushered me into a small room with chairs and a couch. A shrink's office. The guard stayed outside.

David was small and soft, with a gentle, friendly face. He knew I was a reporter. I asked simple questions to get a feel for him. He said he was doing okay, people were nice, he wasn't hearing voices at the moment. But he seemed guarded, stiff. It was a boring chat. Just keep him going, I thought, be cool and smooth. Obviously I wasn't, because he asked, "Why are you so nervous, why are you pointing your pen at me?"

I blurted out the truth. "In case you try to jump me. I'll shove the point right into your throat."

He seemed to like that. "You think I'm dangerous?"

"I do." Emboldened, I said, "In fact, if you have the powers you say you do, how do I know you can't reach out to harm my family?"

He smiled, relaxed, told me he did have the power to send destructive forces into my home but would not. He would send forces to protect me and my family. After a few more minutes, he said he liked me and wanted to write a book with me.

Turned out there was a touch of the Jack Scott bathroom deal in the setup. Though I would get the several-hundred-thousand-dollar advance, I would have to pay Berkowitz's lawyers their hourly billing rate for interviews. It made me uneasy. Since I would thus be paying for his defense, he would be profiting from his crime (this was before the so-called Son of Sam law was created so he and subsequent criminals wouldn't be able to make crime pay). While I was struggling with this, *Times* editor Abe Rosenthal pulled the plug— he didn't want the paper involved in such a shady deal. He was right. A week later, when my agent at the time, Lynn Nesbit, moved the project to a much larger publishing house for much more money, I bailed out. Now I had another phantom blockbuster on my résumé.

On to the new medium. *CBS Sunday Morning*. Again, I approached it as a summer job. I'd get some background for a TV novel, I thought. Or I'd stockpile money for a season. Pillaging again. I never expected to spend the next eight years on three different networks with Gerard Papa as my quintessential subject, as unlikely as he seemed to be at first.

In his everyday costume, then and now—black Flames T-shirt, drawstring white ghetto bloomers, and red sneakers—he looks like a wannabe thuglet. He doesn't read books, he tans himself on beaches all summer, he loves to cruise in his top-of-the-line luxury car. In his Brooklyn accent, he declaims, "There are always good and evil forces in any sea of endeavor. It is up to the leadership as to whether good or evil prevails. I see the world from the bottom up from the kids in the gym and from the interaction with everyday people. Kids play or fight, depending on who is in charge. The same people can do good or bad or be chaotic. It depends on their leaders."

When we first met, Papa was something of a curio to me, one of those "local heroes" occasionally discovered by the media and examined anthropologically. "Look at this," goes the reporter's message, "despite no money, no Ivy League connections, no professional training, and no political office, these natives have managed to do some good in their villages. How wonderful! A lesson for us all! Can you imagine if they had our advantages? They might be CEOs or senators! Or us!"

But Papa had our advantages. Raised by his mother, a schoolteacher, he had a rigorous Catholic high school education and completed Columbia in three years, summa cum laude and Phi Beta Kappa. He commuted but managed to be freshman class president, the advertising manager for the *Columbia Daily Spectator*, a lightweight football player, and an anti-anti–Vietnam War activist in 1968. In his third year at Columbia Law School, he ran in the Republican primary for a New York State Assembly seat. He lost big, and the campaign soured him on elective politics but not on public service through the Church.

As Papa became less of an anthropological object—this guy went to *my* college, he was better educated than I was, probably made more money—he became a subject of troubling comparison. This guy was actually doing something useful in his community that could have citywide, nationwide impact. If I couldn't do things like this myself, at least I could help spread the word. But what he was doing was in the service of religion. And who knew what he was really getting out of it? Dig out the story.

The story began in a world I understood, trying to win basketball games. In 1974, at a local priest's request, he began to coach an all-white team of fourteen- and fifteen-year-olds. He named the team the Flames, after one of his favorite quotations, "Stir into flame the gift of God bestowed on you" (2 Timothy 1:6). The Flames nearly guttered out, failing to win a single game in their first season. Papa took it personally. He had to become a better coach. He studied, talked with other coaches, planned his practices, and spent time drawing up plays. The following season, the Flames won half their games.

By then, Papa, a tax associate at a Wall Street firm, was in what he calls his "innocent" phase; he believed that most people want to do good and that people who do things the right way will always triumph.

Papa was ready to expand. He needed a parish to sponsor him in the Catholic Youth Organization's prestigious basketball program and found the Reverend Vincent J. Termine, at nearby Most Precious Blood. A crusty, twinkly Brooklynite in his early fifties, a kind of movie priest ("Celibacy was never a problem," he told me once, "and I didn't take a vow of poverty. But obedience, ah . . ."), Father Termine seemed to have been waiting for Papa.

He helped Papa paint white lines on the linoleum floor of his bingo hall and erected portable backboards. They held open tryouts. Black kids from the nearby Marlboro Projects ventured across Avenue X, the black-white borderline. When the team was assembled, it was more than half black.

Racial integration was not the original goal. Blacks, Papa told me, "weren't relevant to where I lived. I had essentially no contact with black people, and I didn't really think about 'em too much." Papa just wanted to win. He was surprised when the neighborhood freaked. At the first integrated practice, a van screeched up and a gang of young white men piled out swinging bats. One of them was the son of the local Mafia "man of respect." The Flames piled into Gerard's Thunderbird and raced off to Coney Island, figuring correctly that their attackers would not follow them into a black neighborhood.

That season there were telephoned death threats, and Papa's tires were slashed. His black players were beaten, and most of his white players were pressured to quit. But he refused to disband the team.

He believed in his own righteousness. Apparently, so did Father Termine. Remembering a piece of advice from his own mother—"Better a dead priest than a bad one"—he stormed into the back room of the local social club. Cards and chips flew as Father Termine ("I can be dramatic when necessary") roared about Jesus and justice. When he was finished, the team and Papa were promised safe conduct.

Emboldened, Papa began swaggering into Brooklyn gyms in a black leather jacket, unshaven, wearing his "ghetto stare, where you look at people and show no emotion." The stare fooled people. Papa was scared. "Most tough guys are actors anyway. You get them alone, and they cry just like you."

The Flames became a perennial winner in the CYO, and by the time I profiled Papa for the show, they were a league of their own—some three hundred youngsters from eight to nineteen years old on thirty-two "house" teams that played all winter in the bingo hall and on a handful of CYO traveling teams coached by volunteers. Over the years, thirteen teams from various age groups wearing the Flames' emblem—a black hand and a white hand grasping a torch—won diocesan championships, and Papa personally coached three of those teams.

Watching Flames games, I came to understand how sports can shape young lives positively (I had spent too much of my career in the big-time realms of gold). The style Papa imposed on his teams is a projection of his own personality. No jump shots allowed, no three-pointers, because you might start to depend on them, take shortcuts, and get lazy. Pass only if you don't have a shot. His kids never stop running, with or without the ball, never stop driving to the basket. When they are cooking, the Flames are quick and brash, like Papa—slapping balls out of hands the way he snaps out demands and retorts, rebounding with their entire bodies the way he has elbowed his way through bureaucratic zone defenses. He found supporters, both white and black, in law firms, the district attorney's office, the media, and enlisted them as coaches, advisers, contributors.

He enforces The Rules. No hats, headbands, wristbands in the gym, nothing but uniforms. No girlfriends present at games. In fact, no one is allowed to watch except family members over twenty-three. And they can clap, but they can't cheer. Every player needs to do service to the Flames, contribute at least one hour a week to cleaning up, keeping score, refereeing. Older kids coach younger teams. There is mandatory playing time, even if it means that talented kids sit on the bench and watch clumsy kids get their minutes.

Papa grew along with the Flames. "That first real troublesome year, my problem was coming predominantly from white kids, so I started thinking every black kid was good and every white guy was a problem. Over the next couple of years my feelings matured a little bit, and I've reached the stage now where I just don't notice somebody's color. That's a fact. Racism's a two-way street. More importantly, racial fear is a two-way street."

Papa left Wall Street and set up a small local private practice. "I have everything I need, a great education, the ability to earn however much money I need to earn. When I die I'll have money in the bank, so why do I have to worry about having a little more? A poor kid, his duty isn't to go out and start something like the Flames. It's his duty to get an education if he can; if not, then some kind of trade, a job, a wife and kids, and build himself up. We take things at their own level."

There were echoes of my dad in what Papa said, especially that sense of mission toward his boys and the certainty that the mission would succeed once the boys understood that he was serious, that he wasn't going to give up on them. He was compassionate, but he was demanding. I remembered visiting my dad when he was a principal in tough Brooklyn schools. He had a ghetto stare of his own and a righteousness leavened with an easy rapport with the students. I admired what my dad was doing, the *goodness* of it. Following Papa, even in the early days of our relationship, I was aware that I might be transferring some of my feelings about Dad's work to Papa, so I was especially wary. What exactly *was* Papa getting out of this? Money, prestige, power, some of those perverted priestly perks?

In 1986, the year I moved from CBS to NBC, he ran into big trouble. While scrambling for private grants and city funding for the Flames, he antagonized several local politicians; ever righteous, he blew the whistle on their misuse of funds earmarked for youth programs. There were a *Daily News* exposé and an indictment. The Flames still didn't get any money, and Papa almost got killed.

A few minutes before midnight, Papa was driving his powder blue Lincoln Town Car in Coney Island with a friend, James Rampersant, Jr., the twenty-three-year-old son of a Baptist deacon. A car came toward them the wrong way. As Papa tried to drive around it, the car cut him off and its doors flew open. Long-haired, roughly dressed men with guns leaped out, yelling. Papa threw his car into reverse and crashed into a second car that had come up to block him from behind. More men with guns jumped out. Papa again tried to drive past the first car, but the Lincoln stalled. The men opened fire.

Papa thought he was caught in the cross fire of rival drug gangs. He thought he was going to die. He and Rampersant began praying. They heard a police siren, but their problems were only beginning. The men in civilian clothes—plainclothes cops—dragged them out of the car and beat them. It was hours before Papa was treated for bleeding head wounds and broken ribs, Rampersant for deep bruises. They were arrested and charged with attempted murder, assault, reckless endangerment, and criminal mischief. It was three months before all the charges were dropped.

A year later, a grand jury report reached "the inescapable conclusion that this was a case of mistaken identity by all involved that led to a chaotic situation, frightening and endangering all the participants, police and civilians, for which no one can be held criminally responsible." The report also suggested that police be better trained in the dangerous "suspicious vehicle stop."

When I trailed him in 1988 with NBC cameras, he seemed a little shaky, diminished. He had lost some of his zip, his smart-aleck repartee, and his quick legal logic. He had headaches and bad dreams. He forgot names. He tired easily. He was undergoing physical therapy, neurological rehabilitation, and treatment for post-traumatic stress. Yet he still seemed more focused and determined than most people. He still had hopes and a plan. "The kind of progress that still has to be made is the kind of progress you have to write onto people's hearts, not the kind you have to write onto law books."

It wasn't until the mid-1990s that he seemed to be finally recovering from his injuries. Flames enrollment was at an all-time high, as was his own credibility among street hoodlums and members of the media, two groups he courted relentlessly. To top it off, he was rich. After a two-week trial, Papa and Rampersant won $76 million from the city, the largest award in a civil case in Brooklyn. On appeal, it was reduced to $6 million, which they received in 1994.

Then, once again, times got hard. The Church he had always leaned on began to fail him. Father Termine had retired and the new pastor of Most Precious Blood declared "a different vision" for his sports program, and the CYO leadership found a way to formally exclude the Flames. The next few years were a scramble to find gyms, leagues, opponents. I was back at the *Times* by then, and my notes, mostly from telephone interviews with Papa, are filled with Flames' play dates in Queens, in leagues made up of synagogue teams. To practice, friends of the Flames slipped them into parish and public school courts. They dribbled on.

Papa began to reevaluate his own religious convictions, especially after the Church ignored petitions and protests from white and black parents and from a group of predominantly black ministers from other denominations in the area. "It's one thing," he told me then, "to find out there are bad cops. My kids were always telling me that. But your church?" He barks his ironic signal. "Reading about some guy getting burned at the stake and getting burned yourself are two very different sensations."

Once Papa filed suit to force the Brooklyn Diocese to admit the Flames into the CYO play-offs despite the loss of their sponsoring parish, no one in the clergy would talk publicly about him to me. One bishop had set the official line when he told me for a *Times* story, "He's done a lot of good for a lot of poor kids. No one's denying that. But he's been a thorn in everyone's side. He's not accountable."

Bang! If I'd had any doubts about what kept Papa on my mind, there it was. *A lot of good . . . but . . . a thorn in everyone's side. He's not accountable.* That Bishop Bully was a "whited sepulcher," I thought. He could have been talking about Jesus!

The judge eventually refused to make the CYO admit the Flames because "a court cannot tell a church what to do in matters that affect the practice of the faith." Basketball as faith? I talked to the judge. Nice Jewish guy. The law, he said. He offered himself as a mediator, but the bishops weren't interested.

Papa's Wall Street and Columbia connections came through, and the Flames began playing at a nearby high school. More and more middle-class kids began joining, often the sons of former players. Papa eliminated travel teams, enhancing the experience for kids of lesser talent. These days, when street agents and amateur coaches with sneaker money are running national teams, tournaments, and summer camps for elite players, it is rare for the Flames to attract star talent. They are not, after all, about those kind of hoop dreams.

On a summer Sunday while I was writing this book, with Flames tryouts a month away, we were sitting on Papa's porch, reminiscing. He has mellowed. He is not so restless. He shrugged at that. "Over the years, I think less and less about winning and more and more about instilling discipline and ideals, giving kids some structure, a place to go to feel good."

Regrets?

"Not getting married and having kids," he said. He was in his fifties.

"You never could have run the Flames as a one-man band if you had," I said.

He nodded. "And the other is turning down the book and movie offers when they came around in the early nineties. Talking to the Hollywood guys, I was afraid they were going to change the story, trivialize it. I ended up not giving permission."

"You didn't sell out," I said. "See, I always said you were really a priest. Priests take vows of poverty and chastity."

He glared at me.

I touch base with Gerard more often than I do with any other of my subjects/teachers. We call, attend Columbia functions, eat in Italian joints in Brooklyn. When his mom, Elena, was very sick, he asked me to pray for her recovery because God was more likely to listen to a selfless request from someone who never prayed. "That's the point," I told him. "I never pray. No one has ever asked me before." "I'm asking you now," he said. I could feel the ghetto stare over the phone. I prayed. She got better. "The new medicine," I said. He said, "Who knows?" He threw a lovely eighty-ninth birthday lunch in 2010 for his mom and the half-dozen members of her prayer team at the posh St. Regis Hotel in Manhattan.

Sometimes I think I need Gerard to recharge that spirituality he claims to see in me. This is a good man doing good work. I was right to invest so much air and space in him. His lesson is so profound: you can change the world one kid at a time.

And sometimes I think I am still looking for the flaw, the dark end of the story. I'm a reporter, I don't trust anyone. I'm too hip to be happy.

Chief Oren Lyons at the opening ceremonies of the 1998 World Lacrosse Games in Baltimore. (Photograph by Michael Greenlar)

ELEVEN | The Faithkeeper

Chief Oren Lyons's main attraction at first was that he reminded me of my father: average height, muscular and chesty without seeming aggressive, and calm. Like Dad, he was so calm you couldn't read his mood and thoughts. Unlike most people, neither of them mimicked the expression on your face. Both of them were unfailingly pleasant, confident, yet somehow wary, reserved. When I first met Oren in 1984, Dad was eighty and Oren was fifty-four. So he reminded me of my father when I was just starting out at the *Times*.

I had gone up to the Onondaga Reservation near Syracuse,

New York, after a story I thought would let me move away from the relentless geniality of my *Sunday Morning* sports essays. Something edgier. Dennis Banks, a founder of the American Indian Movement, had become an FBI fugitive after a gun battle on a South Dakota reservation. The Onondagas, as a sovereign nation, had given him asylum. In return, Banks was running health and sports programs on the reservation and had organized the Jim Thorpe Longest Run, a pan-Indian solidarity event that would send young runners from reservation to reservation, starting at Onondaga and finishing at the 1984 Olympics in Los Angeles. It was a long shot, but I thought that might be enough of a sports angle to justify coming back with a producer and crew.

After a long discussion, Banks agreed to an on-camera interview if the Onondaga chiefs approved. I was introduced to Oren, who heard me out, nodding and grunting like Dad. He was just as decisive. "Be good TV," he said. I had no idea he was an international Native American diplomat, a university professor, an artist, and a former all-American college athlete. He was just a chief in running shoes, jeans, and a beaded shirt.

We toured the reservation, a hardscrabble community of 2,000 or less (no census takers admitted) on 7,300 acres of junkyards and vegetable gardens, rusty trailers and suburban-style homes. I noticed elementary school boys and girls slamming hard rubber balls against the brick wall of their school with lacrosse sticks and teenagers choosing up sides for boisterous scrimmages in muddy backyards. Some older men were clearing debris from a sports field. Oren noticed my interest.

"*Guhchigwaha*," he said. "Means 'Bump Hips.' The Jesuit missionaries called it lacrosse because they thought the stick resembled a bishop's crozier."

"You guys still play it?"

"It's the lifeblood of the Six Nations of the Iroquois Confederacy.

It's the Creator's game. There are two times of the year that stir the blood. In the fall for the hunt and now for lacrosse."

He had me at *Guhchigwaha*. Sorry, Dennis, I just found a *Sunday Morning* story.

Banks and his run got into the piece, but it was mostly about Oren and lacrosse. There was a great news peg: the Iroquois were cranking up to compete in the international arena after a long absence (they had been banned on trumped-up amateurism violations when they got too good). Also, white college and club lacrosse was booming, and Native American teams were playing both an indoor and outdoor version. Oren himself was coaching several Onondaga teams, one starring his son, Rex, and his nephews, Scott and Kent, another his grandson Montgomery. Generations.

Even after the piece ran, I kept going back to Onondaga or meeting Oren at lacrosse matches, conferences, the United Nations, where he was an international diplomat for indigenous peoples. He was running a close second to Gerard Papa as a subject who had entered my personal life. Oren slept in my apartment in Manhattan, I slept in his cabin on the res. I wrote magazine pieces and newspaper columns about him. Over the years, what he represented to me changed as I changed, but from the beginning he was symbolic of a masculinity I could admire: tough without bravado, shrewdly self-reliant, generous as a friend and mentor. Like Papa, Oren was a source of positive energy in a world of sucking black holes. Like Papa, he knew who he was, and he was comfortable, almost to the point of being smug. Was it a flaw or just confidence?

Oren attributed his sense of self to his upbringing on the res. Hunting was Oren's first rite of manhood. "My father would give me one shell. If I missed, he'd send me home. If I killed, he'd let me stay. The discipline of the hunt is very important. You've got to eat. You learn to respect skill. And you stay in touch with everything around you."

Sports and art, traditional tickets out of the slum, had given young Oren some early fame on the res. He was a good amateur feather-weight boxer, and his drawings of eagles and wolves were of magazine illustration quality. ("Isn't it interesting," he once said to me, "that the only kind of taxes the United States lets you vote on is school taxes, and then you go out and cut them, which is like cutting off your own foot. And what do you cut, sports, which gives you strength and health, and art, which gives you that balance, sensitivity.")

But it was lacrosse at which he made his mark. He was a teenager then, playing in the shadow of his own father, a renowned goalie who would eventually be buried with his lacrosse stick.

"My father told me, 'You have to concentrate, have to keep your eye on the ball. No matter what happens, don't let them catch your eye, 'cause then you're done.'" Oren paused, cocked an eyebrow to punctuate the metaphor. "That's all I ever took from him, but it's all you need."

Roy Simmons, Sr., then the lacrosse coach of Syracuse University, told me some years later about watching Oren play on the reservation in the late forties. "Oren was sensational. He was quick as a cat, entirely courageous. I wanted him. But there was no way. I think he only had about a year of high school before he dropped out."

"I quit school in the eighth grade," said Oren. "I had such a head on with the teacher, just hostile to me, didn't like me. I recognized it was beyond me because I never offended that teacher. I tried my best. I was lucky to understand early it wasn't about me, it was racism. And resisting it helped me sustain myself."

Oren boxed, drank, sketched, and raised hell until he was drafted in 1950, at twenty. He joined the 82nd Airborne. At twenty-three, he returned to the res and supported his wife and baby daughter by painting boxing portraits on the walls of local bars at $10 each.

Coach Simmons rediscovered Lyons. "My kid, Roy, was entering Syracuse and I was anxious for him to play on a good team. I knew

Roy would score plenty of goals, but I needed a goalie who would keep the other team from scoring. And there was Oren.

"The semester had already started, so I grabbed the dean of admissions and dragged him down to this restaurant, Norm's Arena. There was a painting of Jack Dempsey, looked like he was going to jump out and hit you. That got Oren into the School of Fine Arts, and I got the best goalie I ever had."

Eventually, with Oren in goal and two other all-Americans on attack, Roy, Jr., and the future NFL star Jim Brown, the 1957 Syracuse team went undefeated.

"Oren was different from other Indian athletes," said Roy, Jr., who replaced his father as coach. "He was on time, he accepted discipline. But most Indian athletes are hard to read. Stoic. Never cry or admit pain. Winning and losing are not as important to them. They like to play the game, give and take licks, and when the dust settles, when it's over, just shake hands. They'll accept not being number one. And they'll never admit they made a mistake. That's hard for a white coach to deal with."

"It's perplexing to white coaches," said Oren. "Self-respect and individuality are very important to Indians. They're very sensitive, they expect rejection. You can't yell at them, or they'll just drag up and go. They walked out on British officers who barked orders at them during the Revolution, and they walk off steel when the foreman yells at them, and they'll walk off teams."

After graduation from Syracuse in 1958, Oren moved to Madison Avenue. In ten years he rose from paste-up artist to head planning director for seasonal lines at Norcross Greeting Card Company, an experience, he says, that "grounded me in the American psyche."

Club lacrosse took him into the dark upper reaches of that psyche. The last time Oren went hunting with white men was in the 1960s. A group of his lacrosse teammates, Wall Streeters, organized a Catskill Mountain hunt on the first day of deer season.

"That's a fierce sight, white men unleashed. Twelve-inch knives strapped to their thighs, bandoliers. They almost hit some guy in another party, missed him by six inches, and he fired back. They went to slug it out. I stopped it and volunteered to stay back and cook dinner. White men have all the rules, what kind of guns to use and which dates to use them, but not how you treat each other. I didn't want my kids growing up in that environment."

Oren's disdain for the white world was almost casual, an engaging combination of disgust and amusement. None of that fierce red-man resentment I remembered from the more enlightened Westerns that Dad and I had gone to on Tuesday nights in the summertime. Oren wasn't Geronimo or Tonto. He acted as though he came from a superior culture that hadn't given up battling the bully. With Oren, I never felt sorry for Indians, that it was my duty to stand up for them. They could stand up for themselves, given an equal chance. It was my duty to go after the big assholes who think they can get away with anything.

When Oren was called by the Nation in the late 1960s, it was easy for him to go home. The Clan Mothers had summoned him back to the reservation to take his place on the council. Women select the Onondaga chiefs, then sit behind them in the Longhouse, silent historians. It was a tumultuous time throughout Indian country, as white men and their native henchmen went after Indian lands for casinos, toxic waste dumps, staging areas for gun, drug, and human trafficking.

In 1971, Onondaga refused to allow the state onto the reservation to widen a highway. The head chief, Leon Shenandoah, with Oren at his elbow, drew a line in the dirt and said, "This is where the United States ends." Governor Nelson Rockefeller's presidential ambitions were at stake, and he didn't want to look weak. State troopers were massed for the assault, facing Onondaga rifles, when they were abruptly pulled away to quell the Attica prison uprising.

As a traditional chief, Oren spoke out publicly against Indians selling out their heritage. The Mafia had supposedly put a price on his head. Once, walking across a meadow on the res, we were fired upon from the tree line. Oren said not to worry; they were Indians and would have hit us if they wanted to. They were merely registering displeasure. (Like most Indians I met, he did not ask to be referred to as "Native American." "Indian" was fine, although naming the specific nation was preferred.)

Oren supported himself as an associate professor of American studies at the State University of New York at Buffalo but spent more time at the day-to-day work of the traditional chiefs, including the mediation of long-simmering feuds between neighboring families that often broke out in gunfire. The chiefs wanted to keep Indians out of American courts, as well as hospitals. I found such tales of tribal justice irresistible. My favorite was a dog story from Oren's own past.

Smudgie was a working partner, not a pet, a mean old spayed bitch who hunted with young Oren through the years right after his father left, when he kept his mother, his sister, and his six brothers fed with his gun. He shot pheasant, rabbit, and raccoon, and Smudgie pointed and found them. The woodland was their supermarket. Oren tried not to let Smudgie follow the deer or get a taste for flesh, but somewhere along the way she began to freelance around the reservation.

One night, Smudgie lurched up to the door of the house, her chest blown open. She died in Oren's arms.

The blood trail made it a simple backtrack. The killer, a crabby old neighbor, had waited in ambush. He had let Smudgie get close enough to his henhouse for a clear shot from his doorway. It would have been easy to chase her, even to let her take a chicken and then demand reparation from the Lyons family. The chiefs would have enforced that. But the old man was bitter and had killing on his mind.

So Oren buried Smudgie and hiked out to the meadow where the old man kept the two horses he used for plowing and transport. Oren shot one of them. Simple justice.

Nothing was ever said.

Thirty-five years later, I asked Oren, "You still think you did the right thing?"

"Absolutely."

"And it never crossed your mind to shoot the old man?"

Oren looked amused. "That would have been something a white man might do."

Through Oren, I became a student of Indian history and lore, especially intrigued by the Iroquois concept of Seven Generations, every decision based on its ramifications for children and grandchildren and beyond. As I grew older, I found myself interested in mentoring, in sharing my experience with younger sportswriters and young adult novelists instead of competing with them. But I wondered if that was merely a way for me to opt out of the arena, to give up before I gave out. I watched Oren reaching his big hand out to his nation's youth, and the lesson seemed clear. What could be manlier than to be an elder of the tribe and to help shape its future? Another lesson I could have learned from my father, had I been listening then. Their basic philosophies were similar, too.

At eighty, Oren still reminded me of Dad. In the summer of 2010, with a new hip and a pacemaker, he looked solid and calm as ever. At his birthday party, he called on us all to "share." A few weeks later, as a leader of the Iroquois Nationals, he negotiated unsuccessfully with the British government to allow the team to fly to Manchester for the world lacrosse championships on Haudenosaunee (Iroquois) passports. Was it homeland security or once again were Indians barred for being too good?

Once, while we were sitting on the raw plank deck of his hilltop cabin, Oren said, "There's a moral nut in every human being. We have to keep reminding people, we have to keep exposing them to what's good in themselves. We have to teach the question, the only question. 'Is it right?' So simple. But if people don't want to follow that, the game is up. It's all over."

Ali is briefly down in the first Joe Frazier fight in 1971 (which he lost). The pale face in the crook of his left arm is mine. (Associated Press)

TWELVE | The Onliest (Part Two)

Turns out Ali and I weren't done with each other after all. Though I hadn't forgiven his betrayal of Malcolm X, with time I came to understand how it could have happened. Ali was twenty-two years old, in the bubble of a magical universe beyond all his dreams—he was the heavyweight champion of the world, a sex god, the "onliest boxer that people talk to like he's a senator," and under the fatherly protection of a religious cult's leader, Elijah Muhammad of the Nation of Islam. Ali felt safe and important. The apostasy of Malcolm, cold and real, threatened to prick that bubble. So Ali ran out on him.

Through the early 1970s, while I wrote fiction and then *SportsWorld*, I found myself wondering what he was like now. After he beat George Foreman in the Rumble in the Jungle to regain his heavyweight title, I decided it was time to return to the story that had jump-started my career.

After four years away from him, I was fresh and he was fun again. It was 1975. He was less dogmatic—he was more comfortable in his religion—and more relaxed. He could be kind; I remember almost missing a flight because he'd noticed that a little old lady had left the cap on her camera lens, and after plucking it off he posed for her again. He could be an outrageous hound; at a middle school award ceremony he MCed, he tried to pull a teen queen into our limo. She was willing, but the principal blocked her. "Does he always do this?" the principal asked me. "I'm not always with him," I said.

That was a stop on a weeklong Florida exhibition tour I tagged along on for a freelance *Times* magazine piece. The tour ended in a high school football field near Daytona Beach. He had just finished a jokey charity boxing match, and now he was back in the motor home he used as a dressing room, changing clothes while his bodyguard shooed everybody out, Jake LaMotta, Angelo Dundee, me, everybody except three foxes he had picked out of the crowd. Then two of the foxes were released, and Ali grinned at us as he closed the door behind himself and the chosen fox.

I watched for a while, until the motor home began to jiggle on its springs. I imagined that the champ was floating and stinging.

Members of his entourage looked at their watches—there were planes to catch—and then at me. "Don't even think about it," someone said, and Angelo said, "Don't write about this, Bob," and one of the press agents said, "Not if you ever want to interview him again."

I thought about the scene in *Madame Bovary* when Emma and Leon did it in a carriage that jiggled on its springs. Could I steal from Flaubert? It would be homage, right? Show off that "smooth literary touch" that Talese had mentioned. Eventually, in the *Times* magazine piece, I described the scene clearly enough to ensure that I would never be able to interview him again. This was no discreet quickie, it was in public, part of his performance. I felt a twinge of regret. Too bad. It was over between Ali and me before it really got started again.

The *Times* titled my article "King of All Kings." I thought it was a good enough piece to go out on, my last word on my Big Story. Time to move on.

Yet I wasn't all that surprised that the first thing Ali said a year later when he saw me again was "'King of All Kings,' right!"

Then he invited me to come listen to him some more.

"Nat Turner and Wyatt Earp," he said dreamily, "they was dead a hundred years before their pictures was made. And of course they didn't get to play themselves."

This was in Miami, and he was lounging on a couch in the stern of another motor home, dressed for a morning run in a black sweat suit and black army boots. But he was also wearing makeup for his title role in his autoflick, *The Greatest*. That's why I was there. The *Times'* Arts and Leisure section had sent me down to write about Ali playing himself. I had figured that even if Ali wouldn't talk to me, there would be plenty of people on the movie set who would.

"After this picture I'm going to play Hannibal, hundreds of elephants. I got to have roles equivalent to my life. This face"—he sat up and touched it reverently—"is worth billions. My roles have always got to be number one. I can't be the boy in the kitchen. Some big football star plays the waiter in the movie while some homosexual gets the lead role."

I probably should have known better than to quote him, but it was such a great line and not untrue. Hadn't the closeted Rock Hudson taught my generation how to bag chicks? Ali had always made homosexual jokes, wouldn't this be a way of showing character, much like the jiggling motor home? I didn't care about protecting him. This quasi-accurate movie was based on his quasi-accurate autobiographical book. The Oscar-winning screenwriter Ring Lardner, Jr., told me, "What made the script difficult to write was the facts. We decided not to be inhibited by the facts, to change them if necessary, to adhere to the truth."

Two weeks after Ali's quote about homosexuals in leading roles appeared, the National Gay Task Force, in a letter to the editor, called "Ali's bigotry . . . unconscionable" and wrote that "an interviewer should not let such prejudice ride without comment."

I think the Task Force was right; I should have put that quote into the context of Ali's mindlessly casual and mostly unreported racist, sexist, and anti-Semitic remarks. But still it rankled that, under some pressure, I replied, "I made an error of judgment. My consciousness stands raised." Who wants to admit a mistake? Or have to avoid writing truthfully because of what has come to be called political correctness?

While I'm remembering getting ticked off about that, I remember something else I perceived—in a selfish, careerist way—as a professional humiliation.

That was on a day in 1986, in Atlanta.

"Hello, stranger," murmured Ali. He was sitting on a hotel room couch in the official headquarters of King's Dream, a heavyweight fight between Tony "TNT" Tubbs and "Terrible" Tim Witherspoon for which the new King, Don, had paid the old King of All Kings walking-around money to drum up some press.

But Ali was not walking around. His bare feet were in a plastic pan of water that also contained electric massagers. He was trying to jolt his numbed appendages back to life. It might have been an early symptom of Parkinson's disease. In those days, no one wanted to deal with the possibility that he could be seriously ill or, for that matter, even mildly punch-drunk. He slurred words when he was tired.

I was feeling sad and nostalgic. I hadn't seen much of him, and although friends had commented on his physical deterioration, it was new to me. I was still at *Sunday Morning.* I had come to this warm city for a proposed twelve-minute segment on Ali. With me was a talented young producer, Brett Alexander, a six-foot, four-inch African American I worked with often.

After the usual chitchat to cover the interminable setting of lights and camera angles, I conducted what turned out to be the shortest and worst interview Ali and I have ever had. I started it by referring back ten years, when Ali had been talking about being on a divine mission and . . .

"I have nothing to say," said the man who never had nothing to say. His words were slurred. "Not talking about that."

"What are you talking about?"

"Nothing."

It went on like that for a few minutes. I was hurt and embarrassed. I was supposed to be the Ali-ologist, and it's expensive to send bodies and equipment out of town for a TV story. So I pressed on.

"You are a tricky man, a wise man," he ranted, "and you been sent by the power structure to make me look bad. And they sent along the biggest, darkest nigger they could find."

Now I was angry. We shouted at each other for a few minutes, but it was not even good television, at least not for an artistic, mild-mannered program. After a while, Brett signaled the crew to pack it in and we left. I was furious, but they were nonchalant, concerned about where we would go for lunch. Brett was sympathetic; he figured the poor guy was down on his luck, hurting, and probably a little paranoid. I asked about being called "nigger," and he shrugged. Blacks are allowed.

But I couldn't let it go. I had to go back. The hell with the "I don't have to be what you want me to be" stuff. One thing he has to be is a decent interview for me. It had been part of our social contract for twenty-two years.

It was a bad moment that still makes me squirm. Why should this be all about me? Why wasn't I sensitive to what he was going through? The King of All Kings, down on his luck, vulnerable, having to put up with my egoshit. But I was still fuming. If he didn't come through, I was going to write about this, rip him up and down, expose him for what he was, a mindless pug available to be interpreted into a symbol of anything you need, a blank slate on which to write your own dogmas and dreams. Ultimately, Ali signified nothing.

I stormed back into the hotel room by myself. Two young women were giggling as Ali pulled them into the curtained-off area that was his bedroom. Just before he pulled the curtain, he grinned at me and said, "Just like old times, huh, Bob?"

With that the bad air whooshed out of me. I grinned back at him.

Every time he's seen me in recent years, Muhammad Ali asks the same question: "What's the difference between a Jew and a canoe?"

He starts laughing before answering: "A canoe tips."

Ali knows I'm Jewish—in the old days he often informed me I was so intelligent because I didn't eat pork (wrong). Once he even asked the Jew-canoe question during a fund-raiser for his Muhammad Ali Center in Louisville, then being referred to as the Museum of Tolerance. While his fourth wife, Lonnie, and his handlers winced, the other attendees, all white and mostly Christian, laughed uproariously. They told me later they knew he was kidding—in fact, they said, it was a brilliant send-up of intolerance. After all, Ali had quickly added, "If a black man, a Puerto Rican, and a Mexican are sitting in the backseat of a car, who's driving? Give up? The po-lice."

He followed that with "What did Abraham Lincoln say when he woke up from a two-day drunk?" While his audience blinked, he answered, "I freed who?" and rewarded himself with laughter before they did.

By then Ali was getting the benefit of the doubt as a cartoon saint, nonthreatening and mostly mute. Many of the people who had hated him in the sixties—and there had been plenty, black and white—had come around to admiring his courage and lack of self-consciousness as a Parkinson's patient. Those who loved him most were those who had not wanted to serve in the army during the Vietnam War—his refusal had helped justify theirs and removed the stigma of cowardice—and African Americans, who saw him as a powerful race man who stood up to the white establishment.

His critics say, with some validity, that he has benefited from projection. They point out how his admirers assign him progressive political and social views that he does not hold. His admirers point out his sacrifices for principle; had Ali remained a Christian, jockstrapped through the army giving exhibitions for the troops, and kept his sexual affairs private, he might have become a major corporate endorser.

I can go both ways. I wept in 1996 when he lit the Olympic torch with a shaky hand (he burned himself but never let on), and six years later I cursed when he refused to condemn Al-Qaeda after the 9/11 attacks because "I got business interests in that part of the world."

A Muhammad Ali revisionism is under way. Right-wingers see bashing Ali, whom they consider a liberal icon, as a way of bashing liberals. Ali's mocking of Joe Frazier through the seventies as an "Uncle Tom" and a "gorilla" was certainly an Ali low point, whether or not it was merely to hype the gate of their fights.

Yet whatever Ali was or wasn't personally, he made people brave.

I found it hard to believe that he'd actually pull off that museum of his, although I was in awe of Lonnie's drive and intelligence. She had an MBA and an icy discipline. I should never have doubted the power of Ali's name combined with Lonnie's ambition. In recent years, not only did the Ali Center open but 80 percent of his commercial rights were sold for a reported $50 million to the same company that markets the Elvis Presley image. A book was published called GOAT (Greatest of All Time, his corporate name), a gorgeous gallery of photos that weighed seventy-five pounds and sold for $3,000 (the autographed "champ" edition, with a Jeff Koons plastic sculpture attached, was $10,000). I had contributed an essay and was thus a guest of the publisher, Taschen, which launched the book during Art Basel, an international show of the hot, the hip, and the hustling, at the Miami Beach Convention Center, the site of that first fight with Liston.

So there I was at ringside (I was one of many to make a brief speech), possibly sitting in the same seat I had sat in some forty years earlier for the fight. Only this time I was sitting near Ali and Will Smith, who had played him in the movie *Ali*. It was December, and just like the very first time we met it was cold where I came from but warm here and the popcorn man was making money and I had something to write about. It doesn't get better than this.

Ed Gallagher, the self-described "Queer Quad," who said he gained his soul when he lost his body. (Associated Press)

THIRTEEN | Queer Studies

In the summer of 1999, a *Times* marketing executive, Tom Kulaga, called me with a hot tip off the gay grapevine. In a lifestyle piece about a new restaurant, the *Miami Herald* had outed one of the owners, Billy Bean, a former major-league outfielder. Kulaga thought Bean would be an excellent guest for a series of panels on gay athletes that I was moderating for the *Times*. I'd been back at the paper since 1991.

I called Bean on August 19. He was pleasant but hesitant at becoming a public spokesman while he was barely out of the closet. He had allowed a gay reporter to include his sexual orientation in her story because he could no longer live a furtive life. A former college teammate had recently died in a car crash, and none of their mutual friends had been able to call Billy in time for the funeral. No one had his telephone number or e-mail address. He had pulled away from them to preserve his secret.

We talked about his baseball career. "The whole nine years," he said, "I had one foot in the major leagues and one on a banana peel." We made a date to talk some more.

Two days later, I called again. We agreed that a panel discussion might not be the best next stage of his coming out. I suggested a big *Times* story first. Lay out his life so that when he did appear in a public forum—on that *Times* panel, of course—he wouldn't have to explain himself. He sounded interested, but he wasn't sure, he needed to think about it. We agreed to a third telephone call in a few more days in which we'd talk about the possibility of meeting face-to-face.

I wanted that story. I'd been leading up to it for years. I thought about my bully Willie and the Halsey Junior High hoods kicking our "fag bags" out of our hands, about all the coaches using words like "pussy" and "sissy" to keep straight boys in line. A major-league ballplayer! This would be a chance to crack open the cynical homophobia of Jock Culture.

Ever since the publication in 1977 of *The David Kopay Story*, the autobiography of an NFL running back, I'd thought that gay athletes could provide fascinating insights into masculinity in Jock Culture. An aggressive player nicknamed "Psych" for his ferocious running and blocking, Kopay had written movingly about the terrible shame of homoerotic thoughts in a sport outwardly contemptuous of homosexuals; the emotional isolation; the need to prove "manliness" through heterosexuality, drinking, and reckless play; and the awareness that football itself was a sexual release.

Not only did the *Times* not review the book, but Pulitzer Prize winner Dave Anderson's thoughtful sports column about it was killed. The incumbent editor, Abe Rosenthal, and the publisher, Arthur Ochs "Punch" Sulzberger, were considered homophobic. Gay *Times* editors and reporters were deep in the closet.

Kopay's book became an underground bible for gay athletes, who had few confidants who could understand their two worlds. As eye-opening as the book was for nongays, the book had little early traction; sportswriters enjoyed gossiping about suspected gay sports stars but shied away from writing about homophobia and homoeroticism in the locker room. I was freelancing when Kopay's book was published, and I pitched my agent a book called *Gay like Me*, playing off John Howard Griffin's best seller *Black like Me*, for which he had temporarily darkened his skin and traveled through the Deep South. I would "come out" and observe the response. My agent thought that not only would my book make no money, it might darken the rest of my career. Soon afterward, I was diagnosed with testicular cancer, a manliness test of its own. I didn't get back to gay athletes until 1986, when I did an NBC News piece on the unconquerable Tom Waddell, a decathlete on the 1968 Olympic team. Before he died of AIDS, Waddell created the Gay Games (until the Olympic Committee sued, it was called the Gay Olympics), a sports and cultural festival with no qualifying restrictions. You didn't have to be gay to play.

In 1988, during the lead-up to the Seoul Olympics, I hung out with Greg Louganis, the world's best diver. I use "hung out" advisedly; it was in a restaurant bathroom, away from my producer and crew, that I asked him about his sexual orientation. There were constant rumors, and the man he was living with in Malibu was gay. Greg seemed to enjoy being playfully evasive, neither answering my question nor shutting me down.

Louganis had spent his life fighting slurs; he'd been called "retard" (he had a learning disability) and "nigger" (he was part Samoan). He didn't need "fag." And what more did we need than his courageous performance? At the 1988 Seoul Olympics, I watched him crack open his head on the diving board, then come back a few minutes later, bloody and stitched, to nail a gold-medal dive.

Five years later, now back at the *Times*, I went to see him in an off-Broadway play, *Jeffrey*, in which he played a chorus boy dying of AIDS. I returned the next day before showtime to tell him how much I had liked his performance. "So does this mean you're out?" I asked.

Louganis laughed and recalled our last conversation. Then he said, "You know, the way I deal with my feelings is that if I'm afraid of something, I'll face it. When I was growing up, I had nightmares about snakes biting me. So when I was around ten, I got a boa constrictor. The pet shop guy said it was a girl. We named her Rosie. She was only about four feet long. She lived in my room. And my sister was really terrible about this. She would come in and bother Rosie, and Rosie would start biting me. So I've been bitten, oh, countless times by a snake, my worst nightmare."

"Is this some kind of metaphor for me to figure out?"

"I guess you could also say this play is my Rosie."

The *Times* held the column for a few days, concerned that I was outing Louganis against his wishes. The climate at the paper had changed radically; Punch Sulzberger's son, Arthur, Jr., was a champion of gay rights (as was Abe's son, Andrew, later the editorial page editor). Editors eventually decided to run the column, figuring that Louganis was outing himself, which he confirmed to me several years later and in his autobiography. As usual, my subject was at least a beat ahead of me. Though I thought Louganis was finally declaring himself gay in my column, in fact he was also declaring himself HIV positive. (Which created a brief, retroactive controversy: what right did he have to dive into that Olympic pool with a bleeding wound and endanger others?)

Despite my interest in the subject, particularly as a tool to pry deeper into Jock Culture, it was difficult to write about male homosexual athletes; other than Kopay, no members of a big-league sports team had come out. Then I met Ed Gallagher, who at twenty-seven, in despair over his homosexuality, had rolled his body off the highest point of the Kensico Dam in Westchester, a New York suburb.

Gallagher had presented himself to the world as "meat man," a six-foot, six-inch, 275-pound former offensive lineman who loved to hit hard, drive drunk, and use women like Kleenex. He'd been all-state in high school, gone to the University of Pittsburgh on a football scholarship, and had a tryout with the New York Jets. After he was cut, it got harder and harder to maintain his identity to himself.

"I was a sports hero, but please don't look beneath the surface, I can't handle it," he told me. "No one ever got close. I was moody, sometimes I lashed out. I was so confused: Who am I? What am I supposed to do? I've got these thoughts and feelings a jock isn't supposed to have and these sexual fantasies about men as well as women."

In early 1985, "tanked up on wine," he cruised Greenwich Village bars until he found a man who "coaxed" him into his first homosexual experience. He liked it. But the next morning he felt "filthy." Twelve days later, at the dam, he attempted suicide, two miles from his high school football field. At the bottom of his 110-foot "fall from grace," Gallagher broke his neck.

Later, he would say that in losing his body he gained his soul. He felt liberated as a quadriplegic in a wheelchair. "I used to be emotionally paralyzed, Joe Macho, John Wayne. I tried to match my image to the beer commercials. The jock.

"I feel sorrier for the person I was than for me now. If I could reach back, I'd hug me and say, 'Kid, you're a human being of which there's a wide variety. So just go find people you can share your feelings with and love.'"

By the time I met Ed in 1992, he was thirty-four years old, loud, handsome, bearded, driving his wheelchair like Ben-Hur's chariot.

He lived on full disability in a subsidized housing project. In the seven years since his suicide attempt, he had become a local resource for suicide prevention groups, giving talks at schools, producing and hosting a weekly cable show, and directing a nonprofit self-help group, Alive to Thrive.

"Don't tell me that life stinks," he'd tell a high school audience. "Tell me what part of your life stinks. You don't throw away an apple because it has a bruise. You cut out the bruise and eat the rest of the apple, right? I tried to throw all of myself away."

Ed was smart and open, and his insights into Jock Culture led me deeper into the homosociality (the latest preferred academic phrase) of the locker room, the meaning of all that naked horseplay, dick grabbing, ass slapping I'd seen even in the big leagues. Were these guys so sure of their hetero masculinity that they could mock it, or were they exciting themselves with homoeroticism?

"Both at the same time," said Ed, laughing.

By the time Billy Bean arrived in 1999, I was ready with my questions and comfortable asking them.

For that third phone call, the one in which we were going to discuss a face-to-face meeting, I flew to Miami and told him I was around the corner. There was a slight pause, he laughed, and we made a date to have dinner that night. I knew I had my story.

Bean was simply one of the most charming and engaging people I've ever interviewed, boyishly model handsome, funny, warm. I could easily believe one of his big-league teammates who later told me, "Billy could have been a great player, but he tried too hard to make everyone happy, wanted everyone to like him, he put too much pressure on himself."

Bean's story of isolation and subterfuge may have been familiar to countless gay men and lesbians, and his passion to play big-league ball was shared by countless high school and college baseball players, but, as I wrote in a front-page story, "the combination of those two struggles offers a rare window into the fiercely competitive and hyper-masculinized arena of major team sports."

"I never dated another major leaguer, and I have no idea whether or not there are other gay ballplayers," said Bean. "One would think so, but if they were as deeply closeted as I was, who would know? I went to Hooters, laughed at the jokes, lied about dates because I loved baseball. I still do. I'd go back in a minute. I only wish I hadn't felt so alone, that I could have told someone, and that I hadn't always felt God was going to strike me dead."

High school quarterback, point guard, valedictorian, college baseball all-American, handsome, thoughtful, and a celebrated "babe magnet," Billy Bean was his family's golden child. Yet he was nagged by the feeling that something was missing, that there was an emotional hole at the center of his life. His mother would later describe it to me as "a sadness in him I couldn't reach." Bean had long suspected that he was homosexual despite being heterosexually active since high school. He was married for three years. He didn't have his first homosexual experience until he was twenty-eight.

By that time, the pattern of his baseball career was set. In nine years of bouncing onto and off major-, minor-, winter-, and Japanese-league rosters, Bean logged less than four years of major-league pension time for three different teams. Six feet tall and 200 pounds, he was not considered fast enough to be an everyday center fielder. Left-handed, he was a sound defensive player in the outfield and at first base, but he didn't have enough power to start in those positions. His career big-league batting average was .226 in 272 games. He hit only five home runs. He rarely played three major-league games in a row.

He described himself as one of those "scrappy scrubs who will do anything to stick in the Show," from running extra wind sprints to cheerleading from the bench, even giving teammates free clubhouse haircuts (sixties-style astronaut cuts called "beanies") to boost camaraderie and morale.

His Dodgers experience overwhelmed him. With most of his friends and family in southern California, he was barraged with requests for tickets, for inside baseball gossip, to show up at parties. His parents remember him trying to please everyone. He was thrilled when the Dodgers broadcaster Vin Scully acknowledged his existence by dubbing him "Guillermo Frijoles" on air, then crushed by the avalanche of phone messages he felt he had to answer.

The chilly Dodgers culture was particularly tough on a backup player with a secret fear. Manager Tommy Lasorda considered himself the only true star of the team and was not the warm father figure of his publicity. Bean was told that young players had to knock on the manager's door, and then only when it was open. Bean regarded the nameplaces over the lockers as symbolic—they were erasable chalkboards. He batted .197 in fifty-one games.

When Bean's biological father died suddenly of a heart attack in 1991 at forty-four, Bean says, he felt a sense of mortality that motivated him to deal with his sexual feelings. Within a year, he had left his wife and had his first homosexual experience. He says he still regrets not having told her the truth at the time.

"Something was just drawing me to that other side. I've had good sex with women and good relationships, but something was missing, even with my wife. I wasn't fulfilled, I had a fear of not being understood, not being totally accepted. I was looking for a soul mate, someone I could let my guard down with. I only found that with men."

Interviewing Bean over several days, I felt the excitement I remembered from the early years at the paper, when every story was a new experience, a window opening on a new world. No question this guy was a jock, and a successful one. He'd made it to the top. Yet he was a "fag."

There were midnight walks on road trips to get away from his tomcatting teammates, to work off the stress of being a spy in his own life. There were anonymous sexual encounters after which he'd come back hoping God would forgive him. There were a great deal of guilt and self-hate until he began living with Sam, an Iranian he met at a health club. But he kept the relationship a secret, even refusing to let his brothers stay at his Del Mar house. Sam hid in the car when teammates dropped by.

Then, for the second time, sudden death became a catalyst. On April 23, 1995, Bean returned from an exhibition night game to find Sam semiconscious with a mysterious fever. He died of cardiac arrest in the emergency room the next morning, eight years to the day of Bean's major-league debut. Because Sam's family barred him from the hospital, he never found out what had killed Sam.

Bean remembers calling his mother, crying, "Not fair, not fair," and her urging him to take a shower and go to the ballpark. She had no idea that Sam was more than just a buddy. He felt confused. How could he explain to the club he needed a day off to grieve? Bean got a hit that day. After the game, he was called in for an announcement he knew too well: he was being sent back down to the minors.

"I swore to myself I would never again let baseball take precedence over my life," said Bean. "If I ever fell in love again, that relationship would come ahead of my career."

Later that season, in Florida to play the Marlins, he met the owner of a popular Miami Beach restaurant. In town again four months later, Billy called him up.

At Thanksgiving, Bean went home and told his mother.

"While he was trying to get the words out, I said it: 'You're gay,'" Mrs. Kovac told me. "We left the house and drank coffee in the car, and we both cried. I wondered what it would mean to him."

With dread, Bean went back inside to wake up his stepdad. The tough old homicide cop opened his eyes, listened, nodded, hugged and kissed his son, and said, "Okay, now it's official. Can I go back to sleep?"

Bean did not return to baseball in 1996. He assumes he would have been assigned to a minor-league team. He knew he could no longer live so furtively. To come out while still playing, he thought, would mean lurid headlines and talk shows, and then baseball would find a way "to kick me out." He moved to Miami Beach and worked in radio and television as his relationship with the restaurant owner became professional as well as personal. Precise and methodical, a leader, he began taking over more and more operational duties at the restaurant. Then they opened one together.

It was the third sudden death, of his old college teammate Tim Layana, a former Yankees pitcher, that pushed Bean out to a more public platform. He missed Layana's funeral because none of their mutual friends had his contact information. He had become estranged from his own life. A month later, he succumbed to *Miami Herald* writer Lydia Martin's entreaties and allowed her to make him a public gay figure.

He called another college teammate, Jim Bruske.

"I kinda suspected," Bruske told me. "I wouldn't say anything till he did, no one knew for sure, but he kept shying away from us. I'd come to Miami to play the Marlins, and he always had some reason we couldn't get together and he'd be short and change the subject when it got personal.

"He was right to keep it a secret. The guys would have been brutal. I'm glad it's out. I told him it would have no impact on our friendship."

After the story appeared, Billy had a flurry of TV interviews. He wrote a memoir, *Going the Other Way*. He joined human rights groups and spoke to college and high school students. He was taken up as a hunky poster boy by gay publications. But there was little follow-up or commentary in the mainstream sports media. I was surprised and disappointed that the story didn't have more legs. Billy was no star, but he was a major-league baseball player. There had to be others, and if not there had to be a reason.

I called gay sportswriters around the country. They were disappointed, too, but not surprised. They thought that each coming-out story was incremental progression toward understanding and acceptance. The dream of a major superstar coming out at the height of his popularity was not realistic, they said. What would be more likely and probably more helpful would be sports fans following a gay high school superstar who had gone on to brilliant college and pro careers.

That's what made Corey Johnson's story so appealing. He was no superstar, but he was that masculine icon, the high school football captain. A linebacker, yet.

Less than a year after the Billy Bean story, again following up on a gay writer's local piece—this one by Peter Cassels in *Bay Windows*—I met Corey, who had revealed his sexuality in a series of meetings orchestrated by his school and a Massachusetts gay rights group, while he was still playing. It was a textbook model of how to peel the coming-out onion in a nonconfrontational way. It turned out well; after one big victory in which Corey starred, his Masconomet High teammates gave him the game ball and sang the unofficial gay anthem "YMCA" to him on the bus ride home. It was a feel-good story but hardly typical. A few miles away, a high school football player had been beaten by teammates when he came out. His family was driven out of town.

I thought that because of Corey's age and the iconography of high school football, this story was advancing the stories of Gallagher and Billy Bean. But it would not have been on page one without a fortuitous news peg. The Sunday it appeared, Corey, who had just turned eighteen, was a speaker at the Millennium March for Equality, a gay and lesbian rally in Washington.

For gay activists trying to shatter stereotypes, Corey Johnson was a rare find, a bright, vivacious quick study who also wrestled and played lacrosse and baseball as he won three varsity letters on a winning football team. He was also conscious of his role.

"Someday I want to get beyond being 'that gay football captain,'" said Corey, "but for now I need to get out there and show these machismo athletes who run high schools that you don't have to do drama or be a drum major to be gay. It could be someone who looks just like them."

At five feet, eight inches and 180 pounds, Corey had to make up for his drama club size with the speed and brutality of his blocking and tackling. He suspected his homosexuality by sixth grade but suppressed further thoughts about it. He did not feel part of what he called "the elite jock mix" of heterosexual innuendo and bravado. He didn't go out with girls, he told me, because he didn't want to waste their time. It wouldn't be fair.

In the very first game of his varsity career, as a sophomore starting at both right guard and middle linebacker, his blocking was so effective and he made so many sacks that the line coach awarded him the game ball. Yet he was so afraid that everyone would hate him when his secret was revealed that he was often unable to sleep at night or get out of bed in the morning. He would reach out on the Internet, finding other gay youngsters, even other gay football players. For years, he exchanged e-mails with a gay right guard in Chicago.

Corey's decision to come out began taking shape during his family's 1998 Super Bowl party. One of his uncles pointed at the comedian Jerry Seinfeld in a commercial and called him a fag. He said that such "sick" people needed to be "put into institutions." Another uncle laughed. Corey's mother, unaware at the time of Corey's orientation, chided her brothers and asked them not to use such language.

Corey went into the bathroom and cried. A month later, he told his guidance counselor and biology teacher that he was bisexual. He was a virgin at the time. Later, he told his lacrosse coach that he was gay. All three were supportive. They also began to understand his moodiness and mediocre grades.

He told no one else during that summer and the football season of his junior year. He joined the school's Gay Straight Alliance, which was made up mostly of straight girls. Since he was known for defending kids who were being hazed or bullied, no one found this remarkable. The team voted him cocaptain.

After Christmas vacation, he decided to tell his parents.

His father already knew. He had read an e-mail exchange. For months he had held the secret; he didn't want to burden his wife, who was absorbed in ministering to her dying mother.

"I dropped the ball," he told me. "What if Corey had done something to himself?"

Corey told his teammates that he was gay, that he hoped for their support, and not to worry: "I didn't come on to you last year in the locker room, and I'm not going to do it now. Who says you're good enough, anyhow?"

That lightly dropped remark had been scripted in the preliminary meetings with his teachers and the state's Gay, Lesbian and Straight Education Network.

Corey remembered, "At first the team was meek about it, people didn't talk to me, and when they saw it was still just me they asked all kinds of questions. They wanted intimate details. They thought it would be cool to know more about the subculture. When they heard about a gay bar called the Ramrod, they asked me to get them T-shirts."

There were incidents, quickly shut down. The president of the school's booster club, the father of four past, present, and future players, demanded that Corey be removed as captain to preserve "unit cohesiveness." Coach Jim Pugh told him that he was the divisive one and that it was not an issue. When younger players complained to another cocaptain about having to shower with a gay teammate, he would growl, as he would to most complainants, "You're a football player, toughen up." But then Masconomet football players traditionally never showered at school; they went home from games and practices filthy and smelly. I couldn't figure out how much of that was teenage self-consciousness and how much the nasty condition of a rusty old high school locker room.

After the story ran, Ed Gallagher called me, ecstatic. "This Corey is a pioneer, a leader, but he's up against the hypocritical right-wing hate mongers who want to punish people for being human. I say there are no straights or gays, just 'strays.'"

We both thought the dialogue would begin now. This one was the Big Story, a high school football captain rallying the jocks, smashing the stereotypes. High school was the heart and soul of Jock Culture; it was where the values and definitions of American manhood were imprinted. Sports columnists, talk radio hosts, the latest phenomenon of Internet chatterers (this was 2000) would be all over this story.

It never happened. They didn't want to hear about gay players. It was off message, it complicated the mainstream fantasy. Rumors of gay stars tended to be floated by gay fans who wanted to claim them and antigay fans who wanted to put them down.

My third and final Big Story about an athlete coming out was again about a popular hard worker who tried to fit in, but this time it was a 300-pound NFL defensive lineman, a veteran of nine years in the trench warfare zone of sports. How could you discount this symbolism? Pro football players have been promoted as supermasculine warriors, no women or sissies allowed. So how do you explain Esera Tuaolo living in a suburban house with his adopted twenty-three-month-old twins and the man he described as his husband?

Tuaolo had been a star at high schools in Hawaii and California, and at Oregon State. He'd had a successful rookie year with the

Green Bay Packers in 1991 that included thirty solo tackles and the singing of the national anthem at Lambeau Field before a game.

"I knew when I was young that I was attracted to men," Tuaolo told me. "But once I could give a name to it, I backed off. I had girl-friends as a cover-up, and I made sure I was seen leaving strip clubs. I drank a lot. I was always anxious, always in pain. I was afraid if I was too much of a star I'd be exposed. Once you learn the system, you can play just hard enough to make the team. That's pretty sad. I didn't want to call attention to myself. If I had a sack I'd have a sleep-less night, wondering if now they would catch me."

In the locker room he was the jolly "Mr. Aloha." He says he never suspected that there were other gay football players. ("His gaydar must have gone dead," says Dave Kopay.) Tuaolo's social life play-ing for Green Bay, Minneapolis, and Jacksonville was limited except during the off-seasons, when he returned to Hawaii and to friends who knew he was gay. In 1997, concerned about Tuaolo's suicidal depression, a friend gave him a copy of *The Dave Kopay Story*. The book had just been reissued. It was the first book he'd read since college.

"It confirmed everything, it was eye-opening, I wasn't alone," he said. "It forced me to make choices. I decided I was going to be open to a real relationship."

A segment about Tuaolo on the HBO show *Real Sports* under-scored the rationale for his secrecy. A former teammate and cur-rent ESPN broadcaster, Sterling Sharpe, said that any player who declared himself gay would be driven off the team. Sharpe implied that players would feel threatened; a gay teammate would cast doubts in fans' minds about all players' masculinity and sexual orientation. Sharpe's hostility extended the shelf life of the Tuaolo story, giving commentators a chance to expound on the unit cohesiveness theory used to discriminate against gays in the military.

My story ran in the back of the sports section. Old news. I was disgusted by Sharpe and by the mainstream sports media's refusal to take these stories seriously. Maybe they too were afraid of being called fags.

Once again, I wanted too much. Kopay was thrilled. He said that Tuaolo's coming out had an enormous impact on him. The two men hugged and cried when they met at our "Brokeback Locker Room" panel at the 2006 Chicago Gay Games. By that time, Bean was heading into a big-league real estate career (Alex Rodriguez was a client), Tuaolo was a successful singer, and Corey Johnson was a political operative in New York. They were all out in the world with thousands of Facebook friends.

But progress was still agonizingly incremental, I thought. Bean was disappointed, too. "I talk to too many kids who decide not to go out for the baseball team or the football team, they'll be found out," he told me in 2009. "They're aware of the ramifications, they hear the gay slurs from the stands, and those are mostly straight guys yelling at other straight guys. I've spoken at thirty schools—mostly Division III colleges—and I've met one out person in baseball. A lot of guys still go out for cross-country instead."

It's 4 P.M., May 25, 2001, just before my crew chief said, "You're good to go."
(Courtesy of Richard Petty Enterprises)

FOURTEEN | My Driver

I n my naiveté (Cosell was right about that), I had thought the gay athlete stories would have a more visible impact. But they just rolled off the table. Was I the only straight journalist interested? What was wrong with those sycophantic dummies, too busy fluffing upcoming events and godding up or beating down athletes to follow real issues? Was Jock Culture that impenetrable?

I felt stuck. The *Times* column read stale to me. Like Ishmael, I was feeling "a damp, drizzly November in my soul." Where's Moby Dick when you need him? As usual, I turned to Neil Amdur, the

Times sports editor, a pinwheel of ideas. As usual, he had an idea for me. He tossed me the keys to the car.

Speed thrills.

The Charlotte, North Carolina, racetrack was hosting ride-alongs for journalists, and on Thursday, January 11, 2001, I maneuvered into a line for a driver who seemed a little steadier, more careful than the others, although I have no idea how I could have made such a judgment on my third day covering NASCAR. I had never heard of Mark Martin. I was also attracted by the sponsor for his blue Ford Taurus: Viagra. Even if I hated the ride, I figured, I'd get a few paragraphs out of the brand-new drug, at that time a late-night joke more than a staple of late-night life.

Martin, small, wiry, leathery, at forty-two already old to be the contender he was, barely looked at me as I was stuffed through the window into the seatless passenger side of his car. Hands reached in to fasten a makeshift seat belt and push a red helmet down over my head. The number 6 Viagra growled into life under Martin's foot. The sound, abrasive at first, became comforting as it enclosed me. By the time we burst onto the track, I felt part of the car.

The first one-and-a-half-mile lap, the warm-up, was faster than I had ever gone before, perhaps 100 MPH, but still slow enough for fantasy. I imagined the Speedway skyboxes filled with corporate sponsors eager to bankroll my NASCAR campaign, the 150,000 seats filled with hard-core fans screaming through the roar of forty-two other cars for me to find a hole in the snips of air between our metal skins and drive around them, through them, before I was crushed by the looming wall.

And then we were at speed, the qualifying lap, and I gave myself up to sheer pleasure. My body pressed back against the seat on the straightaway, but my mind lifted out of my head, a balloon freed of thought, and I felt an exhilaration so intense it seemed a white light. At each corner, as Martin braked and the car slipped down the banked track, I thought, Faster! Faster! and then he accelerated out of the curve and I lived again.

Into the last lap, approaching the checkered flag, Bob (Lippy) Lipsyte in the number 6 blue Ford about to make his move, passing the leader on the inside . . .

Martin's hand was out the window as he slowed into the third and final lap. I felt satisfied yet incomplete as we rolled back into Pit Road. The rush had lasted less than two minutes. I wanted more. I thanked him. He nodded and looked for his next passenger.

Back at the garage, I was told that we had averaged 163.64 MPH on that second lap, probably somewhere between 175 and 180 on the straightaways. Someone looked into my eyes. "You okay?"

I raised a thumb. I wasn't ready to talk. I had sensed what NASCAR was all about, and I thought, I am spoiled forever. I have known speed. I want to drive!

Amdur was delighted by my experience, and quite a few readers and colleagues turned out to be closet NASCAR fans, but most Manhattan friends were bemused by my enthusiasm. Some were merely ignorant, some judgmental. Why was I helping to promote a wasteful "sport" of no social value, environmentally destructive, dangerous, obscenely commercial? Isn't oil the root of all international evil? I tried not to be too defensive. After all, did you have to love war to cover it? In truth, I was loving NASCAR for jump-starting my stalled column.

What was supposed to have been another short-term *Times* hitch had already lasted ten years. For six of those years I had also written a column for the *Times'* weekly City section called "Coping," whose conceit was that one man's neighborhood was the city writ small and in my daily rub in the Union Square–Gramercy Park area of lower Manhattan with neighbors, tradespeople, the bureaucracy, I could explore the life of the city.

The two columns, so different in content and tone, created

a wonderful professional balance for me. The city column was so much warmer and more intimate than the sports column that I felt like two Bobs. Or Bobbin and Lippy. Readers thought so, too. I'd meet couples at parties who claimed to be fans of mine. The husband would glance at his wife. "Since when did you start reading sports?" and she would say, "Oh, he doesn't write sports." I loved that, and I loved the opportunity to merge the personal and the political in "Coping." But I came up against a wall because another marriage, my third, was falling apart. Though I could write about my mom's slow death in 1998 and what I learned about the health care system, I couldn't write about the central issue in my personal life, and "Coping," this purportedly personal journal, felt bogus. So I quit it.

I'd been through illness and divorce and raggedy times before, but the sports column—or the new book or the TV show—had always been the guideline that led me through the storm. As Billie Jean King said, no matter what was going on in your life, at least you could lose yourself in the game. But this time I wasn't losing myself in the game. I needed a new game.

Back in 1992, Amdur had suggested I spend an academic year following the boys' and girls' varsity teams of a big, diverse high school in Elizabeth, New Jersey. I met the remarkable former football coach turned principal, Frank Cicarell, who opened all doors for me. I vividly remember being taken by a sixteen-year-old football player to the school's day care center so I could see the baby son he had sired with his former girlfriend. He was trying to impress me and his new fifteen-year-old girlfriend with his manhood.

A year later, Amdur deemed that ice hockey, a sport that I and most *Times* readers thought we knew enough about not to want to know more, was worthy of my intermittent attention. I spent two glorious seasons sporadically hanging out with the amiable rough-necks of the New York Rangers, including the Beowulf of pro athletes, Mark Messier, and came away with enormous admiration for their hardiness, professionalism, and decency. Unlike most baseball, football, and basketball players, who tend to answer simple questions with something like "Why the fuck didn't your editor send someone who knows something?," hockey players seemed delighted to educate a reporter. Besides the obvious fact—that the sport was hungry for major-league publicity—I think the attitude also reflected the traditional, dad-driven, Canadian/midwestern/Eastern European families in which most players had been raised. And I was their dads' age! The two seasons ended in a made-for-Lippy finish—the Rangers won their first Stanley Cup in fifty-four years.

Then, under pressure from soccer fans, Amdur thought we needed to pay some attention to the world's most popular game. That turned into years of stories about the teams of immigrant West African, Caribbean, and South American boys who had turned Martin Luther King, Jr. High School in Manhattan—otherwise known in the tabloids as Horror High—into a nationally ranked power. The coach, Martin Jacobson, a former drug abuser and petty criminal, took control of his life by creating opportunities for his players. As long as they showed up, played hard, and eschewed the hip-hop life around them, Jake would be their father, guidance counselor, college guide, immigration adviser, nutritionist, dating consultant. "We are so good," a Trinidadian player once told me, "'cause Coach Jake got no life but us." It wasn't true, but Jake had created an environment in which greenhorn kids felt safe. Being with Jake is like running inside a hurricane. He is still a recurring character in my life.

For 2001, Amdur came up with the most excellent of our adventures, a sport most *Times* readers were content to know nothing about. Amdur believed, rightly, that NASCAR would be the new century's hot sport. We thought I'd write about stock car racing every six or seven weeks, features, tutorials, a little dilettante anthropology.

But as I had been thirty-seven years earlier on the exotic island of boxing, I was soon enthralled. I met Dale Earnhardt, Sr., the crusty

John Wayne of wheels, learned about restrictor plates and drafting, marveled at the layers of sponsorship and the autocracy of the France family, which had created and owned the sport. From owners to mechanics, everyone was glad to see me, eager to explain their sport to a Yankee from Moneyworld. It felt like hockey, only easier: better weather, more free food and drink, more publicity people, many of them northern corporate operatives. I was surprised to find how interested I became in the economics and the technology. And in the traditional Christian family values, a NASCAR theme. Generations of fans rooted together in the stands, and generations of mechanics passed wrenches in the garages. I was particularly interested early on in the relationship between Dale and Dale, Jr., who was expected to become an even better, and more popular, driver than his dad.

Less than a month after my Big Ride, I went to Florida for the Daytona 500, the first and most celebrated race of the season. It was scheduled for February 18, the same date I'd met Ali and the Beatles in Miami Beach in 1964. The race week buildup felt just like the buildup to a heavyweight championship fight. I was renewed. The Kid Comes Back!

On the eve of the race, the first person I went to interview at length was Mark Martin. It would be his seventeenth 500. He had never won one. I wanted to talk about the love of speed.

"I don't particularly love anything about the sport except winning," he snapped. "Racing's not about speed for me, it's about being better than other people." The drum-tight skin on his pale, sharp-featured face creased with a humorless smile. "You're the one who liked the speed. What did you feel?"

I told him about the pleasure of becoming part of the machine when he hit 175 MPH on the straightaway, about an exhilaration so intense it had become a white light.

"You weren't scared?" He looked skeptical.

"I picked your car because I trusted the way you drove, very methodical, precise. I sensed it was a chore for you, but you were going to do it right, you weren't going to embarrass NASCAR and get me killed."

Martin's smile softened then, and the pale blue eyes seemed to lose some of their locked-in focus. "That's true. I'm compulsive about everything I do. I hate testing cars, it's boring because you're not racing against anybody, but once I start I do more laps than anybody else. I block out the world. Always like that. Tropical fish, ceramics, motorcycles, going from thing to thing until I found stock car racing when I was fifteen."

Martin, I had been happy to find out after our ride, was a NASCAR stalwart, popular with fans and other drivers, steady, a clean racer. He was known as the best driver never to have won the championship. The word around the garage was that Martin was unlucky and that he lacked the killer instinct of the three superstars to whom he had finished as championship runner-up: Dale Earnhardt (twice), Tony Stewart, and Jeff Gordon. Jeff and Tony might wreck you if you were in their way. Dale would wreck you just because he could. Martin might not even wreck you to win. Some people I talked to about Martin seemed disdainful of his innate decency. I admired him for it. He had a prickly integrity. He wouldn't answer a question if he couldn't be honest. The chip on his shoulder from old personal and professional defeats, from too much drinking and the early death of his father, his racing mentor, had been sanded and painted over the years as he made himself sober and competitive. But it was still there as time ran out for him. He said he knew he was old, that he was not the future of the sport. I could put myself in that category, too, I thought.

Earnhardt at forty-nine was pretty much past a prime in which he had won seven championships. Dale—"The Intimidator"—was one of the last of the laconic, hard-charging carburetor cowboys with whom southern workingmen could identify. They flew Confederate flags with his face superimposed. They wore hats and shirts with his number 3 and grew imitations of his push-broom mustache. And they plastered their pickups and rec vehicles with pictures of his main rival, the California-born Gordon. There would be a red slash through Gordon's pretty face and the words "Fans Against Gordon" (FAG). It was the worst they could throw at Gordon, who drove as hard as Earnhardt, who liked and mentored the younger man.

I didn't get Dale. I had spent a little time with him that week in Charlotte. He was gruffly charming, and I found what I considered his contradictions amusing. Here was a rural populist hero whose North Carolina office/race shop complex, the so-called Garage Mahal, contained a curated display of his hunting rifles, mounted animal heads, and pictures of his executive chef cooking up his kills. I was simply too new to the sport, maybe too New York, to appreciate his mythic place and how what seemed like contradictory excesses for a country boy were aspirational to his constituency; someone like them could make it big, could have the northern suits begging for his time.

Dale seemed like a bully to me on and off the track and not a particularly winning father—the tough love he'd practiced with Dale, Jr., wasn't making the kid into a great driver. Did Junior even want to race? He was twenty-six at the time and seemed happier with his video games, his pals, his guitar.

A *Times* reporter had been sent down to cover the Daytona 500. I was doing a long piece on the crowd, the drivers, the scene. Introduce *Times* readers to the smell of NASCAR Nation, gas fumes, sizzling ribs, beer sweat. I'd spent most of the night roaming the infield, the area inside the 2.5-mile track in which thousands camped out in fancy double-wide trailers and the beds of rusty pickups. There were jolly four-generation family groups and packs of surly, stringy, tattooed rednecks. There were concession stands, a lake, tubs of iced Bud. Everybody seemed wasted by midnight, when girls were eager to lift their T-shirts at demands to "Show your tits!"

During the race, I was still typing my long piece when the track exploded in an eighteen-car collision. One car was actually airborne. This was the Big One people were always talking about, a monster wreck. I jumped up in the press box looking for Mark Martin, whose car had been torn up in the crash. Not Mark! I was ready to run down to count the dead. How could anyone walk out of that pileup? But everyone did.

Which certainly lulled me, a few hours later, at the very end of the race, on the final turn of the last lap, when Earnhardt slammed into the wall near where I sat.

I can still hear the frantic voice of Earnhardt's crew chief calling to him through my radio scanner: "You okay, Dale? Talk to us, talk to us."

Minutes later, a blue tarp was thrown over that famous black number 3 Goodwrench Chevrolet. I didn't understand the symbolism of the blue tarp until I heard a terrible moan rise from the 200,000 people in the grandstand. Then people around me in the press box began to cry. Earnhardt's body was being covered.

The office called and asked me to write the story. For page one. There was a shivery moment—Can I still bring it on deadline?—before the adrenaline kicked in and I remembered all those nights at ringside energized by the ticking of the clock. Didn't I used to tell new kids, "Deadlines clear the rust out of your ass"? Let's see what you got, Lippy. It's 1964, and Clay just won the title from Liston and the teletype operator is waiting for you to rip copy out of your little manual Olivetti, paragraph by paragraph. You've got more time now since you only have to press your own computer send button.

By Robert Lipsyte

DAYTONA BEACH, Feb. 18—Stock car racing's greatest current star and one of its most popular and celebrated figures, Dale Earnhardt, crashed and was killed today after he made a characteristically bold lunge for the lead on the last turn of the last lap of the sport's premier event, the Daytona 500. One of the two cars he was trying to overtake was driven by his son, Dale, Jr., who never saw his father smash into the wall.

Popular opinion and most other writers had a different, more poignant spin. They had Dale gallantly blocking the rest of the field for the two front-runners, Dale, Jr., and his protégé and employee Michael Waltrip, a thirty-seven-year-old journeyman who went on to win his first Cup race.

I could have been wrong in my conclusion, which was based on a sense that Dale, Sr., would never not try to win himself. It was my first race, and I didn't know any of the principals well. The legend is fine by me.

More interesting was the clash of reactions to Earnhardt's death—"Oh, God" versus "So what?"—which led me into a political take on NASCAR. This was just a few months after that chad-choked 2000 election in which George W. Bush beat Al Gore. Earnhardt's death became a signifier of America's cultural divide. Red states v. Blue states. Beer drinkers v. wine drinkers. Carnivores v. herbivores. The estimated 75 million Americans who lived through NASCAR, defined themselves by the drivers they followed, the products they bought, the vacations they took v. millions of Americans who thought of NASCAR as numbing Sunday afternoons of gas guzzlers mindlessly snarling around a track while rednecks got hammered. The term "NASCAR dads" replaced "soccer moms" as shorthand for the latest demographic to be wooed by politicians.

Earnhardt's name did not appear in the headline of my page-one story: "Stock Car Star Killed on Last Lap of Daytona 500." The editors decided that not enough *Times* readers knew who he was. They were probably right, yet another indication of the red-blue divide.

In death, Dale not only became a passing political symbol but gave NASCAR a mythological figure, its own Babe Ruth. It also gave NASCAR an increased aura of danger that lifted it above what gearheads contemptuously call "the stick-and-ball sports." And it gave the *Times* more reason to refuse to let me drive a car even when I found a way to do it. It didn't want me under a blue tarp while it supported my survivors.

Despite my rooting, Mark had one of his worst seasons in years, finishing twelfth in the standings. But his main sponsor, Viagra, which paid something like the standard $12 million to finance the season, was racing alone on the erectile dysfunction track and winning big. Racing purists, mostly older writers, were offended by the sponsorship. Next would come hard booze sponsors and then foreign cars, they'd grumble, and it turned out they were right. Fans might have wished that the big *V* on Mark's car still stood for the oil products of Valvoline, his former sponsor, but they didn't quit on Mark. Pfizer, the pharmaceutical company that produced Viagra, set up a medical tent at racetracks offering free blood and urine exams by local doctors for diabetes and other disorders (and sexual performance advice if asked for). I sat in one day and was amazed at the number of overweight men and women with dangerously high glucose and blood pressure levels. For many, this was their only medical exam of the year. Some said they had made a choice between their medicine and their grandstand tickets. "Why live if you can't go racin'?" was the way they put it. The doctors told me they thought the fans were making an understandable—if regrettable—"quality of life" decision.

I ended up writing more than occasional NASCAR columns.

Times editors and readers liked them, NASCAR management was pleased with the attention (it hoped for a New York–area track), and old-timey race writers went out of their way to help me—their stock rose with mainstream coverage. I was no rival for their inside-the-engine fanzine pieces.

Sometimes I wondered if the positive reaction I was getting made me willing to overlook or at least try to justify the dark side of NASCAR, its ostentatious commercialism, its union-busting stance, totalitarian structure, reactionary politics, environmental pollution, and discriminatory exclusivity (there is no racism, homophobia, anti-Semitism, or sexism in NASCAR, I'd say at Manhattan parties, because almost everyone, including Jeff Gordon, is a white Christian hetero male).

Hey, I own a big story, I'm feeling young again. Especially after Friday, May 25, 2001, 4 P.M., when I got the chance to drive.

In retrospect, I probably should have turned it down; there was more than a hint of gift giving, conflict of interest. Publicists from Fox (the network broadcasting the races), Lowe's Speedway, and the Richard Petty Driving Experience—a fantasy day camp that offered a menu of rides and drives from $89 to $2,999 at twenty-four tracks—figured out a way to clear track time after the drivers' regular practice session so I could fulfill my need for speed.

I had no qualms about safety, liability, or ethics, only about performance; my experiences with manual transmissions, in a laundry truck as a college kid at a summer job, and in a U.S. Army jeep, had been unhappy and were at least forty years in the past. I spent the day before my drive grinding the gears of John Jeppesen's modified Volkswagon GTI. John has since become a friend, but at the time he was the Viagra PR guy. I was not exactly a model of journalistic integrity in this. I was obsessed. The day of my drive I found a Gold's Gym and worked out for an hour to get my blood pumping. As Mark Martin did.

The afternoon of my drive was cool and overcast, threatening rain. The Petty guys dressed me in a fire-retardant jumpsuit and talked me through the controls of a race car. It's surprisingly simple once you switch on the ignition and hit the starter: just keep steering left until it's time to brake and come in. Hardly any shifting of gears. Remember to press the talk-back button on the wheel so the pit crew can hear you.

One more thing: they wanted me to meet with Darrell Waltrip, the retired NASCAR champion who had recently made a seamless transition to the Fox broadcast booth. He was famous for talking a lot. His nickname as a driver had been "Jaws."

He was waiting for me in a corner of a garage he used as an office. It felt like an audience. I thought his eyes narrowed as he took in my jumpsuit. He started talking before I sat down.

"There's not a guy on the road who doesn't think he can do what I did. You will never really know what I felt unless you're racin' with forty guys right around you. Stay high on the straightaway, between the white lines and the wall. Take the center of the turn, clip the grass coming down. The car will pull left, trust it. The car knows what to do. No violent moves, you'll only make the car unhappy."

I nodded as humbly as I could. This was a great champion, a Hall of Famer. It wasn't an interview, he was giving me advice. Why was I so anxious to get this over with and drive?

"Do everything slowly, but think ahead, anticipate your moves, anticipate where you want to be. You must always know where you are. Always. *You must always know exactly where you are.*"

I thanked him and said, "Sounds like advice for life."

Waltrip laughed. "When you're out there, you'll be closer to God."

My pit crew was waiting outside, Petty's national quality assurance coordinator and two teenage tire wranglers. I clambered through the driver's window of a blue-and-yellow Cheerios-sponsored Dodge, number 43, Richard Petty's old number. I was strapped in.

My helmet was slipped through the window and fitted on my head. They hooked up the neck brace and turned on the radio, snapped on the steering wheel, and flipped the ignition switch.

The teenagers adjusted the snarling throttle and drilled me on the emergency release of my safety restraint and use of the fire extinguisher. No one had ever needed to do it for real in a Petty fantasy car, they said. No one had ever died or even been seriously injured. One of them said, "You'll have such fun, just don't be nervous."

In the pits, when the green panel light blinked on, my crew chief said, "You're good to go."

The growl of the motor insulated me; my mind was filled with the techniques I had learned. I let the clutch up, accelerated to 1,500 RPM, shifted to second and, once I was up to 4,000 RPM, to third. Now on the track, I pulled down into fourth and followed a pace car. We were the only cars on the track.

My gloved hands were welded to the wheel of the 3,400-pound car. I was surprised by the bumpiness of the speedway, littered with scabs of black tire rubber from the drivers' practice sessions. I used them as markers to find my groove. I worried—although distantly, as if about someone I was watching—about rear-ending the pace car, scraping the wall, taking the turns so sharply I would flip. Over the radio, a crewman said, "Looking good," but I was too absorbed to remember to press the talk button on the wheel when I acknowledged as instructed, "Ten-four."

After eight laps, the checkered flag in the stands snapped. I slapped into neutral and rolled into Pit Road.

They checked my tires and said I'd been averaging about 110 MPH. Now that I seemed in control, the pace car would go faster.

I felt a surge of power. I couldn't wait for the green light, to shift through the gears, to burst onto the track. I didn't want to follow a pace car, I wanted to chase it, and as the car accelerated it became happier and the road was smoother and I was the brain of a gorgeous, howling 630-horsepower machine that lived only to fly on the straightaway and knife down through the middle of the turns and clip the green and rocket back up.

Suddenly I didn't want to chase the pace car—I wanted to pass it. But it stayed three car lengths ahead no matter how hard I mashed the gas. If I had had a coherent thought it might have been *Just give me a few more horses, just a little more road, and I will spin gravel into your windshield, for I was born to run.*

I hated to see the checkered flag. I eased into neutral and coasted home. My pit crew was cheering and waving, there were a couple of photographers, even a Victory Lane beauty, the Petty marketing director. I felt an overwhelming warmth for them all. They seemed bubbly with gratitude that I was alive. Someone estimated that I had reached about 130 MPH.

I swaggered away, brimming with adrenaline, suddenly wanting to eat, drink, smoke, make love, call everybody I had ever met. I was glad I didn't have to give a news conference and remember to thank all the sponsors whose names were on my car.

Two days later, Tony Stewart drove 1,100 miles in two races on one day, the Indy 500, averaging about 153.6 MPH for about three hours, fifty-two minutes, and then the Coca-Cola 600, 138.1 MPH for four hours, twenty-one minutes. All the while dozens of other drivers were bumping and scraping him, trying to run him off the track, and he was remembering to push the talk-back button to discuss gas consumption, tire use, and who was coming up behind him. Watching Stewart bounce and babble after his long day, I thought of my own 24-mile, twelve-minute taste of absolute concentration under incomparably less challenging conditions and was awed by his feat. If I had ever thought that all you needed was a heavy foot and a death wish to drive wide open on a banked track, I was now disabused.

Later on the evening of my run, after my adrenaline had drained, driving a rental car with far less aggression than usual, I felt amused at and offended by road hogs, ragers, and show-offs. They couldn't get to me anymore. I had driven at speed.

For a while after that I found myself writing more about race tactics, but I eventually settled back into my version of anthropology, the circuit-riding NASCAR preachers, the winking attitude toward cheating (after all, NASCAR's heritage was moonshiners outracing revenue agents), and the military culture in NASCAR families. All those brothers, sisters, cousins, and friends on active duty were making satellite calls and sending e-mails back to the garage. The citizens of NASCAR Nation were among the first to raise money to buy armor for Humvees in Afghanistan and Iraq.

I followed Mark Martin, of course, but as he faded that year it was harder to justify writing about him. By the end of that "Year at Speed," as my NASCAR columns were titled, the rest of the country had caught on and I was feeling nostalgic for the old days. I remembered that at my first NASCAR cocktail party I had bellied up to the bar and asked for a white wine. The room had fallen silent. An old-time writer had told me kindly that I could order any kind of Budweiser I wanted. At my last cocktail party of that year, I bellied up and asked for a white wine, and the bartender asked, "Chardonnay, Pinot Grigio, or sauvignon blanc?"

Pour it, pal. Ishmael's damp drizzle was gone, I was smiling. I was living with Lois, clearly the woman for me, sharp, quirky, fun, independent. She wrote about psychology and was not shy about analyzing me. We squabbled, but always worked through it, something I had never achieved before. I wondered why her dog, Rudy, was in bed with us. "Why are *you* in bed with *us*?" she'd snap. It was not always amusing. If I married her, it would be the *fourth*. Analyze that.

My dad thought four was a questionable number, but he loved Lois ("She is your format," he said) and Rudy, too. Mom was dead two years now, and Dad, ninety-six, was living alone an hour away. I went up to see him often, and the blooming of our relationship was a joy. We roamed the county looking for secondhand books, ate in truck-stop diners, retold old stories in a relaxed way we had never shared before. When I slept over, I could count on being awoken to the kind of scrambled-egg or French toast breakfast I'd had as a kid. Only I didn't have to rush off to school. Dad was very independent, and when he let me cut his toenails, I knew he was feeling as easy as I was.

I kept a fan's eye on NASCAR over the next couple of years. I wrote a young adult novel, *Yellow Flag*, about a teenager in a famous stock car family who wasn't sure he wanted to race. Promoting that in 2007 with John Jeppesen got me back to the races, which was fun, although seeing my old writer pals from a new angle was not; they scarfed up copies of my book, promotional plastic coffee cups, and free food as if I were just another sponsor, and for all their promises to mention *Yellow Flag* in their notes columns, few did. I sensed begrudgment. Did they think I had I crossed to the other side, did they resent me as a scorpion who'd gotten out of the barrel? "Bunch of freeloaders," I groused to John, who shrugged. He'd been at this a long time. I thought more about My Great Drive, now six years in the past. Who was I calling a freeloader?

By then Mark had retired after nineteen years with the same team. He raced part-time here and there. Eventually, the recession hit NASCAR. Corporations were reluctant to spend millions of dollars to run a competitive car, and fans were hard-pressed to pay hundreds for tickets.

And then, in 2009, Mark Martin came back. It was the summer of the old dogs. Fifty-nine-year-old Tom Watson came within a putt of winning the British Open; forty-year-old quarterback Brett Favre unretired to lead the Minnesota Vikings to a winning season; thirty-seven-year-old Lance Armstrong, after a three-season layoff, finished third in the Tour de France; and I was the host of *LIFE*

(Part 2), a weekly PBS show about the challenges and opportunities of later life, something I knew about.

Martin had a powerful new owner, Hendrick Motorsports, and a new sponsor, Kellogg's. He seemed happier than he had ever been. The word around the garage was that the mellower culture of Hendrick had something to do with his new mood. And the pressure was off: Mark's teammates now included the superstar Gordon, the three-time champion Jimmie Johnson, and Dale, Jr., still under-achieving but since his father's death the sports's most popular driver. Not much was expected of Martin beyond some mentoring.

I began writing this book as the NASCAR season began. Watching races on TV had become more and more rewarding. There were in-car cameras with a driver's-eye view and little techno-tutorials by former crew chiefs. I could start worrying about tire tread and gas consumption along with Mark, as I now thought of him. That's how you know you're a fan.

"I know that my reaction times are not what they were 15 or 20 years ago," Mark told *Sporting News*. "But I also know that what I do when I react is tempered by those 20 years of experience."

When Mark won a fourth race, the most of any driver at that point in the season, he was suddenly in contention for the Chase for the Sprint Cup, in which the top twelve drivers in the standings enter a ten-race postseason play-off.

I became addicted to Scenedaily.com, the best site for NASCAR news and features. I read it before I read the *Times*. I was feeling more excited than Mark was sounding. "Everybody gets a little too caught up in all this points stuff," he said. "I'm happy to be driving fast stuff."

I had to fill out a publicity questionnaire that day for another YA novel. "I'm happy to be writing new stuff," I wrote. It wasn't until I wrote it that I realized it was true.

Mark said that he was not stressing as much as he used to. "I can't help if we have a flat tire, or we get caught up in a wreck, or a part breaks, or if rain comes at an inopportune time. There's things you can't control that I'm not going to stay awake at night worrying about."

Only an old guy could say that and believe it. Winning may be the payoff, but the real victory is riding to the buzzer.

But it would be nice if he won.

When Mark won the twenty-ninth race of the season, he moved into first place. It was possible! By the thirtieth race he was back in second place, his place. And he was sounding like the perennial runner-up, at least to Scenedaily.com.

"I have learned a lot and I have seen a lot and I have come to realize that I'm no Dale Earnhardt," he said. "My record don't stand up to his, just doesn't. And when you stand me up against Jeff Gordon, it just don't stand up to it, man. I understand that. . . . So I think it's pretty awesome to hold my own against guys like that in the sport. I gave them something to shoot at in the race from time to time. I gave their fans something to be concerned about and I gave mine something to cheer about."

With one race left, Mark was second in the standings, 108 points behind Jimmie Johnson, who seemed to be storming toward a record-breaking fourth straight championship. I began to wishful-think like a fan: if Johnson ran worse than twenty-fifth at the Homestead-Miami Speedway—a little accident, a blown engine, a fuel miscalculation could do it—and Martin finished first . . .

Johnson was a good-looking, amiable cipher, a fine, if boring, emissary for the sport. But I could sense that sentimental drumbeat of hope for Mark. Or maybe it was just my own heart. Can the old guy do it? Can I do it? Do what?

I made some calls to old NASCAR friends to talk about Mark. He really was happy, they said. He had come to terms with his place in the standings. "This has been the best year of my life," he said.

"You know, I found so much peace and happiness . . . as well as success on the racetrack."

The last race was dull. Johnson and Mark drove carefully. Johnson finished fifth, good enough to cruise into NASCAR history. Mark finished twelfth in the race and, for the fifth time in his career, second in the championship standings.

"There's no frustration," he said afterward. "I don't have one of those trophies, so I don't know what one of those things would mean to me, but I can't imagine it meaning any more than the feeling that I felt from so many people, competitors, and fans."

He said there were a few things he would work on for next season.

Way to go, Mark. I don't have the legs I had when I chased Ali, but I have smoother moves now. We'll show the bastards our tailpipes.

Harold Connolly winning a gold medal in the hammer throw at the 1956 Melbourne Olympic Games despite his withered left arm. Or because of it? (Associated Press)

FIFTEEN | ## Shooting Stars

On July 7, 2009, the day Lance Armstrong was two-tenths of a second off the lead of the Tour de France, I injected myself with testosterone, visualizing the oily yellow drug powering me up the Ram Island hills, the steepest on my routine twelve-mile bicycle ride. Those hills are my Pyrenees. For ten years now, when my quads begin to quiver and my mind begs me to kick off the stirrups and walk the bike, I start chanting "LanceArmstrong,

LanceArmstrong, LanceArmstrong," until I reach the top of the hill. It has always worked. It was especially meaningful in the fall of 2005, coming back from weeks of chemo after a second recurrence of testicular cancer, the brand of bully that Lance and I share.

Lance didn't win the Tour in 2009—he finished third—but it was remarkable that he competed at all. He had retired for three racing seasons after winning the Tour a record seven times in a row. He was thirty-seven but as tough and focused as ever. He's the closest I have right now to a celebrity jock hero.

So, Bobbin, let me ask you this: How would you feel if it turned out that the rumors were true about his use of performance-enhancing drugs?

C'mon, Lippy, isn't it time to get past this chemical witch hunt?

Obviously, I have a personal take on PEDs in sports. Since 1991, when a second orchiectomy ended my natural testosterone production, I've been shooting the juice. Filling my prescription is often a hassle, even at Memorial Sloan-Kettering, where my surgeon, Paul Russo, prescribes it; pharmacists like to remind me that muscle pumpers like Arnold Schwarzenegger made the restrictions necessary and Barry Bonds, Marion Jones, Mark McGwire, and A-Rod didn't help matters. I don't blame any of them. Arnold and the next generation of enhanced performers, driven by their ambition and their audiences' lust for spectacular action, have merely affirmed and endorsed the nation's addiction to quick-fix upgrades.

Though I consider myself a prohibitionist for PED use among teenagers, I'm a libertarian when it comes to grown-ups. If Mark McGwire wanted to become a monster, it's his body. As far as the "level playing field" that moralists call for, I think it is level—especially when McGwire was batting against all those enhanced pitchers.

When Roger Clemens's trainer accused him of using steroids, Clemens denied it and filed suit. But my problem with Clemens was not his alleged drug use. It's my old problem, doctor: he is the quintessential jock bully, in this case the big, white Republican who makes his own rules, lies, cheats, and waves phony family values. He manipulated and sacrificed associates and teammates to accomplish his mission. He was a moral black hole, but in Jock Culture Clemens was hailed for intimidating opponents and for winning.

Clemens is a onetime fat boy from Ohio whose biological father walked out, whose adoptive father died when Roger was nine, who was raised by his mother into a socially awkward, sports-obsessed, lifetime adolescent. His trainer said that he had injected Clemens's wife with human growth hormone so she could pose for *Sports Illustrated* in a bikini.

About the drugs. I came out of the Greenie Era, when amphetamines were as common as M&M's in major-league clubhouses and probably more popular. Ballplayers popped speed to jolt themselves awake after nights on the town. I did, too, once or twice, stopped when I found out it made my heart race but didn't improve my prose. I'm still saving myself for the smart pills.

Rumors of widespread steroid use among American athletes surfaced during the 1968 Mexico Olympics, as did the payoffs to wear Adidas or Puma shoes. By that time we knew about drug experimentation as well as state professionalism among Soviet bloc athletes. I was writing a column then and wrote about it but did no serious investigations. I was more interested in racism in sports and the burgeoning, short-lived Athletic Revolution.

Twenty years later at NBC, I suggested a piece to the *Nightly News* on steroid use. I'd been getting good information from Jack Scott, Phil Shinnick, and some others from the old days. NBC News executives turned me down. They didn't want anything that might besmirch the Games, an NBC Sports event. The wall between News and Sports, which was an entertainment division, was not very high. Moving from CBS to NBC in 1988, from Sunday morning to the early-evening network newscasts, doubled my salary, but I was frustrated in the job. I was marginalized in Seoul—the network wanted happy American stories.

I felt some vindication when the Canadian sprinter Ben Johnson came up dirty in Seoul on September 24, and I was awakened in the middle of the night to cobble together a piece from my previously rejected research. Later, Johnson and his coach admitted the steroid use and said they had been doing it just to keep up with everyone else.

My main lessons on performance-enhancing drugs, other than from the tip of my own syringe, came from two of the more complex and interesting athletes I wrote about, the so-called Running Doc, George Sheehan, and the Olympic hammer-throwing champion Harold Connolly.

In late 1991, toward the end of my first year back at the *Times* and only a few months after I began testosterone replacement, the Shrivers and Kennedys, who ran the Special Olympics, took exception to one of my columns and sent one of their executives, Connolly, to New York to reeducate me. I knew him from his competing days.

Harold and I spent the day touring Special Olympics facilities and talking to athletes and coaches. By evening, I liked Connolly. Once an aloof, driven athlete, a master at psyching out rivals and snubbing the press, he had become a friendly, thoughtful quasi-public man. He was sixty years old.

"I think you have to be selfish to be a world-class athlete," he told me that day over drinks. "For more than twenty years my life revolved around throwing the hammer. I think I'm a better person now. Certainly a better father. I've mellowed, matured. Some of it's this job."

And some of it was coming to terms with his own handicap. A birth accident had left him with a crippled left arm.

Connolly remembered struggling to keep from being dumped into classes for the handicapped in working-class Brighton, outside Boston. In his senior year in high school, he managed to pass the football physical by keeping his withered arm behind his back while a bored school doctor listened to his heart. Faced with the permission slip, the coach reluctantly allowed Harold to try out. He "went nuts" on the field, tackling everything that moved, often with his legs since his left arm didn't work. By the fourth game, he was a starter.

He was a mediocre shot-putter at Boston College until his senior year. Trying to hurry up track practice to get a ride home one day, he retrieved the hammers and threw them back to the hammer throwers. He threw them farther than they did.

As he told me his story, I compared him to the pampered, money-grubbing, drug-pumped athletes of the day. Harold, the natural man, was the real role model.

At the 1956 Melbourne Olympics, Harold met Olga Fikotova, the beautiful Czechoslovak gold-medal discus thrower. It was a sensational international love story. They married, raised four children in California, divorced. After retiring from thirty years of teaching English in the Santa Monica school system, Connolly joined Special Olympics.

Well oiled after a relaxed dinner, I said, "You could have been some disabled poster boy. What a role model."

"I think about that," said Connolly. "But times were different. They didn't treat the disabled with dignity then. I couldn't stand to be treated differently. I wish I had been able to talk about my arm then. I guess I might have helped some people."

"It's all timing," I said. "If you'd been born later, taken steroids, you could have won a few more gold medals."

He looked at me incredulously. "You kidding? I was using after 1960. We all were."

I've turned that over in my head ever since. It was right in front of me from the beginning of my career. All those pimply shoulders, known as backne, in pro football locker rooms. (Could I have actually thought the shoulder pads were chafing?) But no one seemed to care about the monster linemen or the sculpted sprinters, women as well as men. The snide remarks in the press box—and there were plenty—always came with a that's-the-way-of-the-world shrug. How you gonna find out? we asked one another. And who was going to print it? Editors weren't interested. Investigations are expensive, and besides, they said, fans don't want to know. But it shouldn't have mattered. Aren't the newshounds who cover beats supposed to sniff out stories?

I had been out of sports in 1973 when Harold told a Senate subcommittee holding hearings on steroids that during the 1968 Olympic trials, "any number of athletes on the 1968 Olympic team . . . had so much scar tissue and so many puncture holes in their backsides that it was difficult to find a fresh spot to give them a new shot."

He told the senators, "I learned that larger doses and more prolonged use increased muscular body weight, overall strength, and aggressiveness but not speed, flexibility, or coordination. My vertical jump went up, but so did my blood pressure and cholesterol levels. Every time I felt unusual physical reactions, a twinge here a twinge there, a headache, disrupted sleep, or diminished libido, I retreated from the testosterone or steroids—too apprehensive to take them regularly."

Despite that, he told me, had his own children wanted to use steroids in pursuit of their athletic careers, he would have helped them. Apparently, either they didn't want to or they listened to his second wife, Pat Connolly, a three-time Olympian, who forbade it. (Harold died at seventy-nine, in 2010, after falling off his exercise bike. We had spoken a few months earlier, and he said he was in great shape and didn't even need "old guy" testosterone.)

Knowing about anabolic-androgenic steroids, which mimic the effects of natural testosterone, even writing about them, is not the same as mounting an investigation, blowing the whistle, pointing fingers at ripped bodies. Count me among the sportswriters who didn't go after the juicers. All that twenty-first-century media rage over 'roid rage felt like the revenge of the nerds. Sports scribes were so ashamed of having blown the only truly big story of their generation that they turned viciously on their former heroes. It was the mirror image of the story about the weapons of mass destruction in Iraq that weren't there. The front-page bigfeet blew that one. The steroids were right in front of the sports scribes, but they were in denial—and in the tank.

Despite the rash of mea culpas, the media failure on the story of steroid use in baseball was inexcusable, because honest stories *were* being written—and ignored. In the 1980s, Thomas Boswell of the *Washington Post*, among others, was already pointing fingers at the juicers. In 1995, Bob Nightengale, then with the *Los Angeles Times*, quoted general managers as saying that steroids were becoming part of the game. In 1998, Steve Wilstein of the Associated Press wrote about observing a bottle of androstenedione in slugger Mark McGwire's locker. He was assailed by many of his colleagues as a snoop.

In 1999, Tom Scocca wrote in the *Baltimore City Paper* that "McGwire is what people in the bodybuilding business refer to, accurately, as a 'freak.' He is bloated and deformed beyond normal human dimensions. His condition is usually ascribed to strength training—as if some free-weight routine could make his cheek muscles swell up like a pair of grapefruits. If he is not abusing steroids, then he is suffering from a pathological endocrine condition."

In 2002, Ken Caminiti, the National League's Most Valuable Player in 1996, admitted he had regularly used steroids. He died two years later. In *Editor & Publisher*, Joe Strupp wrote, "But instead of sparking a wave of follow-up articles or investigations to ferret out the details of steroid use in baseball—who was using it, where it came from, what it did to the body—sportswriters essentially left the story alone."

They left it alone not out of laziness or stupidity but rather in the sweet moral corruption of love. Perhaps even more than entertainment and political writers, perhaps even more than hard-core fans, sportswriters adore the events themselves and the heady access. Love wants to be blind. As Murray Chass, then of the *New York Times*, told *Editor & Publisher*, "I'm not sure that you want to spend every day being suspicious of someone. It might be the journalistic thing to do. But it is not fun."

Fun was the home run–happy summer of 1998. Remember the moment when McGwire, that St. Louis slugger with the Popeye forearms, androed us out of a national depression over Bill's stain on Monica's blue dress? (Ah, for the dreamy days when McGwire, with Sammy Sosa at his heels, was breaking Yankee Roger Maris's record of 61 homers and thus refurbishing the legend of the mighty Babe.)

Of course, Barry Bonds and Alex Rodriguez did not find that summer fun at all. Barry sulked; he was a far better ballplayer than McGwire, yet was being eclipsed by that wide white hormone container. It must have crossed his mind then that he'd better get some of that stuff Mark was using.

Roger Clemens, then thirty-five and on the downside of a fine pitching career, was wondering how he could survive against this new crew of monster hitters. He found a strength coach who somehow was able to help make him a monster, too. And A-Rod, that diva, was having a career season and nobody even noticed. He had used PEDs before. Maybe it was time to try them again.

I feel a certain empathy here, old guys doing whatever was necessary to hang on, extend their careers, satisfy teammates, owners, and fans. Consider a variation on using performance-enhancing drugs, the case of Dr. George Sheehan, who, while dying from prostate cancer at age seventy-four, manipulated his dosage of a hormone that blocked testosterone so he could run faster in races. He was abusing, too, right?

Sheehan had been a guru of the fitness boom of the 1970s and '80s, his practical advice on running refined and thickened with anecdotes from millions of his own footsteps and quotes from the experiential philosophers, poured into newspaper and magazine columns and into seven books including the best-selling *Running and Being.*

We had first met a few hours before the 1968 Boston Marathon. I was trolling for a column among the 890 entrants waiting for their prerace physical in a Hopkinton high school gym. I'm not sure whether I discovered him—those glittering eyes in a pale, hawkish face—or he spotted my notebook. He became a recurring character of mine for the next thirty-five years simply by telling me that morning that he regarded the race as a Greek tragedy. "There is hubris, and there is nemesis. The beginning of the course is downhill, and everyone is charged up. They run too fast, and their pride destroys them. By the time they reach the Newton Hills, they're walking."

My kind of subject. But for all his rhetoric, he was down to earth. When he heard I jogged in my old army boots like the boxers I covered, he suggested that, based on my build, I might do well to concentrate on swimming and cycling. If I did decide to keep jogging, I should wear old Hush Puppies for starters instead of expensive running shoes and drink lots of water, never soda or the new sports drinks.

I enjoyed talking to him, hearing his story. The oldest of fourteen children of a Brooklyn doctor, Sheehan ran at Manhattan College but gave it up for squash and tennis when he became a cardiologist. In 1962, the forty-three-year-old father of twelve, feeling trapped in his life, snapped after getting a 2 A.M. call to the hospital and punched a wall. He broke his hand. To stay in shape while it healed, he began to run again.

He was feeling very good about himself in 1984 when another running guru, Dr. Kenneth Cooper of Dallas, gave him the good news—he had just scored in the 99th percentile on a stress test—and the bad news—he had cancer.

"I was very angry," remembered Sheehan. "Everything was going my way. But I wasn't surprised. I'm a passive type, the kind who die of cancer. And my lifestyle prevented heart attack."

Then he spun his diagnosis into a metaphor: "I think of dying as a blood sport, like bullfighting. The bull, of course, is death, and I am defending myself, dancing with death, creating this beautiful aesthetic. The blood sports show us that death is not defeat."

This was on a day of gorgeous life in the summer of 1993, four months before he died, the sun splashing off the ocean, filling the living room of Sheehan's beachside New Jersey home, glinting off his pale blue eyes. On the road beneath the windows, joggers huffed by.

"Certain qualities are brought out in the race," said Sheehan, clawing through piles of books, notes, mail on the floor beside his chair. "In the contest, what the Greeks called the *agon*, you find out you have what it takes and you're altered by the experience. To meet the challenge of death is now my race."

Prostate cancer rides to metastasis on currents of male hormone. The hypothalamic hormone he took to block his body's production of testosterone, GnRH, performed a chemical castration. For the first time in his life his mind was clear.

"I am the eye in the sky now," he crowed, "and I see how ludicrous men are, acting out a script written by a gland in their bodies. It's all testosterone. The only thing that protects us against it is good manners."

But that was the philosopher talking. The jock had begun tinkering with his dosage of GnRH, which might have been holding back the cancer but was surely holding back George. To run faster, he needed the juice. He cut back on GnRH while in heavy training and skipped it altogether when a race was coming up. He was willing to whittle days off the end of his life so he could run at his best. I wish I could talk to him right now about McGwire and A-Rod and Bonds. Even about Harold and Lance. I'm sure he'd find something in Heidegger or Saint Augustine that applied. And a personal judgment. And a suggestion for what chemical they *should* be taking.

While it was George who suggested I was built for bike riding, it was Lance who got me onto a bike again. (I had ridden as a kid, of course, and while in college I delivered telegrams for Western Union, which I guess makes me a former professional bike rider.)

In July 1999, after he won the Tour de France for the first time, I ran out and bought a Specialized hybrid and began chanting "LanceArmstrong" up hills. I followed him avidly, read his superb book with Sally Jenkins, *It's Not About the Bike*, and in 2001, when he asked me to moderate a Stanford University panel under the auspices of his cancer research and education foundation, I flew right out.

It was a first for me, working for a subject, and I wasn't quite sure of the conflict-of-interest issues. In my old monkish days I would have righteously just said no. But this was Lance and cancer. The fee I charged was a thirty-minute private interview with Lance. We got off to a shaky start when I asked about the allegations against him.

"Drugs, there you go," snorted Armstrong. We were sitting in a sunny hotel courtyard in Palo Alto, California. "The media, including your newspaper, loves to print all these rumors of what I'm supposed to be taking. When my tests come up negative the stories are much smaller, if you print them at all."

It got better. He was direct, engaged, friendly, twitchy. He was clearly the man I had expected, focused on the interview once he realized he had to do it, honest, still the the hard case who grew with psychic pain he apparently still shuts down with self-inflicted physical pain.

His mother was seventeen when Lance was born, and his father left them when the boy was two. Armstrong dismisses him as "a nonfactor" who merely "provided the DNA." When a Texas newspaper tracked down his biological father, Armstrong not only expressed lack of interest in finally meeting him but called the man's expression of pride opportunistic. It was as if he were trying to abandon the old man right back.

Lance described his stepfather, Terry Armstrong, as "a Christian who used to beat me for silly things." Maybe that's why he described himself as an agnostic. At seven, he was liberated by a Schwinn Mag Scrambler. "Cycling is so hard," he says. "The suffering is so intense that it's absolutely cleansing."

He was a perfect candidate for chemotherapy.

The precancerous Lance Armstrong was known as the Texas Bull, an aggressive, disrespectful rider fueled by the rage that covered his fears. He has said he likes himself much better now. Unlike most public cancer survivors, who profess moral improvement, his claim seems to be more than a way of finding something worthwhile in bad luck.

Though he says that cancer made him a better person, more certainly it made him a better racer. Before his months of chemo, he had been a star of one-day races. After chemo, he discovered his forte was in endurance for the long haul, which is what the twenty-three-day, 2,274-mile Tour de France is about. As is life. Without cancer, he believes, he would not have won the Tour.

For all his calls to "Live strong" and his now-ubiquitous yellow bracelets, Lance was no bumper-sticker motivationalist. But he did say one thing that stuck with me: "We can take responsibility for ourselves and be brave."

It seemed like a powerful mantra, in sickness or sport. I gave it my own spin, of course. That doesn't mean that if we win or lose, live or die, the credit or blame is all ours. The kind of cancer cells that ambushed Lance and me were vulnerable to a chemotherapy protocol that wouldn't have helped if we'd had, say, pancreatic or lung cancer. You have to take charge of your health and goals, do the best you can, face what happens. Control what you can control. The rest is luck.

The panel discussion at Stanford, "Athletes Winning the War Against Cancer," went well. Armstrong was joined by Eric Davis, whose seventeen-year major-league baseball career had been briefly interrupted by colon cancer, and Tom Gullikson, the tennis player and coach, who had cared for his twin, Tim, before his death from brain cancer. I can't remember when professional male athletes have offered themselves up so openly as having been frightened, vulnerable, and out of control of their lives. There were no sports questions from a crowd as raptly quiet as a symphony audience.

Davis, Gullikson, and Armstrong, conditioned as male athletes to "suck it up" and play through pain, had waited longer than most male nonathletes, certainly longer than most women, to present their symptoms. Also, despite their celebrity, they all had their problems with patronizing and insensitive doctors. But typically, as athletes, once they submitted to a medical program they were model patients.

"I approached cancer the way I would prepare for the Tour," Armstrong said. "Get in shape. Find out as much as you can, be motivated by small results. The lesion shrinking a little gave me the same kind of encouragement to keep going that I would get when my uphill times get slightly faster."

On our way out of the arena, a woman stopped Armstrong and asked him how his belief in God had helped him as a cancer patient.

"Everyone should believe in something," he said in his direct, almost chilly way, "and I believed in surgery, chemotherapy, and my doctors."

The questioner looked disappointed, but I felt a surge of relief. Armstrong had held his ground. We had agreed that the intrusion of faith-based treatment can be pernicious, almost blaming the victim, and he had pointed out that "good, strong people get cancer and they do all the right things to beat it, and they still die."

As we left, Lance grinned at me. "I guess I won't be able to go into politics when I stop bike racing."

I was charmed at the time, although after eight more years of Lance watching I wasn't convinced he would ever stop bike racing or consider anything, including politics, closed to him. There is a steely, messianic aspect of Lance that never quits—against cancer, against competitors, and against the forces that seem determined to prove he used performance-enhancing drugs and bring him down, including French antidrug authorities, some of the media, rivals such as former Tour champions Greg LeMond and the disgraced Floyd Landis, and the Javert-like federal investigator, Jeff Novitzky, who has made a career of dogging athletes.

I wish they would give it up, do something useful. I'm not sure if this is Bobbin, the fan, talking or Lippy, the scribe, or both of us in concert. The "war" on drugs was lost a long time ago, and you'd have to be a fool to go up the Pyrenees without a push.

Super Bowl "news conferences" like this one are the kind of crumbs the media has settled for in return for being allowed into the testosterone tent. (Associated Press)

SIXTEEN | The Lodge
Brothers

Scenes from the dawn and from the twilight.

The feisty little tabloid columnist Jimmy Cannon, at a press conference in the early 1960s, is screaming "You're blinding me! You're blinding me!" as he kicks over the TV light stands. He believes he can delay the start of the New Sports Order. Less obviously, the *Daily News* baseball writer Dick Young is scurrying around the room unplugging the light-stand electrical cords.

Nearly fifty years later, as endearingly quixotic, the Pulitzer Prize winner and *Friday Night Lights* author Buzz Bissinger is screaming at Will Leitch, the founder of the snarkish sports Web site Deadspin, that "blogs are dedicated to cruelty, dedicated to journalistic dishonesty," which "pisses the shit out of me." This is on HBO. Host Bob Costas, pretending it is not great TV, has his faintly disapproving schoolmarm face on.

When I started on the path from Cannon's kick to Bissinger's rant, athletes still needed off-season jobs and access was easy. The biggest problem interviewing Joe Namath in the days leading up to Super Bowl III was pushing through the kids and old ladies who clustered around him at the hotel pool. That was another country.

The price for that long-gone access was the promise of protection. Athletes could be sure that their binges, brawls, and bimbos would not be reported. The covenant fractured as the economic and social gap between hack and jock widened, as the financial value of sports grew, as newspaper writers became obsolete as brokers between athletes and fans. TV freed athletes from needing print journalists to present them to the public, and most TV sports journalists (my bloggingheads.tv partner, the writer and editor Bryan Curtis, has called sportscasting "a halfway house for halfwits") were thrilled to be part of the show on the industry's terms. Athletes could also control their images through ads and paid appearances. Blogs and tweets and Facebook pages would give teams and athletes direct access to their fans. They could spin their own news. Mass media conferences are tightly controlled now. One-on-one interviews are negotiated with agents and public relations advisers. Sportswriting has become another department of celebrity journalism.

As it should be. I may feel nostalgic about interviewing Namath at the pool or Casey Stengel at the bar, but those memories seem like tribal legends. Of the most famous athletes of this century, Michael Jordan and Tiger Woods, little was known beyond their performances for a very long time. Most reporters didn't report, happy to be allowed to watch them and god them up. When Tiger's facade of chilly control cracked in 2009, the media's predictable response echoed back a century to Grantland Rice's "Gee whiz" and W. O. McGeehan's "Aw nuts."

The Neo Gee Whizzers declared for Tiger's right to privacy; why he had fled from his Florida mansion at 2 A.M. with his wife in pursuit and crashed his Cadillac SUV into a nearby hydrant and tree, knocking himself out, was his business. All he owed us was continued greatness as a golfer. The Modern Aw Nutsies demanded a full disclosure; why was his wife holding a golf club, and was there any truth to the supermarket tabloid stories about his grand-slam philandering? Tiger is too important to us, they implied, not to clear the air and soothe our concerns. Speak to us now!

Most golf writers tended to be quiet at first, soaking in their shame, I'd like to think. What a crew of house pets! All those years of Tiger's remoteness, his often surly on-course behavior, the changes in his physical appearance were never adequately covered. Were they clues?

When the depth of Tiger's decadent life became apparent, there were the usual bleats of betrayal from "the lodge brothers" (as my old "Sports of the *Times*" colleague, Arthur Daley, called his press box brethren) but little about their own willingness to take Tiger's world at face value. Or to make the connection between Tiger and Andre Agassi, whose compelling autobiography, *Open*, I was reading at the same time the scandal broke. The overwhelming message of the Agassi book was the tennis star's hatred for his game and the life it had forced on him. I wondered if Tiger might have come to the same feeling. Both men were child prodigies driven relentlessly by fathers who lived through them. At twenty-one, already marked as the Mozart of the links (and a "chaser," by the way), Tiger was complaining that he couldn't live a "normal" life. (Famously, Arnold Palmer told the kid that if he wanted to be normal, he should start by giving back all the money.)

Another story I blew. In the early nineties, while writing the

Times sports column, I was approached by an old black golfer on a public course in Los Angeles. He told me to drop what I was covering (a women's golf story) and track down this fifteen-year-old phenom who would soon overwhelm the game. The key to his success, he told me, was the furious ambition of his father, a former army colonel. The defining moment had come when the boy was five or six and Dad, in civvies, had taken him to a military course. Two white admirals had spotted the prodigy and said, "That's some golfer you've got there, Sergeant."

By assuming that Earl Woods was an enlisted man because of his color, the black golfer told me, the admirals had reinforced Dad's determination to send his little tiger out to dominate the world. Earl, who died in 2006 at seventy-four, once said of his boy, "There is no limit because he has the guidance. I don't know yet exactly what form this will take. But he is the Chosen One. He'll have the power to impact nations. Not people. Nations. The world is just getting a taste of his power." He sounded like Don King.

I felt sorry for Tiger when he cracked up; he had never seemed quite human to me before. I wondered if the trail of voice mails and sext messages he had so carelessly strewn was an unconscious destructive urge, a cry for help. That will come out eventually, as have the mea culpas of the golf writers who never wondered too hard what Tiger was doing when he wasn't on the course. Tiger was golf's franchise player, and scribes learn early never to attack the sport that gives them work; you can trash most athletes, some officials and owners, a few rules and conventions, but systemic criticism is for "rippers" with other sources of income.

No wonder that most big off-field sports news comes from police blotters and PR releases, not from the lamestream sports media. Mark McGwire's whimpering sort-of admission of steroids use (it was to get healthy, he said, not to hit more homers) was no newshound coup, rather a media tour under the supervision of

President George W. Bush's former press secretary Ari Fleischer. This was twelve years after McGwire's steroid-fueled 70-homer season and five years after he told a congressional hearing on steroid use, "I'm not here to discuss the past." The former St. Louis Cardinals slugger was taking his swing at salvation, an increasingly important theme in the media narrative, especially appreciated when it involves some jock groveling. Alex Rodriguez, never a lodge brother favorite, was thrashed in the media when they found out he had taken steroids. But a weepy confession and then, most critically, a terrific 2009 season that ended in a World Series championship, was all the redemption necessary, a complete A-Rod moral makeover.

McGwire desperately needed a moral makeover in 2010. He wanted to get into the Hall of Fame with its perks, props, and profits after having been rejected by the electorate—veteran baseball writers. He wanted a soft landing into his new job as Cardinals hitting coach (what drugs would he be suggesting?), reuniting him with the manager who had seemingly been blind to his steroid use at Oakland and St. Louis, Tony LaRussa (the subject of admiring books by Bissinger and the conservative political sage George F. Will).

Fleischer's orchestration included a statement to the Associated Press, short interviews with the AP and selected media (the hometown *St. Louis Post-Dispatch*, the *New York Times*, *USA Today*, and ESPN), and then a sit-down TV interview with Bob Costas, who had left HBO to be the lead face on Major League Baseball's own house network. As is his professed style, Costas interviewed McGwire "civilly and politely." He never asked him exactly which steroids he had used and how McGwire knew they were "low dosage." With a certain detachment (Costas often reminds me of straight actors who keep a distance from their characters while playing gay roles), he gently pressed McGwire on his assertion that his years of drug use had been designed to heal his injuries rather than bulk him up and enhance his performance. McGwire was adamant; drugs were only for healing. He sniffled throughout.

The lodge brothers piled on, dismissing McGwire's tears as phony and his confession as incomplete. Among the traditional mainstream media commentaries, I was most taken with a posting by Bernie Miklasz of the *St. Louis Post-Dispatch*. He wrote, "A lot of the holier-than-thou folks who suddenly have found religion on this issue—mostly media people—want me and others to forget the role they played as carnival barkers in 1998. As I have said many times before, at least I am willing to admit to my hypocrisy. I enjoyed the McGwire-Sosa show. And writing about it sold lots of extra newspapers and advertising in the newspaper. I didn't ask any tough questions. I didn't follow up on my suspicions. I had fun writing about the homers; I didn't want to be the gadfly on the clubhouse wall. But at least I acknowledge that today. Pardon me, however, if I snicker just a little at colleagues across our industry who write and say all of these tough, hard-hitting things about McGwire these days. These are some of the same people who were all but cheering in the press box in the summer of 1998. Some wrote books or freelance pieces and actually made money off McGwire. What, did they forget?"

Take that, Mike Lupica! And as for you, Bernie, admitting your hypocrisy is too easy. You ate your cake; did you forget you can't have it, too?

Since 2003, when I stopped practicing daily newspaper journalism and began consuming it, I've felt increasingly disappointed by my old trade, its failures, its cowardice, its emotional corruption. (Not that I think political and business reporters have done much better.) But I can also understand the problems and empathize.

When Coach Bob Knight was annoyed by the best-selling book about him, *A Season on the Brink,* he called the writer, John Feinstein, a pimp and a whore. Feinstein's famous response was "I wish he'd make up his mind so I'd know how to dress."

This was in the eighties, the book was terrific, and Feinstein, a *Washington Post* sportswriter, was and still is an indefatigable reporter. It seemed he was speaking for all of us, bitch-slapping the bullying, sneering bad-boy coach. Yet, over time, I've wondered if Knight hadn't made a point that applied to us all. Just who do we think we are?

There are all kinds of sportswriters, simply because we are not sure if we are supposed to be reporters, critics, analysts, investigators, fabulists, moralists, comics, or shills for the games that make us possible. That identity quest has become more complicated as many of us shuttle among competing platforms—print publications, the Internet, and radio and TV shows, often on networks that have financial relationships with the leagues.

In spasms of bravery and timidity, we sportswriters lurch back and forth between breaking valid news stories about drugs, sex, and college recruiting violations and then rewriting publicity releases for upcoming blockbusters that always seem to sound something like a grudge rematch between smack-mouth regional rivals overcoming the tragedies of heartbreaking defeats. Somewhere in between are reports of games our audience has already seen and quasi-racist feature stories about fatherless delinquents who rose from ghetto hell-holes to become vicious linebackers who, off the field, played bass guitar, surprised Mama with a house, and ran a foundation for kids like they had been.

Now that sports has lost almost all its moral cachet and is accepted as a branch of the entertainment industry, the customers seem to want the same rigorous scandalmongering that music and politics fans enjoy. It was no surprise that *National Enquirer* led the pack in breaking Tiger tidbits. That exposed yet again the lesson we had learned from the steroid coverage: most of the lodge brothers are unable or unwilling to cover news beats as real journalists. This is nothing new. The stories about the 1986 New York Mets as out-of-control bad boys came not from reporters assigned to the club but from female *city-side* reporters looking for features.

Female sports reporters, a growing minority, tend to become lodge sisters when they can, which is understandable. They were treated poorly. When I started out, women were not allowed into press boxes, much less locker rooms, lest the lodge brothers' faux jockhood be threatened. By the late seventies, most teams in most of the major sports had opened their locker rooms, and the only discernible change was that the quality of feature writing perked up. Baseball held out against women, thanks to the stiff-necked commissioner, Bowie Kuhn. In 1977, an accredited *Sports Illustrated* reporter, Melissa Ludtke, was not allowed into the Yankees' locker room during the World Series because, she was told, "the players' wives had not been consulted and, if she entered, their children would be embarrassed in school the next day." This despite a vote by the Yankees ballplayers earlier in the season to open their locker room to women reporters.

Ludtke's successful suit to desegregate baseball reporting was the female sports journalists' equivalent of Title IX. But as with that landmark legislation, enforcement and attitude adjustment lagged. Neanderthal jocks created nasty incidents, and Neanderthal scribes didn't always stand up for their female colleagues. The mediocre ones had a right to feel threatened.

Some of the best female sportswriters of my time, Jane Gross and Robin Finn among others, left for other departments of the paper, as did a number of outstanding women editors. They had to deal with an undercurrent of male resentment in the clubbiness of the sports departments and of the news pack on the road. Men's fears of women seemed to parallel jocks' fears of gays—would fans start thinking all of us were girls? Among the women who stayed are some of the best sports journalists of this time, including Terry Taylor, the sports editor of the Associated Press; Teri Thompson, the sports editor of the New York *Daily News*; and the columnists Sally Jenkins, Christine Brennan, and Gwen Knapp. One of the most talented stylists, Selena Roberts, a former *Times* columnist who went on to *Sports Illustrated*, has a tendency to shoot from the hip, which women still can't do as heedlessly as men. Her coverage of the Duke University lacrosse team's 2006 party with strippers, which culminated in bogus rape charges, was a rush to judgment (shared by many, including the local DA), although her descriptions of the climate of jock entitlement were thoughtful, accurate, important, and, alas, rare.

As I had once hoped that the women's movement would set me free, so I thought the wave of female sportswriters would have a positive impact on Jock Culture by providing a less adoring impression of men's sports. At the least it would increase the coverage of women's sports. Hasn't happened. Naive on my part. Ambitious women journalists understandably want to cover the NFL and the NBA, to compete in the same edgy, often hostile, environment as male reporters while trying to prove they are not diversity hires. Their presence hasn't yet changed the white male agenda that still, though in its final rounds, dominates the sports media as it does the life of the country. The games are still presented as fantasias in a bubble, dissociated from the culture. No wonder that blogs—as they have done in political analysis and restaurant, book, and movie criticism—have risen to offer a kind of rough democracy in commentary, although not, unfortunately, in basic reporting.

The blog monster is ESPN's "The Sports Guy," Bill Simmons. He is post-Media. In 2009, the year he turned forty, the year his *The Book of Basketball* became a number one best seller, his ESPN.com column was attracting 460,000 unique visitors a month, and his weekly podcasts were being downloaded two million times a month. He also had a million followers on Twitter.

Simmons grasps the cozy cultishness of fandom and knows how

to relate it to other forms of pop culture: movies, porn, music, sit-coms, and the Internet, on which he staked an early claim. Raised in Boston, that cradle of fandom, unwilling to wait his turn at the traditional sportswriting trough, Simmons became a blogger before the term was in common usage.

He doesn't go into locker rooms or interview athletes. His fantasy-league teams seem as existent to him as the real ones (perhaps because the real ones exist only as external stimuli to him). His basic histori-cal references are what he was eating or drinking or feeling when the Red Sox or the Celtics or the Bruins or the Patriots surprised or sad-dened or exalted him, which is like remembering how you felt during episodes of *Friends*, which he often does, or the song on the car radio when you were in the backseat trying to get laid. I'm sure he's written that, too.

I remember being at first appalled when Simmons described the only damage of the steroid era for the genuine fan as being "the shadow of a syringe" that would forever linger over memories. He recalled September 18, 1996, when he was smoking and drinking beer alone on a night off from his bartending job. He was watch-ing the Red Sox game on TV while wondering what had happened to his life at twenty-seven. That was the night Roger Clemens, in whom Simmons had lost faith as an effective pitcher, struck out twenty Detroit Tigers. Simmons called his dad, then ran out to his local bar, hugged strangers, and bought rounds. "For one of the few times that year, I had a smile on my face."

I stewed about that for a while. It's all about me, he was saying. He's missing the essence of the games, I thought, he's objectifying the players, he's celebrating his lack of access. But after I read him regularly for a while (a funny, clever writer, he can become addictive) I got the Tao of Bill. The essence of the game is our response to it, not the game itself. Players are not necessarily human since, as the gap between us and them widens, they become archetypes in our minds.

Besides, reporters with media passes are not getting access either; their "inside knowledge" is the gossip they churn among themselves. So why not gaze at your own navel—you can believe in it.

The writer Dave Zirin considers Bill Simmons "1,000 miles wide and ½ inch deep" but credits his bold and creative use of the Internet with inspiring his own career.

It was my old friend David Meggyesy, the former Marxist linebacker, who tipped me off to Zirin in the spring of 2005. In his introduction to Zirin's first book, *What's My Name, Fool? Sports and Resistance in the United States*, Meggyesy had declared, "His writing reminds me of Bob Lipsyte, former sports columnist of the *New York Times*."

Zirin's writing reminded me of only part of me, the soapbox columns I could get away with because I also wrote paeans to women tennis players and NFL linemen and aging outfielders. But I was fascinated by Zirin's rare combination of political passion and love for games, both of which seemed more intense than my own. When I checked the kid out—he was thirty-two at the time—he turned out to be outgoing, funny, sometimes brilliant. He is a former high school basketball player and former Washington, D.C., elementary school teacher whose limitless outrage is matched only by his enthusiastic energy. He badgered his way onto radio and TV shows, Web sites, and conference schedules and never stopped making startling connections: "Hurricane Katrina got all those people into the Superdome who couldn't otherwise afford it."

I wasn't surprised when Zirin told me that his role model as a sportswriter was the late Lester "Red" Rodney, that Commie agitator from the old *Daily Worker*. He picks up where Rodney, a leading voice for integration in baseball, left off.

From a 2009 "Edge of Sports" column:

Last Tuesday night, there were as many African-American presidents at the All-Star Game as players in the starting lineups.

Only the fourteen-year veteran Derek Jeter represented people of African descent. (Jeter, like Obama, is of mixed heritage.)

Baseball players now tend to come in two groups. There are Latino players, scouted before they are 10, signed into baseball academies before their sweet 16 and imported along a global pipeline until they are cast aside or make the majors. Then there are white players, who largely come from suburban backgrounds and college programs. Baseball—in the US context—has gone country club. Like golf and tennis, or their hemp-addled cousins in the X Games, they are sports that require serious bank for admission. In addition, you need parents with the leisure time to be involved. These sports just don't fit the reality for today's working families, black or white.

Here's Zirin on McGwire:

It's hard not to see parallels in the absence of public accountability among the banking titans of Wall Street. For the powerful, profits mean never having to say you're sorry.

It's long past time we reframed the question and asked: what did the owners know and when did they know it? Why have no owners had to speak in front of Congress? Why have owners been allowed to keep every penny from the big money, big bopping 1990s, while players have been put through the thresher? How have no owners even been threatened with punishment for allowing steroids into their locker rooms? And how in the blue hell does Bud Selig still have a job?

Zirin is no likely candidate for lodge brotherhood, although Simmons and his copycats may eventually own the lodge. The ultimate lodge brother of our time is Bob Costas. No one else has ever walked so gracefully the line between journalist and shill. He is one of Jock Culture's most treasured cheerleaders, and that's no pose; just look how happy he seems bantering with those ex-athletes on pregame shows, a terrier playing with mastiffs and Great Danes, or watch how he gazes down benignly at the Olympic Games, a duke on his castle tower. He takes himself seriously. His 2000 book, *Fair Ball: A Fan's Case for Baseball*, pointed out the game's flaws in such statesmanlike prose that people thought he might be a candidate for Major League Baseball commissioner. Why not? We've done much worse.

Late in 2009, fourteen years after the last time we spoke, Costas and I met for lunch at a midtown New York Italian restaurant. The meal lasted three hours and was far more relaxed than our last one. I think I had changed more than he had (emotionally, to be sure, but he also continues to look preternaturally young). We talked about that previous meal. I liked him for being even tougher on me this time.

He again brought up my 1995 column calling for Cal Ripken to sit out a game and avoid breaking Lou Gehrig's record. "Sometimes I thought you were a contrarian just for the sake of being a contrarian," he said. And then he got to the core of the matter. It was "almost churlish," Costas said, when so soon after Mickey Mantle's death I suggested that he had jumped the line for a liver transplant.

I asked him what he wanted of me.

"I wanted a dash of celebration and appreciation along with the excoriation." He paused, almost smiled. "Am I sounding like Jesse Jackson?"

I nodded him on.

"It gives you more credibility for when you criticize. You know, I grew up reading you, hoping to someday win your regard. When I took you to dinner, I still hoped to win your regard. But I wanted you to be less corrosive; skeptical, not cynical.

"In the sixties and seventies the issues were more clear cut—gays, women, Ali—and you were on the right side. When you made your bones on those big issues, the prevailing tone needed a counterpuncher. How Willie Mays caught a fly ball was covered, so Lipsyte was right to pound away at the issues.

"But now the prevailing tone is so mean you have to play it straight. It's not clear cut, black and white. There needs to be more nuance. There's more of a need to celebrate. I thought of you as a smart and independent guy holding his patch of ground, but something blinded you to the appealing stuff. It's not a breach of integrity to find within what you disapprove things that are worthy of approval and celebration."

I listened carefully and took notes. I didn't argue because I was fascinated. He was talking about me. Later I wondered if he had been talking about himself as well, justifying his own celebration of a sports industry that I think needs counterpunching more than ever.

We talked some more about Mantle and that "almost churlish" liver-transplant column. Why couldn't I see the humanity of Mantle?

He asked if I considered him presumptuous, then or now. Both times, I said, although I had resented it then and was grateful now. There were areas where we needed to agree to disagree. It was apparent that I did not consider him the journalist he thought he was. There was no chapter on steroids in his baseball book ("I was talked out of it," he said, "and I regret that now"), and in the absence of "hard evidence" it was not something he thought he could bring up in his broadcasts of games. Once in the late nineties, he said, he had remarked on air to Joe Morgan that something was out of whack in the game. When Morgan said, "Ball may be juiced," Costas replied, "Not as much as the players."

I didn't think that qualified as serious journalism, but I didn't pursue it. By that time, I was liking Costas, and we parted with a promise to meet again. I hope we do. There would be a lot to think and talk about—beyond Mantle. And I wondered if Costas and I were secret sharers in some way, each disappointed in the other and perhaps even disappointed in himself. He doesn't think he has quite "filled out his role." Maybe after 2012, his last Olympics for NBC, he says, he will "break out."

Maybe I do need to be more of a fan, or at least find more to celebrate. The questions for each of us, I think, are the basic ones: Could I have been more?

And, Is there still time?

The Lipsyte lads in 2004. Dad is one hundred, I'm sixty-six, my son, Sam, is thirty-six, and his son, Alfred, is six weeks old. (Photograph by Lois B. Morris)

SEVENTEEN | **The Man**

My father was in his eighties when I found his track medals in the back of a drawer. He had been a school-boy middle-distance champion. A jock! Pressed for more details, he reluctantly told me that he had quit his college track team when the coach wouldn't send him to an out-of-town meet because the Olympic hopeful, whom Dad had beaten all season, was the one the coach had decided to promote. And that had been the end of his sports career. He hadn't spoken about it in nearly seventy years, he said. Not even to his sportswriter son.

The symbolism of those medals has turned out to be a big piece in the jigsaw puzzle of Dad's life, and thus in my own. In some ways, maybe, my biggest sports story. Over the years, Dad had freely expressed his skepticism—even cynicism—about politics, religion, and academia. Dad had opinions about everything. But he had always seemed indifferent to sports on any level, which, given his great interest in individual and mass psychology, seemed odd. I wondered if he felt too intellectual for sports or, later on, if he was subtly putting down what I did for a living. Or was that me putting myself down? He was always telling me, jesting on the square, to take a week off and write a best seller. I'd breezily reply something like "I'm too busy to get rich," but it felt like a needle and sometimes it hurt.

I had no idea that he was still indignant over what he considered an unfair exclusion. He thought he had won the right to go to that track meet. Sports had disillusioned him. He had believed sports was a true meritocracy. Like Cosell, he believed in America's promise to all of fairness, constitutionality, order. Dad just didn't believe that the country always kept its promises.

After I found out about his aborted track career, I asked for his take on the City College scandals of 1951 in which basketball players had conspired with gamblers to fix the outcome of games. (Dad graduated from City in 1927.) He told me that he thought much of life as well as sports was fixed, though not as blatantly as those basketball games had been. In most cases, he said, it's about the wrong people getting the chance to play "for political reasons." He said that we need to make sure everybody gets an equal chance to play on a level field. Then it's up to them.

Now I get it. He was my jock ideal. Fairness was the dominant theme of his life. Most of his career was in underserved districts of New York City, teaching and administering in schools for what were then officially designated as "socially maladjusted" boys. He lived to salvage those boys. The world might see them as juvenile delinquents, but in his writings Dad called them "inadequately protected children" whose "disturbances" had been caused and exacerbated at home and in previous schools where they had been embarrassed and punished. He offered them "an atmosphere of masculine authority" in which their self-esteem would be boosted.

He was hardly a "leftist" or even a "bleeding heart" by any labeling standards. He was an all-American centrist: Give people a fair shake by making sure they have a pair of boots so they can pull themselves up by their bootstraps, which meant health care, education, shelter, food, and psychological support. After that, they were responsible for themselves. Dad had always felt responsible for himself.

I think his worldview began to take shape in 1912, when he was eight years old and heard the SOS calls from the *Titanic* on his brother's crystal radio set. A seed was planted in his mind. If the supposedly unsinkable *Titanic* could go down, could you ever again put faith in technology or in the officials who misspoke with such authority? When his father died in the flu epidemic a few years later, another seed was planted: even God could not be relied on to do the right thing. Yet Dad was an optimist. He believed that things could be made better and he could be part of the solution. But he took nothing for granted.

Whenever disaster struck, from illness in the family to carnage on the evening news, I'd call him. In 1963, when President Kennedy was murdered, I called Dad to make sure he was okay. After all, the old man was pushing sixty. I called him after 9/11 to make sure I was okay. After all, I was in my sixties. Being a frequent subway rider in New York, I even called him after the 2004 train bombings in Madrid. I said I was calling to tell him we were all okay. I knew he would calm me down. After all, he was 100.

Dad would tell me to relax. Don't let your imagination loose unless you're writing fiction, he'd say: "Nothing is ever quite as good as you imagine it will be nor as bad." When I was younger, there seemed something bittersweet, disappointed, even defeatist about that, but now it feels more like Never Give Up. We Can Get Through This. After all, Dad was saying without saying "Look, I'm still here."

Now he's not, but I'm still talking to him, taking both sides of the conversation. He'd have been very interested—I told you so, he would remind silently with his bushy eyebrows—about the housing bust, the oil spills, the latest Wall Street greed implosion. His frugality, born in the Great Depression, had paid off with a fine nest egg for a schoolteacher. His distrust of Wall Street, where he had worked as a teenage messenger, had impelled him to keep every saved penny in Treasury bills. Thanks for that, Dad. Among other things.

When the name Lipsyte first appeared in the *New York Times*, it was his, on June 28, 1936, two years before I was born. The headline read:

BRONX MAN ALSO VICTOR
Sidney Lipsyte Gets $400 for Article

Dad had won first place in a *Times* essay contest on "the Constitution as a living document." He told me he had written it overnight at the urging of his principal. Dad was a junior high school English teacher then. In the *Times* story announcing his prize, he said he was going to use the money, no small change in those days, to "travel." Actually, he bought one-third of an acre some fifty miles from Queens in upstate New York and began to build a house, much of it himself. So he knew that writing pays!

He always encouraged my writing. Sometimes a little too vigorously. He had lots of ideas to make my junior high school science fiction stories more exciting. We struggled for creative control. At the time I thought it was parental bigfooting, and I was resentful. Years later, when he showed me short stories he had written for school magazines about the Imp of the Universe and his henchmen,

Time-on-his-Hands and Mischief-on-his-Mind, I realized that he was living a dream through me, and I was proud. Knowing that, I felt more comfortable allowing myself to live my dreams through Susannah's social consciousness (she's a lawyer) and Sam's fiction; when his 2010 literary comic novel, *The Ask*, hit the *Times'* best-seller list, I fully understood the pleasure of vicarious pleasure.

When I dropped out of the premed program at Columbia and declared English as my major, Dad was supportive, although he urged me to take the junior high school English teachers exam as a fallback position. I refused until his urgings became challenges. All those Columbia courses, he'd say, bet you couldn't pass a license exam I passed a quarter-century ago with mere City College courses. He knew me. Of course, I had to take the test. He didn't seem surprised when I passed, and five years later, during a newspaper strike, he never said "I told you so" when I was able to support myself by substitute teaching at the Rikers Island jail school he supervised.

He was always suggesting stories for me to write for the *Times*. One of my first Publisher's Prizes, an internal newsroom award, came through a tip from him in 1960. Floyd Patterson, the heavyweight champion, had been a socially maladjusted boy. When he made a last-minute decision to visit his old school (another one that Dad supervised) with his championship belt, Dad called me. It was a scoop.

I remember Dad as emotionally remote when I was a kid, but that was the style of the day. He and I shook hands. Sam and I hug. Sam and his son, Alfred, kiss. Dad was uncomfortable with expressed emotions. He and Mom often called me or my sister, Gale, together. When emotions flared, Dad would hang up the telephone extension. I thought of him as insensitive. Many years later, he told me that he had strong feelings but didn't like to let them show. He said he felt bad that people might have thought he didn't feel at all. As a kid and young man, I was never sure of his approval. Mom, on the other hand, was wildly emotional, freely expressive of loves and hates, of approval and disapproval, a spinning weather vane of passionate feelings.

Mom and Dad complemented each other. They hardly spent a night apart through sixty-six years of marriage. She was the fierce guardian of Dad's career, and he was the soft wall she could bounce off. They potentiated each other's distrust and paranoia, resentment of rich people, and posture of intellectual superiority. As children of nineteenth-century immigrants from Russia and Germany who had settled in the Bronx, they came by their suspicions naturally.

Dad was born on April 4, 1904, the fourth of four boys. He was interested in science and wanted to be an engineer like his oldest brother, but he refused to change his name (all his brothers became Lipton) and pretend to be Christian to beat the engineering school quotas against Jews. I'm not sure why. He never gave me a clear explanation. He was not at all religious. I like to think it was some kind of stubborn refusal to cave to bullies. So he became an ambitious, driven public school teacher, working extra jobs weekends and summers to create financial security, build a country house, and assure college for my sister and me. My mother was a teacher and guidance counselor, but it was a mommy-track career—she stayed at home for long stretches.

I loved visiting Dad at work, particularly during the years he was principal of one of those hard schools. He strode those halls like Captain Kirk on the bridge of the *Enterprise* (he would have thought C. S. Forester's Horatio Hornblower or Patrick O'Brian's Jack Aubrey), a beloved, as well as respected, figure. The rough boys vied for his attention. Several times I saw him wallop kids hard on the butt for some infraction; the boys would grin at him as if thrilled by the caring attention they got nowhere else, promise to behave, and swagger off. I thought about my own Halsey gym teachers booting the bullies. Maybe there was more to it than I realized.

When he loosened up enough—we were both old men by then—

to tell me his stories, one of his favorites was of his first command, at forty-four. He was appointed principal of an elementary school near the Brooklyn Navy Yard in 1948. That school was already old when he took it over. He spent much of the summer before classes roaming the ancient vessel. One day he discovered a sagging wall in the basement. Physically strong and fearless, he pushed the wall over to reveal a huge tiled room, the walls and ceilings festooned with rusted pipes. In old school records he discovered that a shower room had been built for a local immigrant community that had no hot running water.

Taking advantage of the brief window of accommodation that incoming principals get, he persuaded the district to hire plumbers and restore the shower room for a student body that still could not wash itself on a regular basis. To remove any stigma, he created the Swim Club and promoted its logo, a fish, as if it were a varsity letter or gang colors. Kids wanted to wear that white cotton fish patch pinned to their shirts, members of a club whose sole admission requirement was needing a hot shower.

Dad was a combination bureaucrat and buccaneer. He always wore a suit and tie (bought by my mother in discount stores), usually with a white shirt. That's where I learned about conservative camouflage; even in a cheap suit you can slip into most places, or could before 9/11, and make most establishment subjects think you are one of them or want to be. Tie snugged to his starched collar, Dad ran schemes to help his boys, one of which nearly got him into major trouble. His schools received subway tokens to distribute to pupils, but only for use going back and forth from school. What about the weekends, he thought, visiting relatives, church, sightseeing, shopping, maybe even a museum or a ball game? He started an illegal program to reward kids for regular attendance, improvement in grades, and good conduct with subway tokens. Attendance, grades, and conduct improved. When an assistant principal who wanted Dad's job turned him in, Dad was called to headquarters. I can imagine him making his case in a pedagogical bluster, his neck and face turning red above the starched collar. We're here to improve and enrich their lives, he'd be shouting, give them a chance to rise above the poor example of family and community. I can imagine "the brass," as he called them, stepping back, waving him away, okay, okay, Sidney, just don't do it again. Or get caught.

Dad ended his career as a director of a bureau in the Board of Education hierarchy, a colonel, I guess. He never made general, one of the various superintendent slots, which I know he would have liked. As so many do, his career ended badly.

In 1968, fifty-six years after the *Titanic* went down, Dad felt betrayed once again. The revolutionary passions that swept through America, even through sports, smashed into the city school system and broke it apart. Teachers went on strike over the issue of community versus central control. It started in the Ocean Hill–Brownsville district of Brooklyn when the local superintendent, Rhody McCoy, who was black, fired a number of white teachers and principals. McCoy believed, as many whites including my father did, that black kids needed black role models. Dad had been in the forefront of hiring, mentoring, and promoting black men and women to be teachers and principals. He had put Rhody McCoy on the fast track in the first place. Rhody was his guy! Rhody danced with Mom at teacher functions! At every one of his promotion ceremonies, Rhody publicly thanked Dad! I had met and liked Rhody.

But now Dad, as an official observer during the strike, was being spat on by black parents, kids, and even teachers. Rhody McCoy saw it and physically turned his back on Dad. The reality and the symbolism of that betrayal devastated Dad, although he tried not to show it. He talked stiffly about politics, not about personal hurt.

Rhody became a controversial and polarizing figure in the city, symbolic of an upheaval that came to be seen variously as a black

power grab, a righteous revolution, and an honest attempt to trans-
fer educational control from a hidebound bureaucracy to the people
it was serving.

Dad was angrier at the white liberal city administration that
allowed it to happen than at his black teachers and principals,
including Rhody. We argued. In my wisdom as a newly anointed
Times columnist, I accused him of having had a colonialist mentality.
Brooklyn instead of India. It was not a good time for us, and I wish
I could take back what I said. Sam was born that year, and Dad's joy
cut me a lot of slack for callowness. Even if I was right, I wasn't.

He retired a few years later and his funk continued, even after
he and Mom gave up their apartment in Queens and moved upstate
full-time. He was lethargic, distracted. He lost interest in his three
greatest hobbies: reading, gardening, and home repairs. He told me
later that he had expected to be dead by seventy-five and sometimes
hoped to be.

Then something changed. Maybe a survival mechanism
switched on, maybe Mom kicked him into gear. Somehow he
reached into himself and restarted his engine. I saw a version of
that strong, distant man reappear, although a little softer around
the edges. He and Mom joined and then ran groups lobbying for
the elderly, volunteered at local libraries, helped neighbors fill out
health insurance forms, edited an increasingly ambitious newslet-
ter for their temple. He started reading three books at a time—
usually one on current affairs, one on ancient history, and one
Patrick O'Brian naval novel. He kept scrapbooks of my writing—
sports, nonsports, he cheered them all. He and Mom roamed local
thrift stores for inexpensive books, old lamps he could rewire, furniture he could restore. He dug out the basement to install shelves
for more books. He patched the roof, mowed the lawn, climbed on
the roof to repair shingles and clean the gutters.

One winter, he refused to let Sam or me shovel the snow in his driveway. It was his job. He said, "If you're not used to doing this, you could get a heart attack." Sam was twenty, I was fifty, and Dad was eighty-four.

He also took increasing care of Mom. Throughout their marriage, she had often been sick, and Dad was quick to shop, cook, clean, launder. He made doing household chores seem manly.

When he himself was sick, which was rare, he would go into a corner and drink tea until he felt better. He refused to go to doctors. He said they just made you sicker. That worked until he was felled by stomach cramps at ninety. Against his will and with my phone support, Mom called an ambulance. I met them in the emergency room of their community hospital. Doctors were amazed—and annoyed—that he had no medical history, no previous doctors, no years of charts. For a week, each specialist poked him and suggested an invasive procedure that we deflected. Dad claimed it was just a piece of bad bologna. He got better without treatment, enjoying a week of jolly roommates and cooing nurses. He was cute as an old man.

It probably was bad bologna, to which he returned with gusto. A moderate eater who had never smoked or drunk alcohol, Dad allowed himself the vice of luncheon meats. The only member of the family happy to share his stash was Rudy, Lois's big old shelter dog. Dad loved Rudy, his first dog friend.

Dad was ninety-four when Mom's mind slipped its moorings. He insisted on taking care of her by himself. He could do it, he said. Maybe he didn't want anyone else to see her without dignity. She was ninety, a diabetic with osteoarthritis, high blood pressure, hiatal hernia, thyroid imbalance, congestive heart failure, and carpal tunnel syndrome, for which she had been operated on twice. Macular degeneration had left her legally blind. She took seven different medications every day, including injections of insulin and an antidepressant that had been prescribed for her diabetic nerve pain some years before. She might have been suffering from depression, as well as vascular damage and Alzheimer's, we were told. Eventually we found out she had a brain tumor.

Dad always went to Mom's doctor's appointments but never into the examining room. That was a job for Gale or me. He just couldn't handle the increasingly hopeless news. He'd be in the waiting room, reading a year-old magazine, ready with some factoid he'd just picked up. I'd give him the headlines of my doctor's notes. He'd nod without comment and write a check for the doctor's bill.

"One hundred and five dollars and sixty-seven cents, you wonder how it is that's one thing they can always figure out so easily." He passed the check to the receptionist, and as the three of us left, he'd ask me, "Should we get something to eat? Need money, Bobby?"

Eventually, it was obvious that Dad couldn't keep up with ministering to Mom alone. He didn't want nurses in the house. He was haggard, fatigued, wearing out. Gale, a Jungian analyst, lived in northern California, and I was finding it harder and harder to give up days to drive Mom to her doctor's appointments. We found a pleasant nursing home that was part of a nearby hospital complex that Dad could easily drive to every day. She was fine there for a while, then collapsed and was moved to the intensive care unit. She was a crumpled heap, a respirator breathing for her. Dad could sit at her bedside for only about twenty minutes before he would have to go into the hall and be alone. He refused to be seen weeping. He would say only, "These tubes have a bad effect on me."

I asked him, "Are you sad?" and he was silent so long I thought there would be no answer. Finally he said, "That's a hard question to answer." For another few minutes I thought the conversation was over.

Then he said, "When you've been with someone for sixty-six years, they are a part of you." Now the conversation was over.

The nurses treated her like a pet, washing and combing her silky white hair. She looked peaceful, except when she twitched reflexively. Dad said he liked to believe that she was having good dreams. And maybe that's why he refused to let her go.

He was her health care proxy. He wanted to keep her alive, despite the living will that Mom had signed a few years before: In the event she suffered from a condition from which "there is no reasonable prospect of recovery to a cognitive and sentient life" and no longer could communicate "meaningfully" with others, she wanted no medical treatments to prolong her life.

I was angry for a while after Mom's heart stopped and was pounded back to life, after massive doses of antibiotics were injected to control the pneumonia. Why not let her rest? But Gale persuaded me that Dad wasn't ready yet; Mom was the campfire at which he kept himself warm. Gale reminded me that Dad would always do the right thing, once he had thought it through. On his timetable.

And then the hospital called. Medicare would be ending payment. Because she was on a respirator, Mom could not go back to the pleasant nursing home attached to the hospital, and if she stayed in intensive care it would cost $2,000 a day. She needed to be moved to a custodial care facility that could handle a respirator, a facility that was a warehouse too far for Dad to visit every day. How many life-and-death decisions come down to money?

We went over all the options with Dad and wrote down questions for us to ask the doctors again. How long would she continue to live on the respirator? Weeks, perhaps months, one doctor told us. How long without it? Hours, days. Was there any hope? No. There were indications her heart was weakening. Nothing was going on in her brain. She might even be in pain.

After a few minutes, Dad suddenly signaled with his hand, a quick chopping motion, that the conversation was over. Gale went out to talk to a passing doctor. After Dad could talk again, he told me that he had just seen the 1997 movie *Titanic* on TV. He said he thought it was a silly movie, although he enjoyed the effects. He talked again about hearing the SOS on his brother's radio when he was eight.

When I recounted the conversation, Gale wanted to know exactly what Dad had said about the *Titanic*. She thought there might be clues to his state of mind.

"C'mon," I snapped, "don't start distancing yourself like he does. Don't start being a shrink in your own life."

Later, I apologized. "You were right," I said. "There was something Dad said that I forgot to tell you. He said that one thing they missed in the movie was a reaction from the shore. He would have liked to know what the families of those passengers were doing and thinking while the ship went down."

We allowed the respirator to be unplugged, and Mom slowly sank. After she died, Dad sat in his house, stared at the piles of books that had always been his comfort, and cried when he thought we weren't watching. He barely ate. He roamed the house through the night. He dismissed any suggestion of talking about his grief, much less with a professional. We thought he wouldn't survive. We remembered the last time Dad had been in a depression. But that had been thirty years earlier and he had lost a job, not his life's companion.

Then one day he made Gale and me French toast for breakfast and urged us to hurry eating because he needed the dining room table to start laying out a family scrapbook. There were two more monster scrapbooks in the six years after that day. He continued to talk about Mom wistfully, but then he would get on with whatever he was doing. How had he been able to reach into himself and start the engine yet again? That's the DNA I want even more than the longevity.

His corners got even softer. He let Gale and me further in. The humor came back, although sometimes with an edge. Reading about Dr. Martin Luther King's philandering, he said in a deepened voice, "I've got a dream . . . girl." Looking at the fetal sonogram of his first great-grandchild, Alfred Major Lipsyte, he said, "He looks just like me." When he finally got to hold Alfred, he looked the newborn in the eye and dramatically intoned, "I am your ancestor."

He was driving around again, looking for bargains in books and food. He paid his utility bills in person so he could have a little chit-chat with the clerks, who treated him as an endearing grandpa. I'd go upstate and hang out for a day or two. It was fun. We'd talk, sometimes just sit and read. I'd usually bring Rudy so the two of them could bologna up together. We'd even watch TV together, especially women's basketball, which he told me he'd "discovered." He couldn't stop talking about the players' passing skills. He urged me to write about it. I could never persuade him that the rest of the world, including me, already knew about women's basketball.

Those were the warmest, closest years. He told me stories I had never heard and would answer any question. He remembered an old friend from college who had introduced him to opera. He became a noted professor, opera translator, and author. He died in 1998. In one of many letters he wrote Dad, he admitted he was gay. In the fearful fifties, Dad told me, he had destroyed all the letters lest they fell into the wrong hands and destroy his friend's career. And his? I wondered. He regretted having lost touch with him. He wished he had the letters.

I asked Dad if he had ever felt physically attracted to another man. He smiled and said, "Not yet."

He was ninety-seven then, and I thought it was the most life-affirming line I had ever heard.

That was also the year he stopped going up on the roof. On his hundredth birthday, he stopped driving. By then he had allowed Gale to hire a former nurse to "drop by" two afternoons a week, check him out, tidy up, and cook a few meals. She and Dad seemed to enjoy each other's company. Dad had his survival skills.

Except for one, it seemed at the time, although now I'm not so sure. He refused to wear one of those I've-fallen-down-and-can't-get-up alarms, a must for old people living alone. He felt that if he fell down and couldn't get up on his own, he wouldn't want to, that it would be the signal that his time was over.

Three months before his 101st birthday, apparently while getting into the shower, probably on a Saturday evening, he fell. By the time he was found on Monday, his organs were failing. Three days later, January 20, 2005, he died peacefully with Gale, Lois, and me at his bedside.

It was while pawing around nooks and crannies in the house that I had found his medals a dozen years earlier and then after his death a letter from his old opera buddy. He hadn't destroyed them all.

The four-page handwritten letter on the stationery of his piano studio was undated. The script was as ornate and whimsical as the words. Operatic. It began, "Sidney, And why the wherefore?" and went on to demand that "my literary executor and Biographer" show up at his Brooklyn home on the coming Sunday to hear "inchoate dreams and plans and Intentions—now Alas! to remain forever unrealized."

He promised a "death-bed scene. Will you do less for me than Dumas fils did for the Lady of the Camellias (the part suits me to perfection, except that I don't use flowers for whooping cough)."

The letter ends "I'll call you up Saturday at 1.00 to make arrangements."

Did he call? Did Sidney go? What year was this?

I love the mystery of this letter and of their friendship. I don't know everything about Dad.

An antiquarian bookseller came to assess Dad's books. Gale thought there were treasures among them, I thought the collection was basically worthless. We were both right.

The bookseller spent several hours reading, touching, even smelling the books for mold, of which there was too much. He lingered over the big art books, the thick old leather-bound histories, the two sets of the 1911 *Encyclopaedia Britannica*.

"Twenty years ago," he said, "this would have been a real find. But in the age of the Internet, all this information is easily available. There are very few important first editions here, and most of them are not in good shape."

He seemed reluctant to leave. "You know, this is not a collection of trophy books, it's a collection of ideas. I know many people who collect expensive books they never open. Your father bought books he wanted to read. I would like to have met him."

I would have liked to have met Dad earlier in the emotional place we found together in the end. By the time I came to appreciate him, to understand his impact on me, we were both old men. But there was time enough.

acknowledgments

I've stood on many shoulders and accepted many helping hands. Some are mentioned in the book. Not all are still alive, although they are to me.

In the big inning, as we sportswriters like to say, there were teachers who gave me confidence: James J. Kernan at Forest Hills High School; George Nobbe, Sr., at Columbia College; and Lawrence Pinkham at the Columbia Graduate School of Journalism.

In the *Times* sports department, among those who reached out to me were my editors/coaches, Jim Roach and Neil Amdur, Steve Cady, Frank Litsky, Bob Teague, Howard Tuckner, Bill Wallace, Sam Goldaper, Jim Tuite, Gerald Eskenazi, Ira Berkow, Dave Anderson, Susan B. Adams, Ray Corio, Steve Tyno, Joe Prisco, Al Levy, Barton Silverman, Tom Rogers, and my fellow copyboys, John Corry and Tom Kenville.

Colleagues along the way included Tom Hauser, Vic Ziegel, Len Shecter, Stan Isaacs, Mike Harris, Lewis Franck, Lee Ballinger, Bud and Susan Lamoreaux, Shad Northshield, Bill Moran, Larry Doyle, Tim Russert, Tom Engelhardt, Karen DeCrow, Lou Charlip, Naomi Boak, Ron Fried, and Glen Nishimura.

I came to depend on the friendship of Peter Levine, Jon Kandell, Joel Millman, Mike Miletic, Joe and Carolyn Lelyveld, Peter Golenbock, and Jay Lovinger.

I'm grateful for love and support from Gene and Layton Borkan and their four daughters, Mara, Rachel, Johanna, and Sasha; Susan Jordan and Ronnie Wong and their daughter, Jenny; and Alun and Fiona Morris and their children and grandchildren, especially Ceridwen, Alfred, and Sylvia.

You wouldn't be reading this without David Hirshey, my brilliant editor; the steadfast and smart Barry Harbaugh; the enthusiasm and wise counsel of Josh Marwell; my commando agent, Jay Mandel; and my three wise readers, Sam Lipsyte, Jay Lovinger, and Lois B. Morris.

And for those who lived in the lights and shadows of this story and actively helped me with it, my sister, Gale; my children, Sam and Susannah; and my wife, Lois, yet another round of inadequate thanks.